Muslim Identities

AARON W. HUGHES

Muslim Identities

AN INTRODUCTION TO ISLAM

Columbia University Press   New York

Columbia University Press
Publishers Since 1893
New York   Chichester, West Sussex
cup.columbia.edu

Copyright © 2013 Columbia University Press

Library of Congress Cataloging-in-Publication Data
Hughes, Aaron W., 1968–
Muslim identities : an introduction to Islam / Aaron W. Hughes.
      p.   cm.
Includes bibliographical references and index.
ISBN 978-0-231-16146-6 (cloth : alk. paper)   ISBN 978-0-231-16147-3 (pbk. : alk. paper)
ISBN 978-0-231-53192-4 (e-book)
1. Islam   I. Title.

BP161.3.H84 2013
297—dc23
                    2012036923

Printed in the United States of America

COVER DESIGN: Martin Hinze
COVER IMAGES: (*top*) Grand Mosque, Mecca, Saudi Arabia (photograph by Basil D. Soufi;
courtesy of Wikimedia Commons); (*bottom*) Mother Mosque of America, Cedar Rapids, Iowa
(photograph by Rifeldeas; courtesy of Wikimedia Commons)

References to Internet Web sites (URLs) were accurate at the time of writing. Neither the
author nor Columbia University Press is responsible for URLs that may have expired or changed
since the manuscript was prepared.

In memoriam

May Alley

(1908–2009)

CONTENTS

PREFACE

RELIGIONS, INCLUDING Islam, mean a great deal to individuals across the globe: they are perceived to give solace to the weak and the oppressed, comfort to the sick and the dying, and memories to the dead. Any book that seeks to introduce readers to a religion must accordingly respect this feature of the religion. In addition, the line between "insider" and "outsider" to the religion, which I discuss more fully in the introduction, is often a very fine one that must be crossed with care.

It is precisely because of these issues that many are either unused to or uncomfortable with speaking about religions using terms and categories normally relegated to explicating more mundane phenomena. Although the latter approach is increasingly becoming normative in introducing aspects of religions such as Judaism and Christianity (e.g., Second Temple Judaism, the historical Jesus), it is only just beginning to enter the "introduction to Islam" classroom. This book attempts to be a part of this process, but in a way that remains sensitive to possible tensions that emerge from such a discourse. Chapters weave both outsider and insider accounts of Islam together so as to appreciate Islam more fully as a historical force.

This book's goal is accordingly to reach some sort of middle ground between what Muslims believe and what certain trends in the academic study of religion tell us to attune ourselves to. The equilibrium required is a very delicate one.

Yet an introductory work that is perceived to be solely about including the traditionally occluded, although interesting, would not necessarily inform us about Islam's staying power. As a result, I have included chapters that deal with beliefs and practices. However, I attempt to show how these beliefs and practices are both historically conditioned and emerge—like all belief and practices—from various contestations and struggles that can be documented historically.

A Word on Sources

I try not to bombard readers with notes. When I do use them, it is to show some of the debates in the secondary literature or to show the source of a particular interpretation. At the end of each chapter, I include a section entitled "Suggestions for Further Reading." The books listed are the sources from which I derived most of my data and are the place to which the interested reader should go to inquire further into a particular topic. Unless otherwise noted, quotations from the Quran come from Alan Jones, trans., *The Quran* (Exeter, Eng.: Gibb Memorial Trust, 2007).

A Note on Transliteration

For better or worse, many scholarly books on religion tend to use diacritical marks to indicate how a word is pronounced in a particular language, especially if that language uses a different alphabet. This is how Islamicists or religionists tend to signal their scholarly bona fides to one another and to nonexperts. I debated whether to use such diacritics in this book and ultimately decided not to, for two reasons. First, I do not want to bombard the beginning reader with pages of unfamiliar diacritical marks on words that may already appear quite unfamiliar. Second, at this stage in technology, diacritics pose all sorts of problems for e-book formatting. For the sake of convenience and for the reader interested in diacritics, however, I have included them in the presentation of terms that appear in the glossary. Words that appear in bold in the text can be easily referenced in this glossary. I occasionally use the ayn (ʿ) and hamza (ʾ) in words. I do this not out of philological precision, but because this is the way that such names and words (e.g., Shiʿi, taʾwil) usually appear.

A Note on Dates

Dating can also pose a host of problems because Muslims use a different system that marks the passing of time, one that revolves around the importance of the hijra, or "exodus," of Muhammad and his earliest followers to Medina (for details, see chapter 2). For the sake of convenience, I have used the Gregorian calendar but reduced it to the Common Era (B.C.E./ C.E.), which is familiar to Western audiences.

ACKNOWLEDGMENTS

IT IS a difficult task to acknowledge the many intellectual debts I owe for a work in which I have involved myself on and off for more than two decades, but I can try. Earle H. Waugh first exposed me to the academic study of Islam when I was a young undergraduate at the University of Alberta. Little did I imagine that his "Introduction to Islam" in the fall and "Introduction to the Quran" in the winter of 1990 would lead me to devote my intellectual life to Islamicate studies. I now find myself in the uncanny position of producing the present volume as a way to introduce a new generation of young minds to this living and dynamic tradition. To my other gifted teachers at the University of Alberta—Ehud Ben Zvi, Francis Landy, and the late Manabu Waida, I am also grateful. They set the stage for what has continued to be a lifetime of learning and intellectual inquisitiveness.

I also thank my other teachers, all of whom taught me much about Islam over the years: Scott C. Alexander, John T. Walbridge, Salman al-Ani, and Suzanne Stetkevych. Although I doubt they would agree with everything that appears in these pages, I do hope they realize what an indelible intellectual mark they have left on me.

In the other direction, I thank the students I have taught over the years. I have continually tested many of the ideas here on them, and many have risen to the challenge. Teaching undergraduate students is truly one of the joys of this great profession.

I also have a large obligation to thank many of my professional colleagues who have either given me encouragement or commented on various parts of this book. I am indebted to Linda S. Adams, Herb Berg, Daniel J. Borsay, Arthur Franklin, Khaleel Mohammed, Russell T. McCutcheon, Martin Nguyen, David Powers, Paul Powers, Steven E. Sidebotham, Erin Stiles, David Valeta, Mark Wagner, and Peter Matthews Wright. I also thank Wendy Lochner, my editor at Columbia University Press, for supporting and believing in this project, and Annie Barva for the care with which she copyedited the entire manuscript.

Finally, I thank my family. My parents, William and Sadie Hughes, have always supported what I have done, even if they did not always understand it. My wife, Jennifer, and my children, Rebecca and Gabriel, continue to inspire me. Last, but not least, I have dedicated this book to my grandmother, May Alley, because her open-mindedness and love made me a better human being. I miss her dearly.

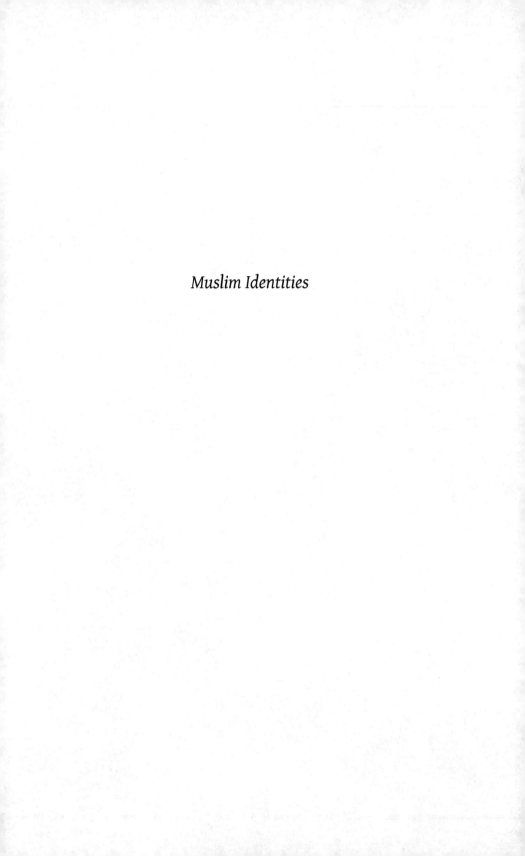

Muslim Identities

INTRODUCTION

Religious Studies and the Academic Study of Islam

THIS BOOK steers a middle path between theological introductions to Islam and works that seek to undermine the religion. Although the latter are rarely, if ever, used in the college classroom, they play a large role in shaping public discourses about what Islam is or, perhaps better, is supposed to be. Their unflattering portrayals conflate Islam and violence or Muslims and terrorists and, as a result, overlook centuries of diversity within the tradition in order to score a political point in the present. The results are both unfair and tremendously inaccurate.

The theological approach is also problematic. Often used in classrooms to introduce the religion of Islam, this approach tends to recycle the basic mythic narratives of the tradition, treating them as if they were historical as opposed to later religious accounts. We are encouraged to appreciate the religion without asking overly critical questions of how it came to be or how it subsequently developed in later centuries in response to various historical, intellectual, and cultural stimuli. The emphasis, in other words, is on a description of the religion and not necessarily on an analysis of it.

This volume maneuvers between the overly critical approach and the apologetic approach, with an eye toward introducing students to the study of Islam in a way that tries to be consistently historical, sociological, and literary rather than theological. Written from the subdisciplinary perspective within religious studies that questions traditional terms and concepts, it also seeks to open up our understanding of Islam across the centuries by using the findings, debates, and methodologies of cognate disciplines, such as archaeology, history, and Near Eastern studies.

September 11 and the Quest for a Normative Islam

Since September 11, 2001, many have called on scholars of Islam to explain the religion in ways that are at odds with what motivated the men who flew planes into the World Trade Center in New York City and the Pentagon in Washington, D.C. This undertaking has been driven by the most noble of intentions that have refused to vilify an entire religion for the actions of a few. However, there is always a danger in defining an "authentic" (or, alternatively, "real" or "essential") Islam at the expense of various "inauthentic" (or "fake") representations. In any such attempt, we must always ask ourselves: Who decides what criteria to use, and what gets to count as a true (or false) expression of faith?

If Islamicists—that is, those of us who study Islam academically—and many believing Muslims are eager to define what constitutes Islam, individuals who are highly critical of this religion have been equally quick to do the same from their own perspective. Yet if the former seek to reveal an Islam that is "just like us" (e.g., liberal, democratic), the latter make Islam ominously synonymous with jihadism, Salafism, and the like. One's version of Islam is contingent on one's political and ideological persuasion. Muslims have been engaged in the process of ascertaining what Islam means or should mean since the seventh century. The overwhelming majority of historical sources that we possess are not objective accounts of what really happened, but attempts to establish various constructions of Muslim belief and practice as normative.

Today, the various sides in the struggle to interpret the *real* Islam—increasingly one of the theaters in the cultural wars in America and Europe—selectively pick and choose their data and subsequently filter these data through the prism of the Islam they desire to create. Liberal Muslims construct a liberal Islam;[1] persons highly critical of Islam create an Islam at odds with the West;[2] individuals who seek a pluralistic America or Europe construct an Islam that fits effortlessly into their agenda;[3] and those who reject such pluralism find no problem imagining an Islam that both is opposed to and seeks to undermine the values of the West.[4]

Yet all these Islams do exist. The goal of this book is not to choose one and hold it up as normative, thereby creating a model against which rival Islams are judged. The struggle to define the *real* Islam is not just a modern phenomenon carried out by Western interpreters of the religion. It is a phenomenon that dates back to the earliest sources of the tradition as various groups struggled to understand Muhammad and his message in the light of various legal, religious, and intellectual paradigms that they themselves both inherited and created.

These twin notions of inheritance and creation—in addition to the manifold ways that they are configured as Muslim actors try to make sense of their social worlds—reside at the heart of this book. Inheritance implies the passing down of property or, in this case, ideas to later generations. It would be a mistake, however, to assume that these ideas are simply handed down and not thought about, adapted, or contested by later generations. Creation comes into play in inheritance: creation is the action that enables subsequent generations to shape that which is inherited in their own image and according to their own needs. The result of this twofold process is the formation of various Muslim identities.

This process is certainly not simple, wherein one size fits all. There are often manifold ways to understand or interpret a religious inheritance, for lack of a better term. The memory of the way things were can often be distorted by the desires of the present. The past studied disinterestedly as history and the past as a theological category do not always correspond to each other. Adding to the complexity is the fact that different groups, even within the same religion, understand the past and its teachings in different ways that are often dependent on their own concerns. So even though students may take a class in religious studies to learn about the beliefs and practices of a particular religion, they should be aware that what constitutes a religion's contents is neither synchronically (at a particular time) nor diachronically (through time) stable. This is why the historical record is so important: it reveals the creative interplay between inheritance and creation. Historical analysis, far from imposing another disciplinary framework on religious data, functions as an important antidote to those who want to claim that Islam (or any religion) is monolithic or that all Muslims (or practitioners of any religion)—past, present, and future—speak with one voice.

Before we examine the creative energies that take place on or around the intersection of inheritance and creation, it might be worthwhile to make a distinction between religious studies (also called the "academic study of religion") and theology. The academic approach to religion is not the same thing as the theological presentation of a religion.[5] Whereas theology sets out to explain religion using terms and categories drawn from the religion itself, the academic study of religion ideally attempts to avoid theology's truth claims and seeks to employ terms and categories derived from other academic disciplines (such as history and sociology). Theology is often done by and for believers; however, nonbelievers or even those from a different religion often teach the academic study of religion to students who come from various religious and nonreligious backgrounds. And whereas theology is usually undertaken, studied, and taught at seminaries associated with a particular faith tradition that necessarily accepts the larger mythic presentation of the religion, religious studies is taught at secular universities and—again ideally, but not always practically—seeks to credit as historical evidence only that which conforms with the laws of nature or with human experience.

When we study a religion academically from the perspective of religious studies, we begin to see something of its diversity across both history and geography. Core doctrines and teachings connect these diverse expressions under a loose canopy that for the sake of convenience we call "Islam" or "Judaism" or "Buddhism." However, it is incumbent upon us, as students of a particular religion, to be aware not only of this diversity, but also of the various legal, political, cultural, and intellectual factors that create and flow from such diversity. In this regard, religions do not exist in hermetically sealed containers that move effortlessly through time, space, and place. On the contrary, they are actively shaped, reshaped, performed, and contested by various historical actors.

The Insider-Outsider Debate

The central question in the academic study of religion is how to understand properly the various texts, actions, behaviors, rituals, and other factors that are described as "religious. The professional religionist is presented with a great deal of religious "data" and must decide how to explain them, interpret them, and ultimately classify them. This decision-making process gives way to a fairly vociferous and potentially healthy debate known as the "insider–outsider debate."

An insider approach—or, alternatively, the emic approach—is one that tries to understand religion from the perspective of religious practitioners. It involves looking at religious texts and religious rituals in order to find out their significance for practitioners and then to describe their contents and performances to others. Many who privilege the insider perspective believe that there is something unique about religion and religious experience that can never be reduced to something else (e.g., culture, society, politics) or explained away. The insider approach represents, in sum, the effort to understand religious thought and behavior primarily from religious persons' point of view.

Inside

The outsider perspective—or, alternatively, the etic approach—is one that refuses to explain religion using the categories and terms of reference that religious people use. It therefore attempts to import categories from the outside in an attempt to interpret or explain religious data. This process can be reductionist; witness Sigmund Freud's desire to "reduce" religion to a psychological function and explain it using the language of psychology or Emile Durkheim's reduction of religion to social processes. This approach tends to question the very appropriateness of the word "religion," preferring instead to see it as a "Western" imposition. Rather than regard religion as something internal to the individual, it prefers to regard religion as a human creation, the site of various contestations and collaborations over ideas and terms that have been signified as divine or transcendent.

Outside

Any attempt to understand religions must necessarily employ both approaches. That is, one must try to give an account of a religion that practitioners recognize on some level, but at the same time one must also endeavor to interpret religious data using the tools and categories of other humanist disciplines. The latter endeavor sometimes causes problems for those who are religious because they no longer recognize themselves or their concerns in such analyses. At the same time, however, we should be careful of assuming that insiders are somehow rendered incompetent to function as scholars of their own tradition. Although insiders of any religious tradition carry a difficult burden when it comes to explaining their own religion in a manner that avoids apologetics, the academic study of religion encourages us to avoid theology in favor of disinterested investigation.

Critics Versus Caretakers

The insider–outsider debate is connected to a related issue in the academic study of religion: the debate between "critics" and "caretakers." There has long been a fairly vociferous quarrel concerning the religionist's job. Is it to describe other religions in order to evoke better understanding of the multicultural, multiethnic, and multireligious world we inhabit? Or is it to examine the ways that religions are invoked to uphold particular ideologies? Are religionists supposed to be "critics" of religion, whose purpose is to undermine the truth claims of religious practitioners by investigating topics in ways that are considered disrespectful or insensitive? Or is it their goal to be "caretakers" by providing another venue for religious individuals to talk to one another and to people who follow other religions?[6]

This debate still rages in the academic study of religion. As in the debate between insiders and outsiders, it is again necessary to take a perspective that combines both approaches. If we are simply critics of religion, we lose sight of how religion functions in the lives of its practitioners. However, if we are only caretakers, we cease to be scholars and are but facilitators of interfaith dialogue. An approach to religion in general and to specific religions in particular must therefore combine the caretaker's sensitivity with the critic's analytic rigor.

The "Authenticity Debate" in Islamic Studies

Both of these debates unsurprisingly play out in the academic study of Islam. Perhaps nowhere is this more evident than in the so-called authenticity debate, the focus of much of part I. This debate concerns how we are to treat the earliest textual sources of Islam. In this regard, the study of all aspects of Islamic origins (from the composition of the Quran and the hadith to the development of law and jurisprudence) is currently at a scholarly impasse.[7] It is important to note, however, that this debate is not simply a matter of Muslim and non-Muslim scholars arguing over the veracity of these sources.

At least three different perspectives are embodied in this debate. The first contends that even though the earliest sources of Islam may come from a later period, they nonetheless represent reasonably reliable accounts concerning the matters on which they comment or describe. For example, the biography (*sira*) of Muhammad, which dates at the very earliest to a couple of generations after his death, is held up as a reliable account of Muhammad's life and times. The **hadith** (the sayings of Muhammad) are accordingly considered to represent authentic accounts of the earliest period. Many scholars have found ways, both constructively and rigorously, to use these relatively later sources to write the history of the second and even first century of Islam.[8]

Another perspective contends that the Muslim historical record of the first two centuries is problematic. The social and political upheavals associated with the rapid spread of Islam fatally compromise the earliest sources, according to such scholars. These sources, according to this position, are written so much after the fact and with distinct ideological or political agendas that they provide us with very little that is reliable with which to re-create the period they purport to describe.[9] Some of these individuals accordingly go to other sources (e.g., non-Muslim accounts, numismatics, archaeology) to try to re-create the earliest period, whereas others continue to rely on the early sources, but do so very skeptically.

The third perspective acknowledges the problems involved with the early sources but tries to solve them using form and source criticism, both of which seek to determine the original form and historical context of a particular text. For example, scholars employing such methods might try to show how early texts may exist embedded in later edited and compounded materials. These early texts can be isolated and removed from the later texts that were written by groups in an ascendant position.[10]

This book is written from the general standpoint that we should approach Islam as sensitive critics and outsiders, which necessarily implies taking a more critical approach toward the early Islamic sources. We should not believe that books fall from heaven, that God exists as an actor in history, or that one set of beliefs is of greater value than any other. Although it is certainly important to examine what Muslims believe, it is also important to realize that such beliefs—like any set of beliefs—are not timeless but take place in history as responses to various stimuli. Taking someone's belief seriously need not always be tantamount to agreeing with everything that person says about his or her religion. Islam is a major religious civilization and, like all such civilizations, includes within itself the noble and the base, the virtuous and the bloody.

Identity Formations

Recent years have witnessed extensive examination of the ways in which group identity is both formed and passed on. This work returns us to the twin notions of inheritance and creation. Instead of regarding any identity—for example, Muslim, Buddhist, or American—as inherited, recent scholarship has attuned us to think about the ways in which that identity is actively created or produced in response to changing social conditions. We should accordingly be cautious of using an ahistorical model of the past as something uniform, in which pristine and clear meanings are simply handed down through the ages until they arrive in the present. Some scholars argue that the very idea of a "stable past" is often a later invention used to serve a particular agenda.[11] Thus, instead of regarding identity as something passive and inherited, we ought to focus on how it has been actively created.

In 1983, Benedict Anderson, a professor of international studies, published the influential book *Imagined Communities*, in which he argued that communities—he had in mind nations, but we can just as easily say religions—are socially constructed or imagined by the people who perceive themselves as part of that group.[12] Because all the members of a nation or a religion lack face-to-face interaction, they must hold in their minds a mental image of their affinity. Through shared symbols and texts, groups are able to imagine themselves as belonging to a community that is much larger than they would otherwise realize. This belonging, in turn, is predicated on perceived borders that distinguish each community from other communities—often other nations or religions. At around the same time, Pierre Bourdieu, a French theorist, argued that how groups imagine themselves is based on a set of criteria that people within these groups internalize at a young age. Taste, he claims, is not—as we would think—an innate disposition, but something constructed by one's social group.[13] People from different classes, for example, are habituated to like certain foods and not others. This social construction of taste and related judgments (what smells good or bad, concepts of beauty) further aids the construction of social identity and group belonging. Another French theorist, the anthropologist Jean-François Bayart, reinforces the notion that identities are fluid and constantly changing in response to numerous political and cultural changes.[14] We must be sensitive to this notion whenever we want to speak of a particular culture—for example, "French culture" or "American culture."

Many of these discussions are highly technical, and their intricacies need not concern us here. I mention them briefly, however, to call attention to modern discussions that inform my understanding of identity formation and to entice the interested reader to pursue them. One thing worth noting is that these theorists and others agree that we cannot take as given traditional models that assume identity is something handed down to us from our ancestors to be passively accepted. Rather, identity is something that was and is actively constructed in response to various needs, and these constructions derive their potency from being projected onto the past, where they are thought to exist in a pure form.

Islam and Muslim Identities

How does this potentially technical discussion of communities and the construction of culture contribute to this book's subject matter—Muslim identities? For one thing, it teaches us that there is no one uniform way to understand Islam. There exist many types of Muslim groups or communities, all of whom have constructed identities for themselves based on their particular understanding of the tradition, which they subsequently deem as the best or the most authentic. As theorists such as Anderson, Bourdieu, and Bayart warn us, such identities—like all identities—represent responses to certain political, social, and intellectual needs. We should thus be cautious of upholding one particular Muslim identity as the most authoritative. When I use the term "Muslim identities," then, I use it primarily to refer to the various understandings of Islam that have existed and continue to exist throughout the course of Islamic history. The word "identity" alerts us to the fact that these understandings are actively constructed based on what the past was and should be, and the plural shows us that there is no one authoritative way to go about this construction. Even within one particular Muslim identity formation—for example, Sunni Islam—there exists much diachronic and synchronic variety.

As noted earlier, inheritance and its creative use in forming religious identity are constitutive features of religion. The past—or, perhaps better, the memory of the past—provides a basic map against which various interpretations of the present are charted and understood. This act of imagination or interpretation creates various religious identities, which include a variety of political, social, gendered, economic, and intellectual forces. If we ignore these forces and simply assume that religious identity is strictly "religious" and inherited, we risk overlooking how and why such identities form. We thus risk assuming that all Muslims believe the same things or that certain forms of Islam are somehow more authentic than others. The use of words such as "authenticity" should alert us that a value judgment is taking place. For example, one never talks about "authentic" Italian food in Italy, but only outside it when we are nostalgic for a particular way of cooking.

Muslim identities are shaped by a host of factors that are dependent on various contexts. It accordingly becomes problematic to speak of a, let alone the, "Muslim identity" (or "Jewish identity" or any other). For this reason, it is more appropriate to speak of an overlapping set of Islams that run the gamut from the mystical to the militant or from the so-called orthodox to the so-called heterodox. Each of these Islams, moreover, claims to offer the correct interpretation of Islam, the Islam that it imagines to be taught by the prophet Muhammad.

These debates over the teachings of Muhammad are certainly not a modern phenomenon. Since Muhammad's death, all movements, sectarian divisions, and the like have made appeals to his message, including the proper way to interpret it. These interpretations include everything from what we today might call (but not unproblematically) the liberal to the literalist. To make the claim that one Islam gets it "right" would be to choose one mode of reading or method of interpretation over others.

As we shall see throughout this volume, Muslims—like any set of religious practitioners—rarely agree on specific matters (e.g., the role of women, the reading of a particular verse, the construction of religious authority). Not only have Muslims believed many different and often contradictory things across history, but there also exist different types of Muslims—Sunnis, Twelver Shiʿis, Sufis, Ismaʿilis, Ahmadis, and so on. How or why should we assume that all these Muslims believe the same things or practice their religion in the same way?

Although on a theoretical level we should not assume that identities are stable throughout history, we can make the practical point that certain Muslim beliefs and practices (e.g., prayer, pilgrimage) have existed throughout the ages. However, we must be aware that numerous actors in various times and places have interpreted and do interpret such beliefs and practices differently. In this regard, Islam—like any other religion or social formation—is both inherited and actively created.

The advantage of an approach that focuses on multiple identities is that it prevents us from reifying Islam or making it into something that it is not. Part 1, for instance, points to the Jewish–Arab tribes, Christian–Arab tribes, and polytheist–Arab tribes that existed at the time of Muhammad. "Arab" identity, in other words, was anything but stable or uniform. An appreciation of this fact prevents us from assuming that modern categories (and the intellectual baggage they carry) such as religion, race, and ethnicity worked in seventh-century Arabia as they do today. Part II charts the various Islams that emerged as Muhammad's message moved beyond the Arabian Peninsula—their historical contexts, doctrinal developments, and attempts to channel that message in its earliest forms. Part III explores some of the manifold rituals, practices, and ideas that many Muslims have believed and performed both in the past and in the present. Finally, part IV examines and tries to classify the complexity associated with Islam—or, better, "Islams"—in the modern world.

Although behind my invocation of the term "Muslim identities" is the complex construction of community, culture, and identity mentioned in the previous section, I do not want to bog down the introductory reader. When I use this term, I do so primarily to call attention to the complexity of Islam as a social formation and the ways in which inheritance and creation contribute to this process of imagining different Islams. Although I try to use Muslim identity formations as the thread that weaves throughout the book, I well realize that this text is an introductory one. And although every chapter does not put identity at the forefront, I trust the reader will be able to appreciate that the breadth and depth of Islam, from its origins in the seventh century until today, is based on particular groups' various interpretations of what they believe to be the true meaning of Muhammad's message.

On Diversity

Any attempt to understand Islam must involve an appreciation of both the religious teachings and the diverse cultural forms of the tradition. Islam today exists on the Arabian Peninsula as well as in Africa, South Asia, Europe, the Mediterranean basin, and the Americas. How Islam arrived in all these diverse places is a historical question. But how Islam is understood and practiced in all these places is a cultural one.

One of the greatest difficulties within religious studies is how to present something of religious practitioners' lived experiences. Perhaps this difficulty stems from the theoretical and textual assumptions that played such a formative role in the establishment of this discipline in the nineteenth and early twentieth centuries. The formation of the discipline in these early years tended to focus on the theological and philosophical texts at the expense of religious practitioners. These texts, however, were often the product of male elites and, as such, they provide insight into only one aspect of religion. They tell us very little of, for example, gender, cultural, or ritual diversity. One of the challenges here is to account for the theological and religious development of the religion, on the one hand, and for the religious lives and practices of real people, on the other.

Yet the movement of Islam into new places and the role of non-Arabs in changing its demographics and social dynamics are not just modern phenomena. They played a crucial role in the first three centuries of Islamic history in the shift from a primarily Arabic to an increasingly diverse community. The needs of non-Arab converts were crucial in shaping Islamic beliefs and practices. Non-Arabs' need to figure out how to be Muslim, for example, shaped the reception of the Quran, the emergence of Islamic law, and theology. This book attempts to include these synchronic and diachronic diversities in the main Islamic narrative.

NOTES

1. See, for example, the collection of essays in Omid Safi, ed., *Progressive Muslims: On Justice, Gender, and Pluralism* (Oxford: Oneworld, 2003).

2. For example, Daniel Pipes, *Militant Islam Reaches America* (New York: Norton, 2003).

3. For example, Tariq Ramadan, *Western Muslims and the Future of Islam* (New York: Oxford University Press, 2004).

4. For example, Samuel P. Huntington, *The Clash of Civilizations and the Remaking of World Order*, 1st paperback ed. (New York: Simon and Schuster, 2003).

5. The line between the two disciplines can admittedly be a very fine one. See, for example, Russell T. McCutcheon, *Manufacturing Religion: The Discourse on Sui Generis Religion and the Politics of Nostalgia* (New York: Oxford University Press, 1997). For an attempt to make the line firmer, see Bruce Lincoln, "Theses on Method," *Method and Theory in the Study of Religion* 8, no. 3 (1996): 225–227.

6. On the problems more broadly, see Russell T. McCutcheon, *Critics Not Caretakers: Redescribing the Public Study of Religion* (Albany: State University of New York Press, 2001), 3–20.

7. On the contours of the "debate," see Herbert Berg, *The Development of Exegesis in Early Islam: The Authenticity of Muslim Literature from the Formative Period* (London: Curzon, 2000), 6–64.

8. Among these scholars and their work are W. Montgomery Watt, *Muhammad at Mecca* (Oxford: Clarendon Press, 1953); Fred Donner, *Narratives of Islamic Origins: The Beginnings of Islamic Historical Writing* (Princeton, N.J.: Darwin Press, 1998), and *Muhammad and the Believers: At the Origins of Islam* (Cambridge, Mass.: Harvard University Press, 2010); and Wael Hallaq, *The Origins and Evolution of Islamic Law* (Cambridge: Cambridge University Press, 2005).

9. A representative sample of scholars who take this position includes John E. Wansbrough, *The Sectarian Milieu: Content and Composition of Islamic Salvation History* (Oxford: Oxford University Press, 1977), and *Quranic Studies: Sources and Methods of Scriptural Interpretation* (Oxford: Oxford University Press, 1977); Patricia Crone, *Meccan Trade and the Rise of Islam* (Princeton, N.J.: Princeton University Press, 1987); Patricia Crone and Michael Cook, *Hagarism: The Making of the Islamic World* (Cambridge: Cambridge University Press, 1979); Gerald R. Hawting, *The Idea of Idolatry and the Rise of Islam: From Polemic to History* (Cambridge: Cambridge University Press, 1999); and Yehuda D. Nevo and Judith Koren, *Crossroads to Islam: The Origins of the Arab Religion and the Arab State* (Amherst, N.Y.: Prometheus, 2003).

10. For examples of works with this perspective, see Harald Motzki, ed., *The Biography of Muhammad: The Issue of the Sources* (Leiden: Brill, 2000); and David Powers, *Muhammad Is Not the Father of Any of Your Men: The Making of the Last Prophet* (Philadelphia: University of Pennsylvania Press, 2009).

11. See, for example, Robert Darnton, *George Washington's False Teeth: An Unconventional Guide to the Eighteenth Century* (New York: Norton, 2003), 60–67.

12. Benedict Anderson, *Imagined Communities: Reflections on the Origins and Spread of Nationalism*, rev. ed. (London: Verso, 2006), esp. 1–6.

13. Pierre Bourdieu, *Distinction: A Social Critique of the Judgment of Taste*, trans. Richard Nice (Cambridge, Mass.: Harvard University Press, 1984).

14. Jean-François Bayart, *The Illusion of Cultural Identity*, trans. Steven Rendall, Janet Roitman, Cynthia Schoch, and Jonathan Derrick (Chicago: University of Chicago Press, 2005).

PART I

ORIGINS

1

SETTING THE STAGE

Pre-Islamic Arabia

P UTTING ANY religion's origins under the microscope is an endeavor fraught with numerous tensions. Are we supposed to believe as true the stories that religious people tell themselves? Or do we attempt to disprove such stories using categories drawn from the secular sciences? The discrepancy between these two approaches symbolizes the tensions inherent to the modern study of religion, representing another variation on the classic theme of the apparent incommensurability between faith and reason. Outsiders usually dismiss religious accounts of origins as "mythic" and of little historical value. Insiders, by contrast, read the exact same stories but regard them as truthful accounts grounded in the historical record.

According to the earliest Muslim accounts—accounts written at least 150 years after the times on which they purport to comment—Islam represents the restoration of an original **monotheism** on the Arabian Peninsula. According to this account, this restoration was the result of Muhammad's fight against **polytheism** and forgetfulness: the Arabs are said to have forgotten their original monotheistic impulse and to have begun to worship other gods. The advent of Islam accordingly represents the triumph of universalism over particularism, good over bad, justice over injustice, and so on.

Like all accounts of religious origins, the rise of Islam is predicated on a sharp disjuncture from its immediate environment. This fledgling Islam, like all new religious movements, had to find a balance between a connection to the distant past, on the one hand, and a shattering of the immediate past, on the other. The former disarms the charge of innovation, and the latter shows the uniqueness of the new message. In the case of Islam, connections were made between Arabs and traditional monotheisms of the distant past supplied by Jews and Christians, and the shattering of the immediate past enabled Islam to differ from its immediate polytheistic context.

All of this, however, takes place against a murky backdrop in which memory and desire, fact and fiction, collide. Because all accounts of religious origins are written only after the fact, they are often filtered and imprecise, describing what should have happened instead of what actually did happen. Scholars of religion usually refer to such stories nonjudgmentally as "myths," or stories that people tell themselves to make sense of their worlds. The end result is that we often lack firm ground from which to perceive origins in any way except imprecisely. We must often take the same texts and narratives that insiders regard as historical and authoritative and subject them to different sorts of analysis.

Religions, like any social formation, do not appear fully formed. It is thus necessary to inquire into the larger contexts out of which religions emerge and against which they subsequently define themselves. As shown in this chapter, those people who formed Islam (whether Muhammad or the final redactors of the Quran or later legists) inherited a larger Near Eastern religious, cultural, and literary vocabulary that they shaped to fit their own needs and an emerging community's needs. Unfortunately, however, we know very little about what was inherited and what was new. Although this question is certainly of interest to us today, it most likely did not concern seventh- and eighth-century followers of Muhammad. As a result, it is very difficult to illuminate the relationship between the rise of Islam and the existence of various Judaisms, Christianities, and other religious forms that existed within the Red Sea basin just prior to the advent of Islam. The Quran, whose dating is not without its own set of problems, offers very little help in this regard.

A second problem that faces the scholar of Islamic origins is the history of Western polemical writings that deal with this subject. Since the medieval period, European scholars have often defined Islam negatively, making it into little more than a seventh-century invention and corruption of more "stable" monotheisms (such as Judaism and Christianity; note that these names are always put in the singular and rarely, if ever, put in the pluralized forms "Judaisms" and "Christianities"). There exists, in other words, a lengthy history of non-Muslims that speaks about Islamic origins as a way to undermine the religion. The alternative, however, is not necessarily more satisfying because it has the tendency to take later Muslim theological accounts concerning the rise of Islam at face value. These later accounts are subsequently projected back onto the earliest period, even though it is a period about which we have very little evidence, and then assumed to provide accurate historical accounts of the period in question.[1]

Although archaeological activity certainly takes place within the Red Sea basin, including the Arabian Peninsula, we still know very little about the early rise of and activity in Mecca (entry to which is forbidden to non-Muslims) and Medina, the two epicenters of Islam's earliest formation. In addition, we possess very few written records that provide us with eyewitness accounts. Some scholars have attempted to use only non-Islamic sources (including inscriptions and coins) to reconstruct the rise of Islam.[2] Despite such attempts, our ability to chart and explain Islamic origins must necessarily be speculative and uncertain.

This chapter has two aims. First, it attempts to provide a historical snapshot of what little we know about pre-Islamic Arabia. What, for instance, *might* the Red Sea basin in general and the Arabian Peninsula in particular have looked like socially, culturally, economically, and religiously? The following problem is indicative of the difficulties in creating a snapshot of pre-Islamic Arabia. We certainly know that Jews (or, perhaps more accurately, Jewish–Arab tribes) and Christians (again, more accurately, Christian–Arab tribes) inhabited parts of Arabia; however, we know very little of these groups' belief structures and religious contours. We should avoid assuming that race and ethnicity (e.g., Jew or Arab) were mutually exclusive cultural markers in the periods before, during, and even immediately after the formative period of Muhammad's movement. There is also a danger of imposing our own theological differences—for example, among Christian, Jew, pagan, and Muslim—on this period. If we look at all these categories as fluid and unstable, we might get a different appreciation and understanding of the period in which Islam arose.[3]

Not unlike most chapters in this book, this chapter offers two often contradictory accounts—insider and outsider accounts—that *attempt* to describe the emergence of various Islams in Arabia in the seventh century.

The insider account tells a narrative of Muhammad's response to the divine message and his skillful navigation of the Arabian tribes from the bonds of idolatry to the freedom of Islam. Muhammad's message, embodied in the Quran, was responsible for the rapid spread of Islam throughout the Mediterranean basin and beyond. The outsider or more skeptical approach, by contrast, argues that any account of origins must be based on historical, archaeological, and philological proof. The projection of later Islamic traditions, according to this approach, onto a period wherein we know next to nothing is largely an ideological project of later centuries and of limited historical value.

The final section of this chapter attempts a synthesis of the two accounts, showing how and why later Muslim thinkers projected various values onto the emergence of Islam.

Pre-Islamic Arabia

The customary presentation of pre-Islamic Arabia is based on a later Islamic myth of its isolation and separation from the larger empires of the area. This trope of a desert people wandering in darkness and receiving a divine message is certainly a common one in ancient Near Eastern religious cultures. However, if we assume the mythic trope as historical narrative, as is frequently done, we miss out on the active involvement of pre-Islamic Arabs and other tribes in these larger empires. It is certainly clear, for instance, that the peninsula functioned as an important nexus on a number of east–west and north–south trade routes.[4] Pre-Islamic Arabia did interact with the rest of the Middle East and did so increasingly as time progressed. The claim that Arabia was untouched by the major empires of the regions *and their religions* is, however, a potentially useful theological claim. The myth of pre-Islamic isolation served a number of functions. First, it allowed Islam to appear miraculously with Muhammad on the world stage. Second, it permitted Islam to emerge untouched by other monotheisms in the area, thereby protecting Islam from later charges that it and its scripture, the Quran, are copies of Jewish and Christian sources. Third, it signals the uniqueness of Muhammad's message that inspired the tribes of Arabia to take up monotheism. Finally, it contributes to the creation of a foundation narrative to rival the accounts of origins found in other religions, most notably various Judaisms and

Christianities, some of whose practitioners undoubtedly formed the core of Muhammad's early movement.

It is important to be aware that Arabia was not monolithic in terms of its cultural, religious, and material practices. It consisted of distinct geographical regions, each of which was settled by various peoples with their own cultural and religious traditions. Scholars who work in pre-Islamic Arabia tend to divide the region into three cultural regions: East Arabia (comprising modern-day Kuwait, Bahrain, Qatar, the eastern coast of Saudi Arabia, the Emirates, and Oman), South Arabia (roughly corresponding to modern-day Yemen), and North and Central Arabia (modern-day Saudi Arabia minus its eastern coast, the Sinai and Negev deserts, and parts of modern Jordan, Syria, and Iraq).[5] The earliest written sources from East Arabia date to roughly 2500 B.C.E., and those from the other regions to roughly 900 B.C.E. The Arabs made up only one group in this area, but they became the most successful, eventually absorbing all the other groups in the region.

The pre-Islamic Red Sea basin occupied a distinctive geographic location that in many ways functioned as a conduit between civilizations and continents. It witnessed the emergence of several civilizations, the relics of which are still evident today. One such civilization was that of the Nabateans, who created the city of Petra in modern-day Jordan (figure 1), one of the seven wonders of the ancient world. Other such Arabian civilizations prior to the fifth century C.E. include the Lakhmid kingdom in the North around the Euphrates River and the Himyar kingdom in the Southwest near Yemen.

The Arabian Peninsula existed between three major agricultural centers: Iraq, Syria, and Yemen. Each of these three lands were connected to what one historian calls "political hinterlands."[6] That is, if one traveled east, north, or south, one would soon come upon some of the major civilizations of late antiquity. In Iraq, for example, there existed the Sassanian Empire; just beyond Syria lay the Greek-speaking Byzantine Empire; and in Yemen there existed the Abyssinian Empire. Subsequent Islamic myths of isolation and separation to the contrary, Arabs seem to have been active participants in the various social, economic, cultural, and religious features of these diverse imperial powers.

Virtually all the inhabitants of pre-Islamic Arabia were members of a tribe, a mutual aid group connected to a larger notion of kinship. These tribes were composed of a hierarchy of overlapping loyalties largely determined by the closeness of kinship that ran from the nuclear family to the tribe and even, in principle at least, to the entire ethnic or linguistic group.

FIGURE 1 Facade of the Treasury, Petra, Jordan. (Photograph by Bernard Gagnon; courtesy of Wikimedia Commons)

Disputes were settled, interests pursued, and justice and order maintained by means of this organizational framework. Early inscriptions from South Arabia mention that tribes were also bound together by allegiance to the cult of their patron deity, in relation to whom they were designated "the children," and by loyalty to their king.[7]

These tribes possessed a strict code of honor that was based on *diyafa* (hospitality), which required that even one's enemy must be given shelter *tax for poor nospotiality* [handwritten]

and fed for some days. Generosity was a related virtue, and even today in many Bedouin societies gifts must be offered and cannot be declined. The community was also responsible for taking care of the poor in its midst, and in many of the tribes tithing (a form of tax) was mandatory. *Hamasa* (courage, bravery) was also closely linked to Bedouin honor, indicating the willingness to defend one's tribe for the purpose of tribal solidarity and heavily bound up with the concept of *muruwwa* (manliness). Although such features may well be pre-Islamic, it is worth noting that they might also be a part of the backward projection of later Muslim virtues onto the distant past.

richer had more connections [handwritten]

The integration of tribes was largely dependent on time, place, and wealth. The wealthier tribes, for example, had a network of clan chiefs and even a paramount (or head) chief who could coordinate tribal members for collective action. Proximity to and trade with the larger powers in the region further increased these paramount chiefs' power and prestige because larger powers often chose to work with them individually. Especially in the rich agricultural-based regions of South Arabia, fairly elaborate kingdoms arose, whereas poorer camel-herding nomadic tribes in the inner deserts tended to consist of little more than loose assemblages of local groups.[8]

Various tribes and tribal configurations existed throughout the peninsula and, depending on the time in question, were tributaries to larger groups located outside Arabia. It was not uncommon for many of these tribes to form various alliances with one another in the pursuit of common causes. There also existed several important towns throughout Arabia. For example, numerous pre-Islamic towns have been located and excavated in the modern kingdom of Saudi Arabia. These towns— for example, Qaryat al-Faw and Madain Saleh—were on important north–south trade routes linking the peninsula to the great economic and cultural centers of Mesopotamia, Syria, and Egypt. Pastoralists who subsequently became involved in trade largely settled these towns; archaeological evidence also links these towns to larger kingdoms in the area (e.g., Nabatea). There is also evidence that such towns were highly literate and had large marketplaces and religious shrines.

highly literate [handwritten]

The existence of such towns is significant because they reveal that Arabia, although largely desert, most certainly was not an isolated oasis. The Arabian Peninsula played an important role in trade; it was on the radar of the region's larger empires; and, most important for chapter 2, it had connections to other regional monotheisms.

Interactions certainly occurred between these towns and the region's larger empires. These empires tended to manipulate the tribes, which increasingly became sedentary in settlements or caravan towns. As the larger powers declined in the late antique period, such towns and the region's nomadic tribes began to reconfigure. Moreover, given the tribal nature of Arabian society, it was not uncommon for various intertribal feuds to emerge, most likely on account of relationships to the larger trade routes that intersected Arabia. This network of trade, feuds, and political struggles tended to "involve the whole of Arabia in a single political complex, if a rather incoherent one."[9]

Pre-Islamic Arabian Religions

The Red Sea basin was closely linked to both the Mediterranean and Mesopotamian worlds. As in those worlds, the major form of religious expression in the basin was polytheism, the belief in many gods and goddesses.[10] We know many of the names of the Arabs' tribal deities because the most common aim of inscriptions was to invoke them, praise them, or give thanks to them. Yet, as Robert Hoyland, a specialist in pre-Islamic Arabia, remarks, "Names do not tell us much, and the brevity of most of these texts makes it difficult for us to understand the nature and function of the gods or to comprehend what they meant to their worshippers."[11] Based on surviving inscriptions, it has been deduced that the main god was Athtar, who seems to have been related to the Ishtar cult in the northern part of Arabia. The cult of Athtar also appears to have been widespread throughout the region, albeit with various manifestations, as attested by inscriptions in various local shrines. One inscription has an individual thanking another god for "interceding on his behalf with Athtar."[12]

If Athtar was a remote deity, many other gods and goddesses were of significance to particular tribes. The popularity of these gods and goddesses seems to have been determined by both the tribe and the particular period in question.[13] From the Quran (e.g., 71:23), we are able to glean the existence of a number of others gods and goddesses, including al-Qaum (the god of war and of night), Wadd (the god of love and friendship), Nasr (the god of time), and Nuha (the sun goddess). Based on inscriptions from South Arabia, we also know that some of these gods functioned as patron deities to particular tribes: Wadd, for example, was the patron of the Mineans, Amm of the Qatabanians, and Sayin of the Hadramites.

In addition to naming deities, inscriptions also tell us of anonymous guardian spirits (*mndht*). They apparently offered protection to encampments, families, and individuals. Inscriptions from North Arabia speak of *ginnaye*, possibly related to the *jinn* mentioned in the Quran. Mention is also made of various malevolent beings and spirits.[14]

In the fourth century C.E., a number of South Arabian inscriptions increasingly began to speak of a monotheistic cult of the deity Rahmanan—the "Merciful One," "the Lord of heaven and earth." Scholars are unsure if this high god is related to the earlier polytheistic structure or a new development, perhaps connected to the increased prestige or importance of Jewish–Arab and Christian–Arab tribes within the peninsula. It is also difficult to determine whether Rahmanan is related to **Allah**, which in Arabic quite literally means "the God,"[15] or, perhaps more familiarly, "God." There is evidence that pre-Islamic Arabs believed in Allah as the high god in the pantheon who gave birth to three goddesses: Al-lat (the Goddess), Manat, and al-Uzza (see, for example, Quran 53:19–23), although no mention is made of a consort. According to some Nabatean inscriptions, however, Al-lat is identified as the consort of Allah.

The supreme cultural expression of Arabian tribal life, whether nomadic or town dwelling, was a highly cultivated body of poetic expression, which in subsequent generations would be referred to as "classical" Arabic. This poetry was highly stylized in terms of its themes, meter, and prosody, and its creators were often tribal spokespersons who received great patronage. Professional reciters recited new poems throughout the peninsula. In Mecca, which will play an important role in the formation of Muhammad's message, there seems to have been an annual poetry competition connected to pre-Islamic religious customs and rituals.[16] It was from this highly literary and poetic environment that the Quran emerged and against which it ultimately had to compete for listeners (see chapter 3).

Pre-Islamic Mecca

By the mid-sixth century B.C.E., there existed at least three major settlements in northern Arabia, along the southwestern coast that borders the Red Sea. The settlements in this area, known as the Hijaz, grew up around oases, or isolated areas of vegetation connected to a spring. In the center of the Hijaz was Yathrib, later renamed Medina. Around 250 miles (400 kilometers) south of Yathrib was the mountain city of Taif, northwest of which lay Mecca. Although the area around Mecca was completely barren, Mecca was the wealthiest of the three settlements, receiving abundant water via the Zamzam Well and occupying a position at the crossroads of a major caravan route.

Even before the rise of Islam, Mecca was an important economic and religious center in the Arabian Peninsula. According to later Muslim tradition, the **Ka'ba**, or "Cube," was originally created by Ibrahim (Abraham) on one of his visits to his son Ismail (Ishmael)—his son by the maidservant Hagar, who, in the Bible's mythic presentation, was subsequently ordered to leave his house after his wife, Sarah, gave birth to Isaac (figure 2). The Islamic tradition, however, remembers Hagar as one of the wives of Abraham. The ground on which the Ka'ba was built, according to Islamic memory, had previously been hallowed by Adam, the first man. It subsequently became a polytheistic shrine when later Arabs forgot its true purpose and began to set up idols to their tribal deities within.

This story interestingly presents Muhammad's message, something that was largely created and spread among town dwellers, as a nomadic story. This presentation may well be the result of the fact that later townsmen were, as Hoyland puts it, "strong on religion, but short on identity."[17] As the followers of Muhammad entered regions with lengthy and venerable religious traditions, they needed their own religious history and identity. They seem to have picked up on the idea—around at least since the time of the Jewish historian Josephus (ca. 37–100 C.E.)—that the Arabs were descendents of Ishmael. This idea enabled the early Muslims to fashion a religious pedigree for themselves. In terms of identity, these early Muslims turned to the nomadic Arabs, "who were short on religion, but strong on identity."

Because it is impossible to prove whether the biblical patriarchs actually existed, let alone visited Mecca and environs, it becomes necessary to look for other possible contexts regarding the origins of the Ka'ba. This task unfortunately proves to be difficult. Several informed guesses are possible. One is that this mythic story was undoubtedly facilitated by a shared

FIGURE 2 The Kaʿba, Mecca, Saudi Arabia. (Photograph by al-Fassam; courtesy of Wikimedia Commons)

cultural history that included a number of themes and motifs found, with different emphases and stresses, in cognate literatures such as the Hebrew Bible or the epic of Gilgamesh (an epic poem dating roughly to the seventh century B.C.E. from Mesopotamia). Related to this shared cultural history is the notion that the patriarchal origins of the shrine could well have provided subsequent generations of Arabs seeking to legitimate their religion with a monotheistic birthright and pedigree. In addition, earlier Greek and Roman authors speak of a fairly widespread cult of stones—both unshaped and carved into various idols—among Arab tribes. Even later Muslim authors comment on this cult and trace it back to the subsequent degeneracy of the tribes descended from Ismail. In its earliest incarnation, the Kaʿba might well have been connected to this type of worship. Early Muslim sources also mention the fact that there were several shrines, several Kaʿbas, round Mecca, which would have made the region and not just the city a religious center.

We can probably assume that historically Meccans, as a settled population, created and venerated gods at fixed shrines. Less transitory Bedouin probably carried their gods with them. The objects they venerated seem to have been stones, other animate and inanimate objects, and the sky—all of which were worshipped most likely because the gods were thought to reside in them.[18] These sacred stones and idols increasingly became fashioned as human likenesses, and by the time just prior to Muhammad they seem to have taken on distinctive names and perhaps even personalities.[19]

The harsh conditions of the Arabian Peninsula indicated a scarcity of resources, which meant a near-constant state of tension between the various tribes. Once a year, however, these tribes would declare a truce and converge on Mecca in an annual pilgrimage, or **hajj**. This pilgrimage, like the one that would later be resignified by Islam, was intended for religious reasons, to pay homage to the Kaʿba, wherein the tribes housed the idols of their deities, and to drink from the Zamzam Well. Poetry, an important part of Bedouin culture, was recited in competitions.[20] Moreover, this pantribal pilgrimage witnessed the arbitration of disputes, the resolution of debts, and the celebration of trade at various fairs. This annual event gave the tribes a sense of identity beyond the tribal unit and established Mecca as an important focus of the peninsula.

Monotheisms in Arabia

Given both the importance of the trade routes to Arabia and the fact that larger geopolitical forces surrounded Arabia, it is certainly unlikely, as previously noted, that the peninsula existed in a religious vacuum or was untouched by the existence of other imperial powers and their monotheisms. Not only were all the political hinterlands connected to monotheistic civilizations, but there is evidence of the existence of Jews, Christians, and Zoroastrians (followers of a monotheistic religion based on the teachings of Zoroaster, who lived in Persia in the sixth century B.C.E.) in Arabia well before the time of Muhammad. More important than asking whether other monotheisms existed in the area, the more accurate and pressing questions are: What were the contours and contents of these monotheisms? And, given the fluid ethnic and religious contexts of sixth- and seventh-century Arabia, is it even possible to assume that these monotheisms represent distinct markers of identity and difference for their adherents?

JUDAISMS

If we accept the historicity of the Arab sources on the existence of Jews in the Arabian Peninsula,[21] Jewish tribes arrived in the Hijaz in the aftermath of the destruction of the Second Temple by the Romans in 70 C.E. There is also clear evidence that by the end of the fourth century there existed a Jewish presence, which seems to have arrived there from Yemen. We also know that in the mid-fifth century C.E. one of the Yemeni kings adopted some form of Judaism as the official state religion. The significant presence of Judaism in Yemen lasted for centuries—long after it ceased to be the state cult. There was also an important Jewish community in Elephantine (on the Nile, part of the Red Sea basin), not to mention Jews in Alexandria. All these Jewish communities apparently had historical and political ties to Iran.

The Jews of Arabia were an integral part of this scene. The Constitution of Medina—a text attributed to Muhammad when he established a polity in Medina/Yathrib—names no less than seven Arab tribes of Jews, and there are other passing references to a house of study (*bayt al-midrash*) there.[22] Moreover, Muhammad Ibn Ishaq—one of Muhammad's later biographers, whom we meet in chapter 2—links the Jewish community of Yathrib to the Yemeni Jews, suggesting that both trade networks and cultural networks ran the length of the Red Sea basin and reached not only into Mesopotamia, but also to the Iranian plateau.

The existence of these Jewish tribes in Arabia apparently predate the codification of the Babylonian Talmud, one of the main documents of rabbinic Judaism, around 500 C.E. Although this codification occurred in the rabbinical academies of Babylonia, which were in relative close proximity to the area, it is unclear how much jurisdiction such academies would have had among Jews in the Red Sea basin. At the same time, however, it is important not to assume an orthodoxy of fixed and ascertainable Jewish identity and practice based on the rabbinic academies of Babylonia and then use this orthodoxy as the standard against which to judge the "authenticity" of Arabian Jewishness. The Talmud, as a product of late antiquity, further reveals the fluid and evolving nature of Judaism in this period.[23]

PRE-ISLAMIC ARABIAN MONOTHEISMS?
THE CASE OF THE *HUNAFA*

An overwhelming majority of scholars working on early Islam claims that the main impetus toward monotheism likely came from the existence of various Judaisms and Jewish-Arab tribes in the Hijaz, especially in Yathrib. However, early Islamic sources, including the Quran, make reference to another group of individuals referred to as *hunafa* (sing., *hanif*). These individuals—interestingly, never defined as a community—professed a monotheism that was neither Jewish nor Christian but was somehow regarded as loosely connected to the figure of Abraham.

It seems most likely, however, that this designation is not historical, but religious. With respect to the latter, it served several important functions. First, it provided a spiritual category in which to locate Muhammad. Making him into a *hanif*, neither Christian nor Jew—which would obviously taint his message—solved the equally unpalatable issue of his being a polytheist. Second, it contributed to Muhammad's mission as being the restoration of a primitive monotheistic cult that the Arabs of his day had largely forgotten.

CHRISTIANITIES

The same kinds of questions arise for the existence of Christianities in the Red Sea basin. If the period just before the rise of Muhammad was one in which rabbinic Judaism was being formulated in Babylonian academies, it was also a period in which the Catholic Church was defining itself and working out what would become "orthodox" belief and doctrine by weeding out what would subsequently become labeled "heretical" movements. Interestingly, all the main forms of Christianity in Arabia were forms of the religion that the church in western Europe deemed more heterodox.[24]

Monophysite Christianity appears to have been one of the more dominant strains of Christianity in the area. Monophysitism adopted the christological position that Jesus has only one nature (*mono* = one, *phusis* = nature), as opposed to the orthodox position adopted at the Council of Chalcedon (451 C.E.) that Jesus possesses two natures, one divine and one human. The other major form of Christianity in the area is Nestorianism, which holds that Jesus existed as two separate persons, the man Jesus and the divine Son of God, or Logos, rather than as a unified person.

The existence of Christian Arabs at the time before Muhammad raises all sorts of interesting questions regarding identity. What, for example, did it mean to be a Christian Arab at this time? Although these tribes may have identified with and even allied with larger Christian empires in the region, the heterodox and even heretical teachings that dominated in Arabia would certainly have limited such identification. Or, again, as we saw in the possible existence of Judaisms in the area, perhaps some form of Arab Christianity—along with other forms of (Arab) Judaism and (Arab) Zoroastrianism, in addition to other local cults—represented the fluidity of loyalties and practices out of which Muhammad's social movement emerged.[25] And, perhaps unlike those religious traditions (such as rabbinic Judaism or normative Christianity) who sought to impose on the tribes the orthodoxies, orthopraxies, and exclusive loyalties to one community or another, Muhammad's movement succeeded because in its formative stages it both appealed to and encouraged a variety of beliefs and practices.[26]

IRANIAN RELIGIONS

Iranian religions were also present in the peninsula. Zoroastrianisms—traditionally the national religion of Iran and the belief that good and evil come from distinct sources—seems to have been present in the area on account of a Sassanian military presence along the Persian Gulf and in South Arabia and on account of trade routes between the Hijaz and Iraq. It also seems that some Arabs converted to Zoroastrianism in the northeastern part of the peninsula. Several Zoroastrian temples were apparently constructed in Najd—whether Iranian colonists or Arab Zoroastrians were responsible for this building activity is unclear.

There is also some evidence for the existence of Manicheans in Arabia. Having its origins in the third century C.E., Manicheanism is also an Iranian religion that seems to have been heavily influenced by Gnosticism. Its cosmology documents the struggle between a good, spiritual world of light and an evil, material world of darkness. Several early sources indicate the presence of people professing *zandaqa*—that is, Manicheanism—in Mecca. Although this term is a loan word from Middle Persian, it later took on the connotation of "heretic." There also exist several Persian loanwords in the Quran—most notably *firdaws* (paradise)—that may well show the influence of Iranian religious thought on the Arabs at the time of Muhammad.

Later Muslim Accounts of Islamic Origins

According to accounts in later Muslim sources—which include the Quran; the hadith (sayings of Muhammad); the biography of Muhammad; *tafsir* (commentary), especially on the Quran; and other genres—the original religion of the Arabian Peninsula, indeed, the original religion of all humanity, was that of **islam**. The word *islam* means "to surrender"—that is, surrender to the will of God. The adjective **muslim**, deriving from the same root, means "one who surrenders." Arabic, like all Semitic languages, lacks capital letters, so one can theoretically and ostensibly submit to the will of God without being a capital M "Muslim." On this reading, although Muhammad or those who came after him brought capital I "Islam" to the Arabian tribes, *islam* has always existed—in some way, shape, or form—in the world. According to this model, everyone from Adam, the first man, to Ibrahim (Abraham), Musa (Moses), Dawud (David), Isa (Jesus), most of the prophets of the Hebrew Bible, and others were *muslims*. According to the Quran 3:67, for instance, Abraham is described in the following terms: "Abraham was not a Jew [*yahudi*] nor was he a Christian [*nasrani*]; he submitted his will to God [*muslim*] and he did not add gods to God."

The later Islamic tradition interpreted such passages to mean that even though Ibrahim may not have been a Muslim and did not practice Islam in the same way Muslims would after Muhammad, he—like all individuals who submitted his will to God—was nonetheless still a *muslim*.

Related to this is the concept of *fitra*, or one's innate submitting nature. According to Muslim tradition, all humans are born with a *fitra*, and it is what predisposes them toward *islam*. As this concept developed, it came to be understood that every human is born a *muslim* and only subsequently "judaized," "christianized," "hinduized," or something else by one's parents.

Perhaps because Muhammad's message spread so quickly in the years after his death, it immediately entered a large marketplace of religions that could claim much older pedigrees. Religions and religious practitioners tend to put pride of place on antiquity, so the concept of *fitra* could be employed to argue that Islam, rather than being the newest of religions, was in fact the most ancient—the *true* religion of the Hebrew prophets, Moses and Jesus.

The question now arises: If, according to the Islamic tradition, Islam is the original religion of humanity, why were many of the Arabian tribes polytheist? How, in other words, did Arabia largely become polytheist and idolatrous? The answer developed by Muslim theologians of the eighth century and beyond is that through time the tribes of Arabia subsequently forgot their original submitting natures and gradually began to worship idols and other deities. It would be up to one individual, an Arabic prophet, to restore the Arabs to their original *fitra*. This Arabic prophet, encountered in greater detail in chapter 2, was Muhammad. Later portrayed as an illiterate prophet, Muhammad was someone unschooled in these prior monotheisms, not tempted by traditional monotheisms, but who, like Abraham, left the religion of his forefathers in order to carve out new religious space for himself and for his followers.

The religion of pre-Islamic Arabia was monotheistic in the ancient past, but it gradually gave way to a period of chaos, which, again, the later theologians sharply constructed so as to juxtapose it against the newness of Muhammad's message. The time immediately preceding the advent of Muhammad was known as the *jahiliyya* (period of ignorance). Despite the fact that later Muslim sources claim a watertight border between the *jahiliyya* and Islam, that border was most likely anything but.[27] Borders, given their very nature, admit of porosity and therefore need to be policed. The unstated goal behind the construction of this border between *jahiliyya* and Islam seems to have been to create a genuine Muslim myth that could be configured in a way that was diametrically opposed to the ideals and imagination of pre-Islamic Arabia. For example, whereas the *jahiliyya* had poetry, Islam has the Quran; whereas the *jahiliyya* had idolatry and mythology, Islam possesses pure monotheism; whereas those living in the *jahiliyya* practiced female infanticide, Islam recognizes the positive role of women; and so on. The border between them, like all borders imposed retroactively, is more apparent than real. In fact, the presence of the *jahiliyya* clarifies that which Islam must be seen both as abrogating and as fulfilling. Without the *jahiliyya*, there could not be Islam. The goal should not necessarily be to show how the latter is distinct from the former, but how the former permeates and influences the latter.

Outsider and Skeptical Approaches to Islamic Origins

In the introduction, mention was made of the "authenticity debate" and, in particular, of how to treat the sources that deal with the formation of

Islam. A skeptical approach to these sources regards them as historically very problematic and as the attempts by later generations of Muslims to justify and legitimate their vision of what Islam should be. Such an approach questions all the "facts" recounted in this chapter. The result is a very different account of the emergence of Islam. This section provides an overview of some of these theories as a way to show the diversity of opinions and research on these sources.

The previous section recounted the basic account of Islam's rise that Muslim sources tell and that many Muslims take as true. This story represents the gradual movement from idolatry to monotheism, from forgetting to memory, from *islam* to *jahiliyya* to Islam. It is, however, a religious account and, like all religious accounts, should not necessarily be taken at face value. Like the myths of Moses's receiving the commandments on Sinai and the death and resurrection of Jesus, this account is how Muslims explain their faith. From the perspective of an outsider, however, it is nothing more (or less) than religious stories that do not accurately reflect the mundane record because those who wrote them did not necessarily claim to be creating such a record. Although speculative, the theories regarding the rise of Islam presented here nonetheless help us to think about it using different paradigms and other theoretical models.

Patricia Crone, for example, argues that it has always been assumed that Mecca at the time of Muhammad was the center of a far-flung international trading empire. She questions this assumption, arguing that the state of our knowledge about Meccan trade is so vague and the information provided by the sources so contradictory that any attempt at reconstruction is impossible. She further questions the assumption that Mecca lay close to the Incense Road, which she argues had largely shifted to the sea from overland routes. Moreover, the fact that Mecca is not mentioned in any non-Islamic sources leads her to conclude that it was not the center that later sources claimed it to be. Based on an analysis of sources and trade routes, she concludes that Mecca did not exist in its present location in southwestern Arabia, but in the Northwest. The implication of this theory is that it calls into question the entire narrative edifice on which scholars have constructed Islam.[28]

The late John Wansbrough has also argued—based on a survey of early Islamic manuscripts, including the Jewish and Christian imagery in the Quran—that the rise of Islam represented a version of a Judeo-Christian sect trying to spread in Arabia. As time evolved, he argues, Judeo-Christian scriptures (i.e., the Hebrew and Christian Bibles) were adapted to an Arab perspective and eventually mutated into what became known as the "Quran," a pastiche of sources cobbled together from various Arab tribes. Wansbrough argues even more extremely that the traditional history of Islam was ultimately a fabrication by later Muslims who desired to create a religious identity for themselves—presumably an identity independent of Judaism and Christianity. Within this context, he regards Muhammad as a literary trope or a literary creation to provide the Arab tribes with their own Arab version of the Judeo-Christian prophets.[29]

In another theoretical take on Islamic origins, Patricia Crone and Michael Cook disregard all Muslim sources as later projections and instead focus solely on what they consider to be more reliable non-Muslim historical, archaeological, and philological evidence. According to them, the followers of Muhammad—who claimed descent from Abraham through Hagar—emerged as a heretical branch of Jews intent on retaking Jerusalem from the Byzantine Empire. Fearing assimilation into normative Judaism, this group, which the authors call "Hagarenes,"[30] eventually decided to create their own religion. Driven by the need for an independent theological identity, the Hagarenes created a version of Abrahamic monotheism that included various elements of Judaism, Samaritanism (an early offshoot of Judaism), and Christianity and that eventually crystallized in the late eighth century as Islam. Like Judaism, this new religion possessed a scripture (the Quran as opposed to the Torah), a prophet (Muhammad as opposed to Moses), and a holy city next to a holy mountain (Mecca as opposed to Jerusalem).

One of the most extreme accounts of the origins of Islam presented in recent years may be found in the treatment by the Israeli archaeologists Yehuda Nevo and Judith Koren, who argue that there seems to be little archaeological, epigraphical, and historiographical evidence that Islam existed before the late eighth century (two hundred years later than is customarily presented as the time when Islam emerged). Based on such evidence, they claim that traditional narratives of Islam's emergence are later constructs that neither can be historically confirmed nor stand up to rigorous historical examination.[31] They further argue that the Arabs were pagan when they assumed power in the seventh century in the regions formerly ruled by the Byzantine Empire and that they created a simple monotheism based on the forms of Judaism and Christianity that they encountered in their newly occupied territories and only gradually developed that monotheism into an Arab religion, which culminated in Islam in the mid-eighth century.

Once again, these theories represent some of the more extreme accounts that attempt to provide a theoretical paradigm for the rise of Islam. Many other scholars or practitioners of the faith have criticized such theories as either ludicrous or hostile to Muslims. The evidence these scholars present is certainly not without its problems, and, as we have seen time and again, they must face the same lack of sources that all who deal with these issues encounter. Yet a theory that proposes the creativity and the task of inventing a cultural and religious identity in the face of rival monotheisms should not strike us as completely farfetched.

Islamic Origins: A Synthetic Approach

It is worth reiterating that we know very little about the origins of Islam. We have neither eyewitness accounts nor, as yet, holistic archaeological data. Most of what we do know does not emerge until the late eighth and early ninth centuries—roughly 150 to 200 years after the death of Muhammad—when Islamic records begin to appear. These records are interested in understanding Islam and in constructing an "orthodox" Islamic identity. They are, as such, what we would largely label as theological or insider accounts. So although they may tell us a great deal about the ways that Muslims represented the origins of their movement to themselves, they tell us precious little about what may actually have happened. This confusion between the representation of Islam's origin and the reality of that origin, of course, is no different from the confusion regarding the origins of any religious or sectarian movement. Accounts of Islamic origins, like the accounts of religious origins more generally, are largely projections by later groups attempting to read their own agendas into or onto the earliest period with an eye toward legitimation.

As a result, pre-Islamic Arabia up until the second Muslim century is a blank canvas on which later historians and theologians sketch various projections. They all, however, are precisely that: projections that at best can only imagine what happened.

In the final analysis, at least until a major manuscript or archaeological discovery appears, the most pressing question we can try to articulate and then answer is: How and why did early Muslims come to write their own history? It would seem that the Islamic historical tradition arose as a response to a variety of challenges facing the Islamic community during the first several centuries of its existence (eighth to tenth centuries C.E.). The narratives that they produced—biographies of Muhammad, the sayings of Muhammad, and so on—focused on certain themes of Islamic origins that they undoubtedly selected to legitimize particular aspects of the Islamic community and faith. These themes included the status of Muhammad as a prophet, the affirmation that the community to which they belonged was the direct descendant of the original community founded by the Prophet, Muslim hegemony over vast populations of non-Muslims in the rapidly growing Islamic Empire, and the articulation of different positions in the ongoing debate over political and religious leadership within the Islamic community itself.

But these developments came later. What we must be aware of at this point— what this chapter has tried to present—is the fluidity of identities, religions, and categories in the period immediately before and during the time of Muhammad. The populations of the Red Sea basin seem to have engaged in a variety of religious practices that we now associate with Christianities, Judaisms, Zoroastrianisms, and other local cults. Muhammad's religious movement apparently emerged from these overlapping and not necessarily mutually exclusive beliefs, loyalties, and practices. As long as Muhammad's movement conformed to a vague notion of monotheism, its inclusiveness achieved success.

NOTES

This chapter owes much to Peter Wright of Colorado College, who gave an earlier version of it a very judicious and careful reading. Although I acknowledge his comments in various notes, I also thank him here for his very helpful remarks.

1. This paragraph owes its formulation to comments by Peter Wright.

2. Most notably, Robert G. Hoyland, *Seeing Islam as Others Saw It: A Survey and Evaluation of Christian, Jewish, and Zoroastrian Writings on Early Islam* (Princeton, N.J.: Darwin Press, 1997). A more experimental attempt at using only non-Islamic sources may be found in Patricia Crone and Michael Cook, *Hagarism: The Making of the Islamic World* (Cambridge: Cambridge University Press, 1979).

3. This paragraph owes its formulation to Peter Wright.

4. For an archaeological and historical treatment of pre-Islamic Arabia, see Robert G. Hoyland, *Arabia and the Arabs: From the Bronze Age to the Coming of Islam* (London: Routledge, 2001), esp. 1–12.

5. Ibid., 11.

6. Marshall G. S. Hodgson, *The Venture of Islam: Conscience and History in a World Civilization*, vol. 1, *The Classical Age of Islam* (Chicago: University of Chicago Press, 1974), 151.

7. Hoyland, *Arabia and the Arabs*, 115.

8. This paragraph is based on ibid., 113–138.

9. Hodgson, *Classical Age of Islam*, 154.

10. For the existence and contours of religion in pre-Islamic Arabia, I have drawn on the following works: Gerald R. Hawting, *The Idea of Idolatry and the Rise of Islam: From Polemic to History* (Cambridge: Cambridge University Press, 1999), 20–44; Hoyt, *Arabia and the Arabs*, 139–166; Michael Lecker, *Muslims, Jews, and Pagans: Studies on Early Islamic Medina* (Leiden: Brill, 1995); and Tilman Seidensticker, "Sources for the History of Pre-Islamic Religion," in Angelika Neuwirth, Nicolai Sinai, and Michael Marx, eds., *The Qurān in Context: Historical and Literary Investigations in the Quranic Milieu* (Leiden: Brill, 2010), 293–322. It is also worth pointing out that these scholars are not in agreement when it comes to the "authenticity debate" mentioned in the introduction.

11. Hoyland, *Arabia and the Arabs*, 139–140.

12. Ibid., 140.

13. Joseph Heninger, "Pre-Islamic Bedouin Religion," in Merlin L. Swartz, ed., *Studies on Islam* (New York: Oxford University Press, 1981), 3–22. This study has been surpassed by Hoyland's *Arabia and the Arabs*.

14. Hoyland, *Arabia and the Arabs*, 145.

15. See the comments in H. A. R. Gibb, "Pre-Islamic Monotheism in Arabia," and W. Montgomery Watt, "Belief in a 'High God' in Pre-Islamic Mecca," both in F. E. Peters, ed., *The Arabs and Arabia on the Eve of Islam* (Aldershot, Eng.: Variorum, 1999), 295–306, 307–312.

16. On the notion that these poetry contests or at least certain aspects associated with them might be a later invention, see A. F. L. Beeston, "The Mu'allaqāt Problem," in A. F. L. Beeston, ed., *Arabic Literature to the End of the Umayyad Period* (Cambridge: Cambridge University Press, 1983), 111–113.

17. Hoyland, *Arabia and the Arabs*, 243.

18. See the comments in Ulf Oldenburg, "Above the Stars of El: El in Ancient South Arabian Religion," *Zeitschrift für die Altetestamentliche Wissenschaft* 82 (1970): 187–208.

19. For a much fuller discussion of these sacred stones and deities, see F. E. Peters, *Muhammad and the Origins of Islam* (Albany: State University of New York Press, 1994), 57–76.

20. For a selection of poems recited, see the translation in Michael A. Sells, *Desert Tracings: Six Classic Arabian Odes by 'Alqama, Shanfara, Labīd, 'Antara, al-A'sha, and Dhu al-Rumma* (Middletown, Conn.: Wesleyan University Press, 1989).

21. This sanguine approach toward the sources is utilized by scholars such as Michael Lecker and Gordon Newby. See in particular Michael Lecker, *The Banū Sulaym: A Contribution to the Study of Early Islam* (Jerusalem: Institute of Asian and African Studies, Hebrew University of Jerusalem, 1989), and *Muslims, Jews, and Pagans*; and Gordon D. Newby, *A History of the Jews of Arabia: From Ancient Times to Their Eclipse Under Islam* (Columbia: University of South Carolina Press, 1988).

22. See, for example, Nadia Abbot, *Studies in Arabic Literary Papyri* (Chicago: University of Chicago Press, 1967).

23. This paragraph owes its formulation to Peter Wright.

24. J. Spencer Trimingham, *Christianity Among the Arabs in Pre-Islamic Times* (London: Longman, 1979).

25. Hawting, *Idea of Idolatry*, 20–30.

26. For the most recent work, see Fred Donner, *Muhammad and the Believers: At the Origins of Islam* (Cambridge, Mass.: Harvard University Press, 2010).

27. See the comments in Jaroslav Stetkevych, *Muhammad and the Golden Bough: Reconstructing Arabian Myth* (Bloomington: Indiana University Press, 2000).

28. Patricia Crone, *Meccan Trade and the Rise of Islam* (Princeton, N.J.: Princeton University Press, 1987), 24–26. For a highly critical review of Crone's book, see R. J. Serjeant, "*Meccan Trade and the Rise of Islam*: Misconceptions and Flawed Polemics," *Journal of the American Oriental Society* 110, no. 2 (1990): 472–486.

29. John E. Wansbrough, *The Sectarian Milieu: Content and Composition of Islamic Salvation History* (Oxford: Oxford University Press, 1977), 1–15.

30. Hence, the title of their book: *Hagarism*.

31. Yehuda D. Nevo and Judith Koren, *Crossroads to Islam: The Origins of the Arab Religion and the Arab State* (Amherst, N.Y.: Prometheus, 2003), 1–22.

SUGGESTIONS FOR FURTHER READING

Berkey, Jonathan. *The Formation of Islam: Religion and Society in the Near East, 600–1800.* New York: Cambridge University Press, 2003.

Crone, Patricia. *Meccan Trade and the Rise of Islam.* Princeton, N.J.: Princeton University Press, 1987.

Crone, Patricia and Michael Cook. *Hagarism: The Making of the Islamic World.* Cambridge: Cambridge University Press, 1979.

Donner, Fred. *Muhammad and the Believers: At the Origins of Islam.* Cambridge, Mass.: Harvard University Press, 2010.

——. *Narratives of Islamic Origins: The Beginnings of Islamic Historical Writing.* Princeton, N.J.: Darwin Press, 1998.

Hawting, Gerald R. *The Idea of Idolatry and the Rise of Islam: From Polemic to History.* Cambridge: Cambridge University Press, 1999.

Hodgson, Marshall G. S. *The Venture of Islam: Conscience and History in a World Civilization.* Vol. 1, *The Classical Age of Islam.* Chicago: University of Chicago Press, 1974.

Hoyland, Robert G. *Arabia and the Arabs: From the Bronze Age to the Coming of Islam.* London: Routledge, 2001.

——. *Seeing Islam as Others Saw It: A Survey and Evaluation of Christian, Jewish, and Zoroastrian Writings on Early Islam.* Princeton, N.J.: Darwin Press, 1997.

Insoll, Timothy. *The Archaeology of Islam.* Oxford: Blackwell, 1999.

Lecker, Michael. *Muslims, Jews, and Pagans: Studies on Early Islamic Medina.* Leiden: Brill, 1995.

Lewis, Bernard. *The Jews of Islam.* Princeton, N.J.: Princeton University Press, 1984.

Neuwirth, Angelika, Nicolai Sinai, and Michael Marx, eds. *The Qurān in Context: Historical and Literary Investigations in the Quranic Milieu*. Leiden: Brill, 2010.

Nevo, Yehuda D., and Judith Koren. *Crossroads to Islam: The Origins of the Arab Religion and the Arab State*. Amherst, N.Y.: Prometheus, 2003.

Newby, Gordon D. *A History of the Jews of Arabia: From Ancient Times to Their Eclipse Under Islam*. Columbia: University of South Carolina Press, 1988.

Peters, F. E., ed. *The Arabs and Arabia on the Eve of Islam*. Aldershot, Eng.: Variorum, 1999.

——. *Muhammad and the Origins of Islam*. Albany: State University of New York Press, 1994.

Shoemaker, Stephen J. *The Death of a Prophet: The End of Muhammad's Life and the Beginnings of Islam*. Philadelphia: University of Pennsylvania Press, 2012.

Stetkevych, Jaroslav. *The Zephyrs of Najd: The Poetics of Nostalgia in the Classical Arabic Nasib*. Chicago: University of Chicago Press, 1993.

Wansbrough, John E. *The Sectarian Milieu: Content and Composition of Islamic Salvation History*. Oxford: Oxford University Press, 1977.

2

THE MAKING OF THE LAST PROPHET

B OTH INSIDERS and outsiders agree that the Quran is inexplicably bound up with the personality of Muhammad. Where they differ, of course, is in what they consider to be the nature of the relationship. For many believing Muslims, Muhammad is the vehicle of divine revelation, the carnation of the perfect man, illiterate of other scriptures, and the individual whose life and actions embody the ideal response to the Quran's challenge. Although Muslims do not worship Muhammad in the sense that Christians see Jesus as God incarnate, they nevertheless regard him as a sanctified individual, sinless, whom God chose to be the mouthpiece of his message. As such, Muhammad's actions and words become paradigms for future generations of Muslims. Moreover, his actions and words are called on to justify competing—one might even say contradictory—ways of being Muslim, from the mystical to the fanatical.

Outsiders, especially those with a more skeptical perspective, are less willing to accept as objective the religious status that Muhammad enjoys among Muslims. As noted in the previous chapter, the tensions that emerge from insider and outsider portrayals are often very difficult to mediate. Many Muslims regard a skeptical and historical account of Muhammad as invasive, whereas skeptics believe that an account of Muhammad's life that simply portrays him as believers do is biased and subjective. The goal of this chapter, much like that of chapter 1, is to try to strike a balance between these two perspectives. It seeks to show how Muhammad functions in Muslim belief and practice but at the same time speaks to the biographical and textual problems of reconstructing the historical Muhammad. The Muhammad of history and the Muhammad of faith, at least from a nontheological perspective, are certainly not easily reconciled.

A historical approach to the study of Islamic origins must apply the categories of historical scholarship to the persona of Muhammad. This application includes contextualizing what, if anything, we know of the real Muhammad who lived and walked in sixth- and seventh-century Arabia and looking critically at the various ways later sources imagine him. Such an approach necessarily works on the assumption that human agents actively produce all discourses, even those constructed or sublimated as divine.

We again run into the problem of sources here. We possess very little textual or other evidence that dates to the period in question. Because Muhammad is generally considered to be the most important person in Islam, we possess reams upon reams of material about his life and times. However, virtually all this material comes from a later period that retroactively sought to project onto the character of Muhammad what were later considered his virtues and messages. Perhaps a more interesting question than asking about or assuming the existence of the historical Muhammad would inquire into the ways that Muhammad as a textual trope figured in the creation of such identities. When the subject is framed in this manner, we can witness how this textual Muhammad has been cast and recast, shaped and manipulated, to fit any number of competing and often contradictory paradigms of what it means to be Muslim. Otherwise, the historical Muhammad and the legendary Muhammad collide, with the result that it becomes very difficult, if not impossible, to separate them from each other. Although this chapter does its best to undertake this task of separation, its main goal is more modest: to introduce Muhammad and then show how and why his biography became an important part of Muslim self-definition.

After a brief and critical discussion of the various sources that claim to provide us with evidence of Muhammad's life, this chapter presents the basic narrative of this life as it emerges from these sources. The goal is not to take these sources at face value, but to explore some of the potential reasons behind their constructions. For whom were they produced? Why? What functions did they serve? This discussion then segues into the importance of Muhammad's life as one of the constitutive ingredients in the formation of the subsequent Islamic tradition.

Sources

The main sources that we possess for understanding Muhammad's life emerge from the Quran (the subject of chapter 3) and the later biographical tradition. Both of these sources are problematic, however. Although the Quran—at least according to the master narrative of the Islamic tradition—may provide a glimpse at the changing historical circumstances that Muhammad faced as an individual, on the whole it presents us with very few specifics. Moreover, as indicated in chapter 3, there is considerable debate as to the dating of the Quran's final recension. As for the biographies of Muhammad, they present other problems: they were written roughly 150 to 200 years after his death in 632 C.E. As a result, they are often highly stylized, and, unlike historical biographers of the modern period, their authors were not interested in writing accounts firmly embedded in the historical record. It is thus quite impossible to know how accurate they are. Coeval with these biographies, there also exists a related body of literature comprising various sayings and deeds attributed to Muhammad, but, again, modern historians are not convinced that this literature provides an accurate historical source, if for no other reason than that their original goal was not to be an accurate historical source.

Several outside accounts of Muhammad can also be found scattered in various Greek, Syriac, Armenian, and Hebrew sources. Again, however, most of them come from a period after Muhammad died. One of the earliest of such sources, written by the seventh-century Armenian bishop Sebeos, does provide us with the first narrative account of Muhammad to survive in any language.[1] This source seems to confirm what later Muslim sources tell us: that there was a Muhammad, that he was a merchant, that he preached a message that centered on the figure of Abraham (Perhaps a religion of the *hunafa*?), and that he established a community of Arabs and Jews based on common Abrahamic descent. With respect to this claim, however, we would do well, as mentioned in chapter 1, to remember that there is little historical evidence that names such as "Arab" and "Jew" were mutually exclusive cultural markers at this time. And so we should be cautious of projecting modern sectarian notions of "Arabness" and "Jewishness" on seventh-century Arabia.

Despite the existence of such Arabic and non-Arabic sources, our ability to create a historically reliable biography of Muhammad is still virtually impossible. One scholar of Islamic origins sums up this situation accurately: "At present, the study of Muhammad, the founder of the Muslim community, is obviously caught in a dilemma. On the one hand, it is not possible to write a historical biography of the Prophet without being accused of using the sources uncritically, while on the other hand, when using the sources critically, it is simply not possible to write such a biography."[2]

Framing this dilemma in terms of the "authenticity debate," some scholars—including the author of the previous quotation—contend that it is quite possible to isolate what they consider to be historical kernels or fragments from the legendary traditions found in the later biographical accounts of Muhammad.[3] W. Montgomery Watt, for example, argues that the legendary aspects surround only the motivational accounts of Muhammad's actions, but not the actual external acts, which we can take to be largely true.[4] Others, however, contend that the Islamic traditions about Muhammad's life are nothing more than literary products by subsequent generations and not expressly historical documents about the life of *a*, let alone *the*, historical Muhammad.[5]

Perhaps it is best to regard the biographical literature about Muhammad as not the work of historians or even biographical historians, but of creative storytellers or myth makers seeking both to understand and to explain Muhammad—and thus themselves—in light of narratives that were part of a shared or common Near Eastern religious, literary, and cultural heritage. Furthermore, these stories tell us more about the concerns of the people in eighth- and ninth-century Iraq and other cosmopolitan locations than they do about seventh-century Arabia. The biographical literature enabled these later Muslims not only to differentiate increasingly normative Islams from Judaisms and Christianities, but also to show the miraculous nature of their own tradition. Most important, and this point must not be understated, the entire enterprise of creating a biography of Muhammad was to establish and explain the various contexts in which Muhammad was perceived to have received the Quran's revelation—contexts that lasted over a twenty-year period.

In this regard, the biographical literature also seems to be intimately connected to another later genre meant to ascertain the "circumstance of revelation" (*asbab al-nuzul*). That is, subsequent commentators sought to reconstruct the "historical" contexts in which particular verses were revealed to Muhammad. Some modern commentators argue that this literature had a legal function and that its main goal was to determine the order of revelation (an important project to determine what verses abrogate [cancel] or are abrogated [cancelled] by others, as discussed in chapter 4);[6] other commentators connect the genre to the attempt to "historicize" or structure the Quran's otherwise amorphous narrative.[7]

Muhammad at Mecca

According to tradition, Muhammad was born in 570 C.E. in Mecca to the Banu Hashim family within the larger Quraysh tribe. The Banu Hashim were a prominent, if not dominant, part of the Quraysh. Muhammad's parents and grandfather died when he was relatively young, and he then came under the care of his uncle Abu Talib, the new leader of the Banu Hashim.

While still in his teens, Muhammad accompanied his uncle on trading journeys to Syria, gaining experience in commercial trade. According to the later biographical tradition, it was on one of these trading expeditions that he met a Christian monk by the name of Bahira, who is said to have foreseen Muhammad's career as a prophet of God. We read, for example, in the biography (*sira*) redacted by Abu Muhammad abd al-Malik Ibn Hisham (d. 833):

> Then [Bahira] looked at [Muhammad's] back and saw the seal of prophethood between his shoulders in the very place described in his book. When [Bahira] had finished he went to his uncle Abu Talib and asked him what relation this boy was to him, and when he told him he was his son, [Bahira] said that he was not, for it could not be that the father of this boy was alive. "He is my nephew," [Abu Talib] replied, and when [Bahira] asked what had become of his father he told him that he had died before the child was born. "You have told the truth," said Bahira. "Take your nephew back to his country and guard him carefully against the Jews, for by Allah! If they see him and know about him what I know, they will do him evil; a great future lies before this nephew of yours, so take him home quickly.[8]

Such stories undoubtedly increased Muhammad's prophetic pedigree. We can glean from them how they would be useful to later Muslims because they reveal that earlier monotheistic traditions—symbolized by the Christian Bahira in the story—recognized (and thereby acknowledged) Muhammad's future prophecy and in so doing were worried that their own traditions would be superseded by this new dispensation.

Muhammad subsequently married a wealthy and older widow, Khadija, who was heavily involved in the camel-caravan trade. At the age of forty, perhaps owing to a pre-Islamic custom, Muhammad went on a solitary retreat into the hills around Mecca, and on Jabal al-Nur (Mountain of Light) in the Hira cave, he encountered the angel Jibril (Gabriel). Later Muslim tradition marks this event with the phrase that is customarily said to begin Muhammad's revelatory career: "Recite in the name of your Lord who creates" (Quran 96:1). Muhammad went up Jabal al-Nur as a man and returned a prophet in the classic paradigm common among Near Eastern monotheists.

After periods of self-doubt, Muhammad began to preach the message of God's oneness to the inhabitants of Mecca. Other than the conversion of Khadija and of his cousin and future son-in-law Ali ibn Abi Talib to his message, he seems to have had very little success. Because he preached monotheism, his message would have immediately alienated the elites of the Quraysh tribe, who were heavily invested in the economic and religious status quo in Mecca (a large part of which hinged on the polytheistic shrine to the Arabian tribal deities housed in the Ka'ba and celebrated in the annual pilgrimage).

Some sources claim that Muhammad would have seizures when he received revelations. Such occurrences may well have been a mechanism that he (or the later Islamic tradition) employed to differentiate the Quranic revelation from his own thoughts. However, medieval and even some modern European critics of Islam would claim that Muhammad had epilepsy and that the Quran is actually a product of this illness. It should go without saying, however, that a diagnosis of epilepsy by nonphysicians and especially by those living fifteen hundred years after the fact is neither historically possible nor particularly helpful.

THE "NIGHT JOURNEY"

The Quran relates the following very brief sentence about Muhammad: "Glory be to Him, who carried His servant from the Holy Mosque to the

Further Mosque the precincts of which we have blessed, that We might show him some of Our signs" (17:1-3). This verse, although sparse in details, would subsequently be read by the later theological tradition with other verses in the Quran that deal with the twin themes of ascent and vision: "By the star when it plunges, your comrade is not astray, neither errs, nor speaks he out of caprice. This is not but a revelation revealed, taught him by one terrible in power, very strong; he stood poised being on the higher horizon, then drew near and suspended hung, two bows' length away, or nearer, then revealed to his servant that he revealed. His heart lies not of what he saw; what, will you dispute with him what he sees?" (53:1-12).

Such verses would have received much exegetical expansion in the Islamic literature that came years after Muhammad's death. This literature pinpointed the event ascribed to one night in the year 620 (although some sources place it even earlier) and expanded on it so that it became one of the defining moments of Muhammad's prophetic career. One such example of later expansion can be found in the writings of Imam Najm al-Din al-Ghaiti, a fourteenth-century thinker who describes Muhammad's journey in the following terms:

There then came over [Muhammad] a cloud containing every color. Gabriel stayed behind, but he—upon whom be God's blessing and peace—was taken up to a lofty place where he heard the scratching of pens [that are writing God's decrees]. There he saw a man [sitting] concealed in the light of the throne. Said he, "Who is this? Is it an angel?" The answer came: "No." "Then who is it?" The answer came: "This is a man whose tongue in the world was always moist with mentioning God, whose heart cleaved to the mosque, and who never at any time abused his parents." Then he saw His Lord—glorified and exalted be He—and the Prophet—upon whom be God's blessing and peace—fell upon his knees in obeisance.[9]

Although later commentators would debate whether this journey was a physical one or an internal one, it would come to play a crucial role in establishing Muhammad's prophetic credentials. In the first part of this journey, referred to as the *isra*, he traveled from the Ka'ba in Mecca to the "the farthest mosque" (*al-masjid al-aqsa*), identified with the Temple Mount—where the temple of the ancient Israelites stood—in Jerusalem and with the al-Aqsa mosque, which stands there today,

FIGURE 3   Al-Aqsa Mosque, Jerusalem. (Courtesy of Wikimedia Commons)

eventually taking its name from the larger precinct in which it was constructed (figure 3).

On the second part of the journey, referred to as the *miraj*, Muhammad is said to have toured the various heavenly realms, wherein he spoke with earlier prophets such as Abraham, Moses, and Jesus. This story is significant for several reasons. First, it established a justification for subsequent Islamic connection to the city of Jerusalem and thus connected the message of Islam to the ancient Jewish prophetic tradition. Second, it shows how Muhammad met and was greeted by earlier Jewish and Christian prophets, thereby further cementing his stature as the "seal of the prophets,"[10] an appellation that would be interpreted in various ways over the centuries.[11]

THE "SATANIC VERSES"

Another significant event that occurred during the Meccan period is the so-called satanic verses incident. In his desire to convert his kinfolk to the new message, Muhammad at one point apparently allowed potential "converts" to pray for intercession to three pagan goddesses (Al-lat, Uzza, and Manat) who were associated with the polytheistic Meccan cult. Some Meccans apparently believed that these three goddesses, as we saw in the last chapter, were Allah's offspring. According to an account preserved in the later commentary by Muhammad ibn Jarir al-Tabari (838–923), Muhammad originally received a verse that read:

> Have ye thought upon Al-lat and Uzza
> and Manat the third, the other?
> These are the exalted eagles, whose intercession is hoped for.[12]

Hearing this news—again, according to the later account found in the writings of al-Tabari—many of the Meccans rejoiced and began to accept Muhammad's message. Muhammad eventually seems to have realized the problem of this intercession for his monotheistic message, however, and we then have the revelation of the following verse:

> Have you thought upon Al-lat and Al-Uzza
> And Manat, the third, the other?
> Have you males and He females?
> That indeed were an unjust division!
> They are but names that you and your fathers have named
> God has set down no authority concerning them.
> They follow only surmise, and what the souls desire.
> Yet guidance has come to them from the Lord. (Quran 53:19)

Because this story obviously has repercussions for Muhammad's infallibility, many subsequent commentators reject it and argue that it was the result of a "satanic" intermediary or Muhammad's Meccan enemies spreading rumors to slander him and discredit his message. Some non-Muslim scholars, however, use stories like this one to explore the redaction or editorial history of the Quran to show how the text underwent various modifications through Muhammad's lifetime.

As Muhammad continued his criticisms of Meccan polytheism and the political status quo, the Quraysh kept up their attacks on him and his growing community of converts. Matters intensified when Muhammad's uncle and patron, Abu Talib, died in 619, whereupon the new leader of

SALMAN RUSHDIE AND
THE SATANIC VERSES CONTROVERSY

In 1988, the Anglo-Indian author Salman Rushdie published a novel titled *The Satanic Verses*. This critically acclaimed book is inspired in part by the life of Muhammad. Despite the inspiration, Rushdie made a number of choices that struck many Muslims as offensive. For example, he refers to Muhammad by the name "Mahound," which medieval Crusaders used; refers to Mecca as "Jahilia," which means "ignorant"; has prostitutes in a brothel in Jahilia take the names of Muhammad's wives; and has a scribe make changes to the text of the Quran that Muhammad misses.

When the book was published, it was banned in many Muslim countries. In 1989, the Ayatollah Khomeini issued a **fatwa**, a legal opinion issued by a religious authority, ordering that Muslims had an obligation to kill Rushdie, the great insulter of Islam, who at this point went into hiding. The issue was not so much that the fatwa had been formulated, but that substantial numbers of Muslims were motivated to act on it and that their actions received a great deal of media attention. Many bookstores throughout the United Kingdom were bombed; the Japanese translator of the novel was killed; and the Italian translator was badly wounded. Many bookstores that did stock the book did not display copies of it, and interested parties had to purchase it "under the counter." Some estimates indicate that as many as thirty people were killed in events related to protesting the novel.

Needless to say, this event created major tensions not only between the so-called Islamic and Western worlds, but among European and American Muslims. Many Europeans were surprised that Muslims, including those living in their midst, would take such offense at an artistic work. Many Muslims were surprised that so many non-Muslims would jump to defend someone whom Muslims considered to be a "blasphemer." This defense was further evidence, if any was needed, that the West was hostile to Islam and Muslims.

At issue in all of this was a divide between some Muslims and some Europeans. At stake for the latter were freedom of expression and the belief that no one should be threatened for writing fiction. At stake for the former, however, was the core belief that no one had the right to insult the prophet and scripture of Islam. In recent years, this divide has returned over issues such as the Danish cartoons depicting the Prophet and an American pastor's threat to burn copies of the Quran on the recent tenth anniversary of the events of September 11, 2001.

Salman Rushdie is alive and still publishing critically acclaimed works. He no longer lives in hiding, although the fatwa against him has never been removed because the original issuant, Khomeini, passed away. In 2007, Rushdie received a knighthood for his services to literature, which created a further outcry from some Islamic groups, several of which renewed calls for his death.

the Banu Hashim refused to offer Muhammad his support and protection. Interestingly, tradition also tells of a small group of his followers who immigrated to Abyssinia, presumably either to find asylum among Christian groups there or to seek potential converts from other monotheisms in the area. Things eventually got so bad for Muhammad and his followers in Mecca without the protection of his clan that in 622 he made arrangements to leave and establish a new home for his community in Yathrib (Medina), where he was invited to function as a mediator between rival tribes. Yathrib had no less than seven Jewish tribes that composed a significant portion of the town's population. Perhaps Muhammad was encouraged to settle there because he thought that such a large community of Jews—fellow monotheists—would naturally recognize and readily accept his message. Because of his migration to Yathrib, the oasis would subsequently be renamed "Medina," short for "Medinat al-nabi" (City of the Prophet).

Indeed, so important was this move to Yathrib that it became known in the later Muslim tradition as the *hijra*, or "exodus," an event about which the Quran is largely and perhaps surprisingly silent. It was later used to mark the beginning of the Muslim calendar, with 622 C.E. equaling 1 A.H. (*anno hegirae*).

Muhammad at Medina

Muhammad's followers might well have connected Muhammad's inclusive or generic message of monotheism, including the centrality of Abraham, to the Jews in the area and thus felt some sort of kinship with their fellow monotheists. We know, for example, that during this time Muhammad and his followers prayed facing Jerusalem (as Jews do), kept the Jewish Sabbath (Friday sundown to Saturday sundown) in some manner, and fasted during the Jewish holy day of Yom Kippur. It is worth pointing out that early Christians (so-called Jewish Christians or Jewish followers of Jesus) in the first century C.E. also prayed facing Jerusalem. We should also avoid assuming, imposing, or retroactively ascribing rigid sectarian differences between groups, especially between "Muslim" and "Jew," in the seventh-century Arabian Peninsula.

An important question that arises in this context is, At what point did the followers of Muhammad come to self-identify as Muslims and not just *muslims* (those who surrender)? This question is difficult to answer and most likely resembles the question about when the Jesus movement developed into something that we would now recognize as Christianity. Some scholars of early Christianity contend that what would eventually emerge as orthodox Christianity most likely took several centuries to develop in response to various doctrines that only after the fact would be labeled as "heretical." In the case of Islam, we should probably assume something similar: Islam emerged only after roughly a two-century process of self-definition, as legal traditions and other matters were gradually developed and worked out in response to various conflicts and controversies. For the early stage of Islam, it is probably more preferable to speak of a "Muham-mad movement" or a "nascent Islamic polity" as opposed to Islam in the way that we or later Muslims would come to think of it.

At Medina, the followers of Muhammad were no longer persecuted and increasingly began to imagine themselves as an **umma** (community)—one that ceased to be defined along the traditional tribal structures common to the Arabian Peninsula at that time. This community was defined according to the so-called Constitution of Medina. Although some scholars contend that this constitution is in fact a later document—the earliest copy we currently possess dates to several centuries after Muhammad's presence in Medina—it claims to date from the years immediately following the *hijra*. Whatever its provenance, it deserves mention because it acknowledges all the inhabitants of the city—Jews, pagans, and followers of Muhammad—as belonging to one community. This fact might well testify to an earlier dating because it does not significantly differentiate between Muslims and non-Muslims: all possess the same rights so long as they follow the rules and obligations set forth for them. For example, the Constitution of Medina states, "This is a document from Muhammad the prophet [governing the relations] between the believers and Muslims of Quraysh and Yathrib, and those who followed them and joined them and labored with them. They are one community [*umma*] to the exclusion of all men."[13]

It became increasingly clear to Muhammad, however, that some of the Jews of Medina would never accept his message, although this conclusion may well be a projection of later interpretations of Muhammad's position at this time. In the ensuing years, it seems that Muhammad gradually an-ticipated a return to Mecca and that, by making raids on the Meccans' caravan trade, he and his followers sought to increase their power and prestige in the eyes of the other tribes of Arabia. The most famous raid was known as the Battle of Badr in 624, which is mentioned in the Quran as the work of divine assistance. According to later sources, Muhammad and his followers were greatly outnumbered, so their subsequent victory was interpreted as a sign of God's favor. The *Sirat Rasul Allah* (*Biography of the Messenger of God*), for example, records several poems heralding the victory, including one attributed to Ali:

Have you not seen how God favored His apostle
With the favor of a strong, powerful, and gracious one;
How he brought humiliation on the unbelievers
Who were put to shame in captivity and death,
While the apostle of God's victory was glorious
He being sent by God in righteousness.[14]

Muhammad and the Jews of Medina

The situation between Muhammad and some of the Jewish tribes of Medina deteriorated fairly quickly. Perhaps, as seen at least in retrospect, these tribes would have had little patience for the still largely generic and inchoate monotheistic statements professed by Muhammad. Although Jewish tradition forbade the existence of new prophets and lawgivers, certain Judaisms were open to messianic figures and movements. At any rate, it was around this time that some of these Jewish tribes were accused of conspiring with Muhammad's enemies in Mecca to overthrow him. Muhammad confronted these tribes and gave one, the Banu Qurayza, a choice between conversion and death, and they seem to have chosen the latter. Later accounts tell that all the men of this tribe were murdered and their wives and children sold into slavery. However, it is worth pointing out that other sources mention the existence of Jewish–Arab tribes in Medina long after the Banu Qurayza's alleged treason. Perhaps these tribes were eventually absorbed into the Muhammadan polity. Sources also tell us that the sanction imposed on the Banu Qurayza was decided on in consultation with Jewish–Arab tribal leaders. Finally, there exists no corroborating evidence as to the historicity of these events outside of Muslim sources; as a consequence, we are on no firmer historical ground when discussing these events than when discussing anything else alleged to have transpired during the early period of Islam. We should thus be cautious of using such accounts, as some modern political commentators do, to show the inherent anti-Semitism or anti-Judaism of Islam.

The later biographical literature, however, has the following to say about the Jewish tribes of Medina:

About this time the Jewish rabbis showed hostility to the apostle in envy, hatred, and malice, because God had chosen His apostle from the Arabs. They were joined by men from al-Aus and al-Khazraj who had obstinately clung to their heathen religion. They were hypocrites, clinging to the polytheism of their fathers denying the resurrection; yet when Islam appeared and their people flocked to it they were compelled to pretend to accept it to save their lives. But in secret they were hypocrites whose inclination was towards the Jews because they considered the apostle a liar and strove against Islam. . . . It was the Jewish rabbis who used to annoy the apostle with questions and introduce confusion, so as to confound the truth with falsity. The Quran used to come down in reference to these questions of theirs, though some of the questions about what was allowed and forbidden came from the Muslims themselves.[15]

Later Muslim tradition suggests that it is with respect to this time that the Quran (e.g., 2:112, 5:56, 9:182) begins to speak of the Jews (al-yahud) in negative terms, often associating them with hypocrites (al-munafiqun). Most important for Islamic self-definition, it is also around this time that Muhammad (the biographical tradition says God) switched the *qibla*, or direction of prayer, for his followers from Jerusalem to Mecca, told his followers not to rest on the Jewish Sabbath, and instituted the fast at **Ramadan** to replace Yom Kippur.

Muhammad's Wives

According to tradition, Muhammad was married to eleven (other sources say thirteen) women over the course of his life. His first wife was the businesswoman Khadija, to whom he was monogamously married for roughly twenty-five years. It is said that for two years after Khadija's death, Muhammad refused to remarry as a testimony to her memory.

Muhammad eventually married other women, though, and did so polygynously. There was certainly precedence for this polygamy in contemporaneous tribal culture, wherein marriage was generally contracted based on the tribe's larger needs, especially the need to form alliances within the tribe and with other tribes. Some of Muhammad's better-known wives (discussed in greater detail in chapter 11) include the youthful Aisha, who played an important role in the transmission of Muhammad's sayings and deeds, and Hafsa, who was said (by some sources) to have played an important role in the collection of the Quran. Some of Muhammad's widows were active politically in the Islamic state after his death. Safiyya, for example, was said to have aided Uthman ibn Affan, one of Muhammad's successors, during a siege of his house. Aisha also seems to have been involved in some sort of unsuccessful revolt against Ali, another of Muhammad's successors (for more details, see chapter 4).

After Muhammad died, no one was allowed to marry any of his widows (Quran 33:53). To this day, his wives are referred to as *umm al-muminin* (the mothers of the believers [see, for example, 33:6]).

The Return to Mecca and Death of Muhammad

With the growing strength of Muhammad and his followers and the concomitant marginalization of the Quraysh throughout the Arabian Peninsula, negotiations were started to establish a truce between the two competing parties. The signing of the so-called Treaty of Hudaybiyya in 629 would allow the Medinans to enter Mecca the following year for the annual pilgrimage (hajj). By 630, Muhammad's followers had become so numerous and powerful that they were able to march on Mecca with a large army and take control of his former hometown. Muhammad declared an amnesty for past offenses, and most Meccans, many of whom had been his former enemies, converted to his message of monotheism. He subsequently destroyed all the statues of Arabian gods in the Ka'ba. The pilgrimage was now presumably devoid of the pagan practices that had characterized it earlier, and, framed from the perspective of later sources, the monotheistic pilgrimage that first characterized the hajj was reinstituted. Muhammad spent the last years of his life consolidating his position by establishing treaties with the other tribes in Arabia, which often involved, at least nominally, conversion to his message. What would become the normative tradition would have him die in Medina in 632, where he is said to be buried (figure 4). Another tradition (attested to in both early Islamic and non-Islamic sources), however, has him die several years later, after the invasion of Palestine.

The Making of the Last Prophet

Such is the life of Muhammad as presented to us by the later sources. These sources, as mentioned, are known in Arabic as *sira* (manner of life, biography)

FIGURE 4 Tomb of Muhammad, Medina, Saudi Arabia. (Photograph by Yozer1)

or *sira* literature. Among the earliest authors of *sira* compilations, which seem to have been edited from materials that likely originated in various regions among different groups, are Muhammad Ibn Ishaq (d. 767), whose biography exists in several recensions, the most important of which is by Ibn Hisham (d. 833). Other important authors–compilers of early *sira* material include Abu Abdullah ibn Umar al-Waqidi (d. 822), Muhamman ibn Saʿd (d. 844), Ahmad ibn Yahya al-Baladhuri (d. 892), and al-Tabari (d. 923). As mentioned, such individuals were not interested in composing what we would today call "historical biography." They were interested in understanding the life of Muhammad, using a set of inherited criteria and categories meant to explain his life to others. The biographical literature, in particular, tends to read more like hagiography than history.

It seems that the pool of available converts to Muhammad's movement in the early period consisted largely of Arab Christians and Arab Jews. It should come as no surprise, then, that the early biographers drew on a largely oral body of literature, collectively known as "Israiliyyat"—that is, stories about the ancient Israelites. Such stories represent the creative reworking of existing Jewish and Christian traditions in an effort to "correct" what they considered to be inappropriate trajectories of those traditions as they were worked out among earlier monotheists.

Many of these authors–compilers were writing from the perspective of the new cosmopolitan center of Baghdad, the capital of the recently established Abbasid Empire. They would undoubtedly have encountered in Baghdad many Jews and Christians in what was an increasingly competitive religious marketplace. Hearing the miraculous stories that Jews and Christians told themselves about their founders and the reception of their scriptures might well have led to a desire among Muslims to create their own mythic portrayal of Muhammad. In the biographers' hands, the oral traditions circulating about Muhammad were redacted and embellished not only to create a prophet in the more familiar Near Eastern sense, but even more symbolically to establish the credentials of the "final prophet" or the "seal of the prophets."[16]

We have already seen, for example, how the biography relates that both Jews and Christians recognized in Muhammad, even at a young age, the signs of prophecy. We have also seen how the narrative expansions of Muhammad's night journey witnessed his encounter with and acknowledgment from other prophets. Much like the emergence of the cosmic Christ from the historical Jesus, the historical aspects and suprahistorical aspects of Muhammad's personality eventually become fused and indistinguishable. This Muhammad now became the perfect prophet and lawgiver, the bravest general, the best military tactician, the most liberal thinker, and so on. This characterization of him, however, took centuries to develop and was undoubtedly connected to the increasing self-definition required by Muslims as they interacted with other monotheistic religions in the area and as various Muslim subgroups sought legitimation for their ideas and doctrines in the earliest period.

Because Muhammad's personality is intimately connected to the Quran, the creation of a cosmic Muhammad makes perfect sense. This Muhammad had to be described as living a life of "protectedness" (*isma*), which the later tradition interpreted as "sinlessness," to indicate his inerrancy lest his message somehow be contaminated. Although this cosmic Muhammad may make perfect sense from a religious point of view, the end result of its formation is that it is probably impossible to uncover the historical Muhammad.

To get a sense of just how important Muhammad is in Muslim piety, many Muslims today continue to celebrate Muhammad's birthday and to regard him as an intercessor on the Day of Judgment. A thirteenth-century poem from Egypt, for example, shows to just what extent Muhammad functions in the lives of the faith's practitioners. The poem, only part of which appears here, is an acrostic, with the first line of each verse beginning with a letter of the Arabic alphabet:

> *Alif:* Adoration do I have for my intercessor in the hereafter
>> He who is that gentle morning sun, that moon of the cosmos,
>>> Muhammad
> *Ba:* Because he was chosen, strife and enmity have vanished
>> The world is filled with purity, genuine affection, and devotion
>>> Through Muhammad
> *Ta:* Truly the Exalted One, the supreme God in His Greatness
>> Has adorned the heavens with the light of
>>> Muhammad
> *Tha:* Thanks to him, the sky is graced with a pair of moons
>> For the cosmos is resplendent with the light of
>>> Muhammad
> *Jim:* Join the whole creation in witness
>> Its warp and weft arise from the design and guidance of
>>> Muhammad
> *Ha:* Having shielded true religion with his sword
>> The faith waxed triumphant by virtue of
>>> Muhammad
> *Kha:* Culminating as the Seal of the Prophets
>> That seal has the exquisite fragrance of musk:
>>> Muhammad.[17]

The poem continues in the same tenor until it reaches the end of the alphabet. Despite the popularity of this type of literature in the premodern and modern Muslim world, various modern reform movements, such as **Wahhabism** (or, to use the name that the followers of this movement use, **Salafism**), roundly condemn such beliefs and such poetry as heretical. According to them, no one—not even Muhammad—can stand as an intermediary for the individual Muslim when he or she appears before God on the Day of Judgment. However, even these literalist and reform-minded interpretations of Islam model their identities on particular understandings of Muhammad.

Regardless of such critiques, it is important to be aware that in both the past and the contemporary period this cosmic Muhammad is extremely pliable. It often becomes necessary to ground one's identity in him as the vessel of revelation on account of (1) his personal conduct as inscribed in the tradition's collective memory and (2) his function as an exemplar in all mystical, legal, liberal, and militant versions of Islam.

Polemical Literature Against Muhammad

Medieval polemical literature produced by Europeans accused Muhammad of being an epileptic—in other words, saying that his prophecy was not really prophecy, but the product of an illness. Other sources claim that he died in 666 as opposed to 632, thus alluding to the number of the beast and pointing to an obvious sign that he was somehow connected to the devil. Others changed his name to "Mahound," implying that he was a demon that instituted a false religion; yet others attacked him for the number of wives he had and the ages of these wives when he consummated his marriages to them; and still others even charged him with being a former Christian monk. In more recent times, especially after the events of September 11, 2001, and the so-called war on terror, conservative commentators and fundamentalist preachers, such as Jerry Falwell, have called Muhammad a "violent terrorist."

Such comments and labels are certainly connected to larger geopolitical conflicts both in the past and now and need to be understood within such contexts. In particular, they construct Muhammad as a foil for Jesus or someone else who is imagined as instituting a "true" religion." On this theme of religious polemics, it is also worth noting that some modern Muslims, in response to events such as the attacks on the World Trade Center and the Pentagon and to the criticisms leveled at Islam in their wake, seek to make Muhammad into a peacenik or feminist.[18] What both critics and apologists share, of course, is the desire to create a Muhammad who functions as a placeholder for their ideas of what Islam is or should be. Both are constructions ultimately based on the commentators' specific interpretations and, as such, have little or no backing in the historical record because words such as "terrorism" and "feminism" are of a distinctly modern provenance.

The Deeds and Sayings of Muhammad: The Genre of Hadith

Because Muhammad is seen as the perfect embodiment of the response to the Quranic message, later generations of Muslims were necessarily interested in what he said and did. This interest gave rise to a related body of literature that was eventually regarded as important by those who sought to define themselves by preserving and transmitting Muhammad's response to the Quranic challenge. Known as hadith (pl., *ahadith*, but often pluralized in English as "hadiths"), this genre refers to various reports about Muhammad's sayings or actions, including his tacit approval or disproval of something said or done in his presence. These actions can run the gamut from the seemingly mundane (e.g., how he wore his beard) to what we would consider to be more religious concerns (e.g., when and how he engaged in prayer or silent contemplation). Several examples of hadith reports should suffice to illustrate the genre: "Ishaq told me that Ubayd Allah told him on the authority of Shayban on the authority of Yahya on the authority of Muhammad ibn Abd al-Rahman, client of the Banu Zuhra, on the authority of Abu Sama on the authority of Abd Allah ibn Umar that he [Muhammad] said: The messenger of God said to me: 'Recite all of the Quran in one month.' I said, 'But I am able to do more than that!' So [Muhammad] said: 'Then recite it in seven days, but do not do it less than that.'"[19]

This hadith, like all hadiths, is divided into two parts. The first is called the **isnad**, or "chain" of transmission from Ishaq to Abd Allah ibn Umar, with the last individual in the chain considered to be the person closest to Muhammad in time. The second part is referred to as the **matn**, or the actual text handed down in Muhammad's name. Both parts are equally important and, according to the later tradition, a *matn* without a proper *isnad* is considered to be invalid.

Another hadith deals with the importance of proper intention during the Ramadan fast: "Muslim ibn Ibrahim related to us, saying: Hisham re-

lated to us, saying: Yahya related to us from Abu Salama, from Abu Hur-
aira, from the Prophet, upon whom be Allah's blessing and peace—who
said: 'Whosoever rises up [for vigil and prayers] during the night of al-
Qadr, with faith, and in hope of recompense, will have all his previous sins
forgiven him, and whosoever fast during Ramadan with faith, in hope of
recompense, and with [sincere] intention, will have all that is past forgiven him.' "[20]

These reports not only refer to spiritual and legal matters but can also
transmit more mundane features, such as Muhammad's clothing prefer-
ences: "Hudba ibn Khalid al-Azdi has related to us, relating from Ham-
mam, from Qatada, who said: 'We asked Anas what kind of garment the
apostle of God—upon whom be Allah's blessing and peace—liked best, or
which was the most pleasing to him, and he answered : "The *hibara* [i.e.,
striped garment]." ' "[21]

Subsequent experts in Islamic law judged and evaluated hadith reports
to be "sound" (*sahih*), "acceptable" (*hasan*), "weak" (*daif*), or "fabricated"
(*mawdu*) based on criteria such as the verifiability of the *isnad* or whether the *matn* contradicts other narrations. The process by which the *isnad*
is verified is determined by *ilm al-rijal* (literally, "the science of men"),
wherein it is ascertained whether the chain of transmission in the *isnad*
is chronological or not and, most important, whether all the individuals
within it are proved to be of good and reliable character.[22]

Taken together, these hadiths give later Muslims insights into the
Sunna (custom or practice) of Muhammad's life. Again attesting to the
centrality of Muhammad in Islam, his Sunna became a major basis in the
subsequent formation of Islamic law (**sharia**), second only in importance
to the Quran. As a result, the figure of Muhammad was used to develop
various legal positions that subsequent Muslim jurists contended reflected Muhammad's practices and should as a result be binding on the entire
Muslim community. The crucial question that we must ask ourselves (as
discussed in chapter 5) is, When exactly did Muhammad emerge as this
source of legal authority? And, equally important, how is it possible to
know, let alone prove, that Muhammad did all the things that were reported in his name?

The early Islamic tradition also recognized another special type of hadith known as the *hadith qudsi*, or "divine saying." These sayings fit in between the Quran and the hadiths because they were believed to be direct
revelations from God but couched in Muhammad's own words.[23] These

sayings tend not to be concerned with legal matters, but with religious or spiritual matters. A typical example is the following: "I heard the Apostle of God say: 'Your Lord delights in a shepherd on top of a remote mountain peak who give the call to prayer and then performs the prayer. Thereupon God says "Look at this servant of mine! He gives the call to prayer and then performs the prayer. He fears me. So I forgive my servant, and I shall cause him to enter paradise." ' "[24]

In the eighth and ninth centuries, bodies of hadith literature were collected and codified into six authoritative collections by Muhammad ibn Isma'il al-Bukhari (d. 870), Muslim ibn al-Hajjaj (d. 875), Abu 'Abdillah Ibn Maja (d. 887), Abu Dawud (d. 889), Abu 'Isa al-Tirmidhi (d. 892), and Ahmad al-Nasa'i (d. 915). It is worth noting that the two main denominations of Islam, Shi'ism and Sunnism (discussed in chapters 5 and 6), have different collections of authoritative hadith, although there is certainly a sizable body of hadith upon which they agree. Sunnis regard the collections by the men named previously as canonical, whereas Shi'is regard the collections by Muhammad al-Kulayni (d. 939), Muhammad ibn Babuya (d. 991), and Muhammad al-Tusi (d. 1067) as canonical. Many Shi'i hadith also archive the sayings and deeds of individuals who are important to the Shi'i movement, most notably Ali.

Hadiths, like all other materials forming a religion, are not without problems. Chief among them is the fact that one can, in theory, attach a "sound" isnad to any concept, written in the form of a matn, that one wants to prove. The result is that an individual saying by Muhammad can be employed to argue opposite positions, and many of them are. In other words, one can subsequently employ ready-made isnads to justify virtually any principle in Islam and, because hadiths are such an important part of Islamic law, to give such a principle almost immediate legal justification,

Modern Western scholars have also argued that hadiths tend to "grow backward." That is, it is possible for sayings attributed to other individuals (e.g., companions of Muhammad) or even unattributed maxims to show up later as sayings by Muhammad with complete isnads. This factor seems to indicate that isnads became important later in the historical development of Islam and that only then were they required to establish a report's authority, in which case they "grew backward" to include Muhammad and thereby to invest a saying or an opinion with his authority. In this case, hadiths tell us about later Muslims and what was important to them but become problematic when it comes to telling us about a historical Muhammad.

Representing Muhammad

On September 30, 2005, the Danish newspaper *Jyllands-Posten* published twelve editorial cartoons depicting Muhammad in various situations, bellicose and otherwise. Not only did the contexts of the cartoons bother many Muslims, but they considered the fact that Muhammad was portrayed at all to be deeply offensive to Muslim belief, which maintains that portrayals of Muhammad in particular and of humans in general is a form of idolatry. The subsequent protests throughout the Muslim world and beyond became increasingly violent. Charges of **Islamophobia** and racism were leveled at the paper that published the cartoons, at the Danish government, and eventually at all Western nations and individuals that came to the paper's defense. The artist behind the cartoons, however, argued that they drew attention to criticisms of Islam and self-censorship. It is worth pointing out that there is certainly historical precedent for creating images of Muhammad. The uproar created by the Danish cartoons is more likely connected to the current tensions in Europe between Muslims and non-Muslims and to the perceived place of religion (or at least Islam) in society. Hundreds of thousands of Muslims signed a petition sent to *Wikipedia* to remove all images of Muhammad—whether by non-Muslims *or Muslims*—from the Web site. Such conservative Muslims are apparently equally critical of historical Muslim portrayals of Muhammad, and they blame these representations on Persian "cultural" influences that corrupted a pristine Arab monotheism. This argument is, of course, grounded more in memory and desire than it is in the historical record. This and related topics are discussed in later chapters devoted to Islam in the modern world.

This chapter has both shown something about the life of Muhammad, at least as reconstructed through much later sources, and described how this life informs Muslim identities into the present. Whether Muhammad perceived himself to be the "seal of the prophets," or subsequent theologians ascribed this moniker to him, the centrality of Muhammad within both the formation and subsequent development of Islam cannot be denied. Muhammad's importance flows largely from the constructed cultural memory of him that subsequent generations cherished. In addition, his persona becomes intimately connected to the message of the Quran.

NOTES

1. An English translation of Sebeos's account can be found in *The Armenian History Attributed to Sebeos*, 2 vols., trans., with notes, by R. W. Thomson (Liverpool: University of Liverpool Press, 1999). See also Robert G. Hoyland, *Seeing Islam as Others Saw It: A Survey and Evaluation of Christian, Jewish, and Zoroastrian Writings on Early Islam* (Princeton, N.J.: Darwin Press, 1997), 124–132.

2. Harald Motzki, "Introduction," in Harald Motzki, ed., *The Biography of Muhammad: The Issue of Sources* (Leiden: Brill, 2000), xiv.

3. In addition to Motzki, scholars who make this claim include W. Montgomery Watt, *Muhammad at Mecca* (Oxford: Clarendon Press, 1953), and *Muhammad at Medina* (Oxford: Clarendon Press, 1956); and M. J. Kister, "'A Bag of Meat': A Study of an Early *Hadith*," *Bulletin of the School of Oriental and African Studies* 33 (1970): 267–275.

4. Watt, *Muhammad at Mecca*, xiv.

5. See, for example, Uri Rubin, *The Eye of the Beholder: The Life of Muhammad as Viewed by the Early Muslims* (Princeton, N.J.: Darwin Press, 1995), chap. 4.

6. John Wansbrough, *Quranic Studies: Sources and Methods of Scriptural Interpretation* (Oxford: Oxford University Press, 1978), 200–211.

7. Andrew Rippin, "The Exegetical Genre *Asbab al-Nuzul*: A Bibliographical and Terminological Survey," *Bulletin of the School of Oriental and African Studies* 48 (1985): 1–15, and "The Function of *Asbab al-Nuzul* in Quranic Exegesis," *Bulletin of the School of Oriental and African Studies* 51 (1988): 1–20.

8. Muhammad Ibn Ishaq, *The Life of Muhammad: A Translation of Ibn Ishaq's "Sirat Rasul Allah*," trans. Alfred Guillaume (1955; repr., Oxford: Oxford University Press, 2009), 80–81.

9. Najm ad-Din al-Ghaiti, "The Story of the Night Journey and the Ascension," in Arthur Jeffrey, ed., *A Reader on Islam: Passages from Standard Arabic Writings* (The Hague: Mouton, 1962), 634.

10. On the malleability of the symbology associated with the "night flight," see the collection of essays in Christiane Grubar and Fredrick S. Colby, eds., *Exploring Other Worlds: New Studies on Muhammad's Ascension* (Bloomington: Indiana University Press, 2010).

11. See, for example, Yohanan Friedmann, *Prophecy Continuous: Aspects of Ahmadī Religious Thought and Its Medieval Background*, new ed. (New Delhi: Oxford University Press, 2003).

12. Muhammad ibn Jarir al-Tabari, *Taʾrikh*, ed. M. J. de Goeje, 3 vols. (Leiden: Brill, 1879–1901), 1:1192–1193. See also the discussion in G. R. Hawting, *The Idea of Idolatry and the Emergence of Islam: From Polemic to History* (Cambridge: Cambridge University Press, 1999), 130–149.

13. Ibn Ishaq, *Life of Muhammad*, 231–232.

14. Ibid., 341.

15. Ibid., 239.

16. On making Muhammad a prophet, see the comments in the introduction to Gordon D. Newby, *The Making of the Last Prophet: A Reconstruction of the Earliest Biography of Muhammad* (Columbia: University of South Carolina Press, 1989). It is worth pointing out that Newby does take a very sanguine approach to the historicity of these sources.

17. "In Praise of the Prophet Muhammad," trans. Earle H. Waugh, in John Renard, ed., *Windows on the House of Islam: Muslim Sources on Spirituality and Religious Life* (Berkeley: University of California Press, 1998), 120–121.

18. On Muhammad as a "peacenik," see Tariq Ramadan, *In the Footsteps of Prophet: Lessons from the Life of Muhammad* (Oxford: Oxford University Press, 2007), 148. On Muhammad as a feminist, see Lynda Clarke, "Women in Islam," in Leona M. Anderson and Pamela Dickey Young, eds., *Women and Religious Traditions* (New York: Oxford University Press, 2004), 187–217.

19. Al-Bukhari, *Al-Sahih kitab fada'il al-Quran*, 20 vols. (Cairo: Dar al-Arabi, 1955), 6:114, translated as *Sahih al-Bukhari*, trans. Muhsin Khan, 5th ed., 9 vols. (New Delhi: Kitab Bhavan, 1984), 6:517–518.

20. "The Section on Fasting from the *Sahih al-Bukhari*," in Arthur Jeffrey, ed., *A Reader on Islam* (The Hague: Mouton, 1962), 91.

21. Ibid., 132.

22. For a recent in-depth discussion of the criteria and names of reliable hadith transmitters, see Scott C. Lucas, *Constructive Critics, Hadith Literature, and the Articulation of Sunni Islam: The Legacy of the Generation of Ibn Saʿd, Ibn Maʿin, and Ibn Hanbal* (Leiden: Brill, 2004), 287–369.

23. For a study of the *hadith qudsi*, see William A. Graham, *Divine Word and Prophetic Words in Early Islam: A Reconsideration of the Sources, with Special Reference to the Hadith Qudsi* (The Hague: Mouton, 1977).

24. Quoted in ibid., 198.

SUGGESTIONS FOR FURTHER READING

Berg, Herbert. *The Development of Exegesis in Early Islam: The Debate over the Authenticity of Muslim Literature from the Formative Period.* London: Routledge/Curzon, 2000.

Brockopp, Jonathan, ed. *The Cambridge Companion to Muhammad.* Cambridge: Cambridge University Press, 2010.

Brown, Jonathan. *Hadith: Muhammad's Legacy in the Medieval and Modern World.* Oxford: Oneworld, 2009.

Cook, Michael. *Muhammad.* Oxford: Oxford University Press, 2003.

Donner, Fred. *Muhammad and the Believers: At the Origins of Islam.* Cambridge, Mass.: Harvard University Press, 2010.

——. *Narratives of Islamic Origins: The Beginnings of Islamic Historical Writing.* Princeton, N.J.: Darwin Press, 1998.

Friedmann, Yohanan. *Prophecy Continuous: Aspects of Ahmadi Religious Thought and Its Medieval Background.* New ed. New Delhi: Oxford University Press, 2003.

Graham, William A. *Divine Word and Prophetic Words in Early Islam: A Reconsideration of the Sources, with Special Reference to the Hadith Qudsi.* The Hague: Mouton, 1977.

Ibn Ishaq, Muhammad. *The Life of Muhammad: A Translation of Ibn Ishaq's "Sirat rasul Allah."* Translated by Alfred Guillaume. Oxford: Oxford University Press, 1955. Reprint, Oxford: Oxford University Press, 2009.

Hoyland, Robert G. *Seeing Islam as Others Saw It: A Survey and Evaluation of Christian, Jewish, and Zoroastrian Writings on Early Islam.* Princeton, N.J.: Darwin Press, 1997.

Lucas, Scott. *Constructive Critics, Hadith Literature, and the Articulation of Sunni Islam: The Legacy of the Generation of Ibn Sa'd, Ibn Ma'in, and Ibn Hanbal*. Leiden: Brill, 2004.

Motzki, Harald, ed. *The Biography of Muhammad: The Issue of the Sources*. Leiden: Brill, 2000.

Newby, Gordon D. *The Making of the Last Prophet: A Reconstruction of the Earliest Biography of Muhammad*. Columbia: University of South Carolina Press, 1989.

Peters, F. E. *Muhammad and the Origins of Islam*. Albany: State University of New York Press, 1994.

Reeves, Minou. *Muhammad in Europe*. New York: New York University Press, 2000.

Rodinson, Maxime. *Muhammad: Prophet of Islam*. London: Tauris, 2002.

Rubin, Uri. *The Eye of the Beholder: The Life of Muhammad as Viewed by the Early Muslims*. Princeton, N.J.: Darwin Press, 1995.

——. ed. *The Life of Muhammad*. Ashgate, Eng.: Variorum, 1998.

Schacht, Joseph. *The Origins of Muhammadan Jurisprudence*. Oxford: Clarendon Press, 1950.

Stetkevych, Jarolsav. *Muhammad and the Golden Bough: Reconstructing Arabian Myth*. Bloomington: Indiana University Press, 1996.

Stetkevych, Suzanne Pinckney. *The Mantle Odes: Arabic Praise Poems to the Prophet Muhammad*. Bloomington: Indiana University Press, 2010.

Watt, W. Montgomery. *Muhammad at Mecca*. Oxford: Clarendon Press, 1953.

——. *Muhammad at Medina*. Oxford: Clarendon Press, 1956.

Zeitlin, Irving M. *The Historical Muhammad*. Cambridge: Polity Press, 2007.

3

THE QURAN

The Base Narrative

THERE IS a danger of falling into an overly Protestant assumption that each and every religion possesses a written scripture that, unmediated by tradition or interpretation, functions as the essence of that religion. The goal of the spiritual life, according to this Protestant model, is for the believer to read the scripture alone as a way to attain salvation. This model, however, fits neither Islam nor most of the world's religions. Because many Muslims cannot read Arabic, and because the Quran can be a very difficult text to understand, it is received within various communities of believers mediated through centuries of interpretation and tradition. And, despite the importance of the Quran in Islamic life, it is important to acknowledge the persona of Muhammad, as noted in chapter 2. Because of his personal conduct, his response to the Quran's message, emulation of Muhammad is deemed worthy in and of itself. Indeed, there is a hadith attributed to Aisha that the Prophet was a "walking Quran."

Although the Quran's contents are readily and easily summarized, the history of how it came to be the text it did is not nearly as easy to ascertain. The Quran was an oral text, originally embedded in the collective memory of the early community, that was not transcribed into a written text until a later date. The oldest complete manuscript of the Quran in our possession dates to the late tenth or early eleventh century, although there do exist earlier fragments that occasionally provide textual variants from what would eventually emerge as the authoritative codex. Like other aspects of Islamic origins, we know very little about the Quran during the first two hundred years after the death of Muhammad. The details given here are gleaned from later Muslims sources and modern Western scholarship. The goal of this chapter is to present something of the competing accounts of how the Quran came to be and to provide a brief overview of its major forms, themes, and contents.

Overview

Although the full revelation was believed to be complete before Muhammad's death, tradition tells us that he did not assemble the material into a definitive text. This assembly was left to his successors, whose task it became to redact the revelatory materials into what would become known as "the Quran" (literally, "the Recital"), in the generation immediately after his death.

The book itself is divided into 114 **suras**, or chapters, with individual verses referred to as *ayas*. Suras are arranged roughly from the longest to the shortest: sura 2, for example, has roughly three hundred ayas, whereas sura 114 has only about five. Suras are traditionally classified as Meccan or Medinan based on the place where the verses were first revealed. Suras that tend to be shorter, highly rhythmic, and concerned with the end of times are generally thought to be Meccan in provenance. For example,

Idha	zulzilati	l-ardu	zilzalaha
Wa	akhrajati	l-ardu	athqalaha
Wa	qala	l-insanu	ma laha
Yawma'idhin	tuhaddithu	akhbaraha	

When quakes the earth in her quaking
And bears forth the earth her burdens,
And says the human, "What is with her?"
On that day she will tell her news
As the Lord revealed to her. (99:1–5)[1]

By contrast, suras containing narrative content and legal material tend to be classified as Medinan. This clearly reflects the context of the message: in Mecca, Muhammad preached an inclusive monotheistic message based on reward and punishment; in Medina, however, he became leader of a community in need of guidance and specific legal pronouncements.

Prefacing each chapter, with the exception of sura 9, is the *basmala*, a shortened Arabic term for "b-ismi llah al-rahman al-rahim" (in the name of God, the Compassionate, the Merciful). In addition, at the beginning of twenty-nine suras (e.g., 11, 12, 21) there exist seemingly random letters of the Arabic alphabet. Much has been written about these letters in both traditional and modern scholarship on the Quran, with some scholars arguing that they function as mnemonic devices to aid in the memorization of the oral text, and others contending that they refer to some sort of mystical or scientific code. The names of the suras do not necessarily reflect the contents of the entire chapter but instead seem to reflect a word (e.g., the title of sura 16 and the word *bees*) or theme (e.g., the title of sura 24 and poets) that appears, often fleetingly, somewhere in the sura. The only sustained narrative discussion occurs in sura 12, titled "Joseph." The Quran also has a liturgical division into thirty equal parts that are recited each night during the month of Ramadan (see chapter 8). This division is also used to encourage Muslims to read the Quran continually and is often used as a guide for children to memorize the text, an act that is regarded as highly meritorious.

The Quran invokes many biblical stories, undoubtedly contributing to the impression that Muhammad or the final redactors of the Quran were familiar with Jewish and Christian materials. However, the Quran does not take up these themes in the same kind of sustained narrative found in these other sources. When it does mention such earlier stories, it is more interested in the religious message than narrative details. Because of its arrangement, from longest to shortest suras, as opposed to thematic or chronological content, the Quran appears to lack any real beginning, middle, or end, with the result that there is very little narrative continuity in the work.

Words such as "borrowing" and "influencing" may not adequately account for the historical, religious, and literary context of seventh-century Arabia, however. As we have seen in the previous chapters, themes such as desert dwellers, illiterate prophets, revelation, and the hope for ultimate redemption form part of a larger Near Eastern cultural legacy. In this regard, "borrowing" from a shared cultural matrix is not necessarily borrowing at all, but instead using existing and common discourses to articulate particular features. Read on this level, the Quran is not simply the sum of its parts but shares in a broader Near Eastern religious and mythic heritage. Consider, for example, the Quranic version of the flood story, which essentially becomes an altogether new Islamic story:

> We sent Noah to his people, saying,
> "Warn your people, before a painful punishment comes upon them."
> He said, "O my people,
> I am a clear warner to you.
> Serve God and fear Him, and obey me,
> And He will forgive you some of your sins
> and defer you to a stated term.
> God's term, when it comes, cannot be deferred
> If you did but know it."
> [Noah] said, "My Lord,
> I have summoned my people night and day,
> But my summoning has increased them only in flight
> Whenever I summon them so that You might forgive them,
> they put their fingers in their ears
> and draw their garments over them
> and persist and are full of pride." (71:1–8)

Although the name "Noah" is certainly familiar, as is the basic narrative presupposed in it and in Quran 11:25–50, the emphasis on the sending of a prophet, the people's unwillingness to listen to him, and their gradual destruction are much different from what we encounter in other Near Eastern flood stories, such as in the Epic of Gilgamesh or in the Bible.

Although this chapter attempts to summarize the Quran's contents and message, we must not confuse later Muslim accounts of its origin and formation with historical fact. Because of the paucity of sources, the information given here can only at best raise important questions about the Quran's origin. It most certainly cannot solve the messy historical problems surrounding the Quran.

THE QURAN IN TRANSLATION

Most Christians and non-Orthodox Jews read their respective scriptures in translations. The result is that it is customary for such individuals to believe that because scriptures can be and, indeed, have to be translated, their message and contents can be understood in any language. The matter of translation is somewhat more complex in Islam than in Judaism and Christianity because Arabic is regarded not just as the original language of the Quran, but part and parcel of its very textual fabric and the ultimate presentation of its message, even though most Muslims are not native speakers of Arabic. It is for this reason that many modern English translations do not call themselves the "Quran" but often use titles that imply that the translation is only an interpretation of the original Arabic, such as *The Koran Interpreted* and *The Meaning of the Glorious Koran.*[*] Because the Quran describes itself as "an Arabic recitation"—in other words, it is, from a theological point of view, the "speech of God," meaning that God spoke Arabic—to translate it and to call a translation the "Quran" are to alter God's words.

Many Muslims acknowledge that the sense of the Quran can be rendered, albeit imperfectly, in other languages. In this regard, as early as the tenth or eleventh century the Quran was translated into other "Islamic" languages such as Persian. And today there exist translations into many vernaculars, including Chinese. The goal, however, is for Muslims not to mistake the translation for the Quran itself. As a result, every Muslim is encouraged to learn Arabic so that he or she may read the text in its original.

This dogma that makes the Quran unreproducible has hindered all meaningful attempts to create an authoritative translation, something like the Luther translation of the Bible into German or the King James translation into English.

[*] A. J. Arberry, trans., *The Koran Interpreted* (New York: Macmillan, 1955); Marmaduke Pickthall, trans., *The Meaning of the Glorious Koran: An Explanatory Translation* (London: Knopf, 1930).

Traditional Accounts

As shown in chapter 2, the Quran is perceived to be inextricably connected to the persona of Muhammad. The doctrine of his *isma* (sinlessness) and his purported illiteracy—both later theological developments—would secure for his revelation a pure and unique status. According to Muslim tradition, the Quran is the very word of God as revealed to Muhammad over the span of twenty-three years, from 610 to 632. Because of his illiteracy, it is held that Muhammad did not write down the text; his followers, called "Companions" (**sahaba**), did.

It is worth focusing briefly on the claim that Muhammad was illiterate (*ummi*), which becomes particularly important in the early biographical traditions. Some scholars wonder why Muhammad could neither read nor write even though he was actively involved in the caravan trade in the Arabian Peninsula. Although the later Islamic tradition would construe the term *ummi* to mean complete illiteracy, other Muslim sources suggest that it refers to his illiteracy with regard to other religious scriptures. *Ummi* can thus on this reading be translated as "unscriptured."[2] Regardless, the trope of illiteracy seems to be intended to enhance the miraculous nature of the Quran.

Despite the fact that the Quran is intimately bound up with the person of Muhammad, he is surprisingly excluded from playing a role in its actual collection. There do exist some accounts that tell how he and Ali, his cousin and son-in-law, went over the whole text; however, the dominant tradition puts the leaves of the Quran in the hands of Hafsa, one of Muhammad's widows.

The later tradition is also somewhat unclear about who actually was responsible for the Quran's final redaction. According to some, Abu Bakr (r. 632–634), Muhammad's immediate successor (discussed more fully in chapter 4), was concerned about the status of the "text" after a number of individuals who had memorized the Quran perished in battle. Fearing that the Quran might be forgotten or corrupted, Abu Bakr formed a committee headed by Zayd ibn Thabit and including individuals who had memorized the Quran to assemble all its verses in one place. This committee compared the versions of all those who had memorized Muhammad's teaching, and after they were satisfied that they had not missed or overlooked any verse or made any mistakes in collating them, they presented it in book form to Abu Bakr.

Another tradition claims that at the time of Muhammad's third successor, Uthman ibn Affan (r. 644–656), one of the Companions was worried about the divergences in the oral recitations of the Quranic text that he noticed throughout the growing empire. To rectify the problem, Uthman is said to have collected the pages of the text from Hafsa. He then instructed a group of men to copy these leaves into a single volume, which would eventually become known as the "Uthmanic recension." This text quickly became the authoritative text and is the one that remains so until the present. A different version of the story tells how Uthman subsequently sent out his redaction to all the provinces and ordered that all variants be destroyed.

The Critical View

Because the modern Western historical record works on the assumption that "sacred" books do not fall from heaven, scholars cannot take as their default position the notion that the Quran (or, for that matter, the Bible or the Vedas) is the word of God. It is a text like all texts and, as such, the product of human hands. We must accordingly begin our historical investigation into its origins with the following set of questions: Was the Quran redacted from earlier sources in, for example, the way that biblical scholars say that the Old Testament and New Testament were? If so, who redacted the Quran? And from what sources did they collect it? Such questions return us to issues raised in previous chapters. It seems likely that the material that the Quran draws on is the pre-Islamic poetic tradition and various Jewish, Christian, and perhaps even Zoroastrian sources, all of which seem to have formed part of a larger Near Eastern religioliterary "repository." This conclusion certainly does not reduce the Quran to the sum of its sources. As Norman Brown has nicely argued, for example, the genius of the Quran is that it filters all these earlier sources through its own unique prism.[3]

The overwhelming majority of Muslims believe that the text of the Quran has never been changed and that it has existed in its present form since either Abu Bakr's or Uthman's recension. This belief makes very difficult any attempts to inquire into the redaction of the text on historical grounds.

The most important scholar of the skeptical tradition is the late John Wansbrough. It should be recalled that Wansbrough, using an analysis of the genres and words within the Quran, highlighted the persistent use of monotheistic imagery stemming from Jewish and Christian sources. He interpreted the rise of Islam as the subsequent development of what was originally a Judeo-Christian sect. As this sect evolved and differentiated itself from its Jewish and Christian roots, it produced the Quran to legitimate itself. The book, Wansbrough maintains, evolved and was continuously in flux for more than a century, and what we today recognize as the Quran and Islam did not emerge until the late eighth or early ninth century, more than 150 years after the death of Muhammad, even though some of the materials within it may be of pre-Muhammadan origin (e.g., the poetry and oral traditions).[4]

Because the Quran became increasingly important to Muslim self-definition in the same period as the need to compose Muhammad's biography and to establish various legal schools (see chapter 5), establishing a fixed text became paramount. Once again, according to the skeptical approach, all of this occurred roughly 150 to 200 years after Muhammad's death.

What happened before this point, however, is unclear. As we have seen, there are conflicting accounts in the Muslim sources themselves as to who assembled the "final" version of the Quran: Was it Abu Bakr, Uthman, or Hafsa, the daughter of the second successor, Umar ibn al-Khattab (r. 634–644)? If Abu Bakr, for example, had already established a written codex by the end of his rule in 634, why would Uthman need to collect the leaves from Hafsa? The leaves would presumably no longer have been loose, but instead an integral part of Abu Bakr's recension.

Several other minor problems exist with respect to the Quran's traditional literary sources. As mentioned, the oldest extant version of the Quran dates to the late tenth or early eleventh century. There do exist, however, numerous fragments that predate this version, the earliest of them believed to date back to the late eighth century. The variants in these fragments appear to be much greater than we would expect if we take the Muslim traditions about the collection of the Quran at face value, although it is certainly conceivable that these fragments come from variant texts that the Uthmanic recension superseded.

Many elements within the Quran generate further redactional problems. For example, the Quran seems to presuppose knowledge of seafaring (e.g., 24:39–40), yet the biography of Muhammad mentions no familiarity with seafaring on his part. Some scholars use such examples to posit that the Quran was edited later than originally thought as the Muhammad movement spread throughout the Mediterranean basin (where seafaring would have been an important activity). Again, if we assume that the Quran is the word of God, the mention of seafaring in it certainly does not pose a problem because the sea in such verses can be interpreted as referring to the desert. Or, again, if we assume a common Near Eastern mythic heritage of which the Quran partakes, such terms or concepts might not be out of place at all.

Perhaps more interesting, numerous inscriptions have variations on the Uthmanic text. According to Michael Cook, an early theological letter written by Hasan al-Basri around the year 700 includes the following verse from the Quran: "Thus the word of your Lord is realized against the ungodly that they are the inhabitants of the fire." This verse, however, is not in any version of the Quran that we now possess. It does bear a certain resemblance to 10:33, "Thus the word of your Lord is realized against the ungodly that they believe not." It also appears to resemble 40:6, "Thus the word of your Lord is realized against the unbelievers; that they are the inhabitants of the fire." Cook suggests that it seems unlikely that the difference is simply a matter of carelessness on the part of a later copyist because Hasan al-Basri's explanation of the verse turns on his explication of the term "ungodly."[5] The variations thus indicate that the text of the Quran may not have been as firmly fixed after Uthman as the literary tradition would have us believe.

As Cook also shows, numerous coins possess slightly different versions of Quranic materials. For example, a coin minted in Kufa (northern Iraq) around the year 700 has a variant on sura 9:33 ("It is He who has sent his messenger with the guidance and the religion of truth, that He may uplift it above every religion, though the unbelievers be averse"): "He sent him with the guidance and the religion of truth, that He may uplift it above every religion, though the unbelievers be averse."[6] These variations might be the result of later authorities using recensions other than the Uthmanic codex, or these authorities may well have felt free to paraphrase the codex as they saw fit. It is quite simply impossible to tell from a historical point of view.

In the recent monograph *Muhammad Is Not the Father of Any of Your Men*, David Powers argues that in the first generations after the death of Muhammad, sections of the Quran dealing with Muhammad and his adopted son Zayd were altered to establish Muhammad as the "seal of the prophets." Powers holds that because the Quran portrays prophecy through the lineage of Abraham, it was important for the early Muslim community to ensure that Muhammad died sonless, lest later claimants to prophecy arise. The Quranic narrative, despite its silence when it comes to detailing events of Muhammad's life, has Zayd die on the battlefield. Powers further hypothesizes that later generations changed the actual text of the Quran to suit their needs. For example, the verse in 33:40, "Muhammad is not the father of any of your men," clashes with an earlier verse in 33:6, "The prophet is closer to the believers than they are to themselves, *he is their father* and his wives are their mothers" (italics added). This latter verse was subsequently changed so that the clause in italics ("he is their father") was omitted. Although the phrase "he is their father" was removed from all the codices, it continued to circulate in the later commentary tradition.[7]

One final example from Powers's work should suffice to demonstrate the issue at hand. In Quran 33:27, permission is granted to Muhammad to marry his daughter-in-law (divorced from his adopted son Zayd). This

MANUSCRIPTS OF THE QURAN FOUND IN SANA, YEMEN

In 1972, construction workers who were renovating a wall in the attic of the Great Mosque of Sana in Yemen came across large quantities of old manuscripts and parchments, including Quranic materials. They packed them up and left them in storage. In 1979, the president of the Yemeni Antiquities Authority realized the potential importance of the find. He showed them to a visiting German scholar, who in turn persuaded the German government to organize and fund a restoration project.

Subsequent radio-carbon dating has revealed that these manuscripts are very old, dating to as early as the late seventh century, making them perhaps the oldest extant version of the Quran. Those Western researchers who have been privileged to examine the manuscripts suggest that there is much here: unconventional verse orderings, minor textual variations, and rare styles of orthography and artistic embellishments. In an interview with the *Atlantic Monthly*, one of these German researchers, Gerd Puin, remarked:

> My idea is that the Koran is a kind of cocktail of texts that were not all understood even at the time of Muhammad. Many of them may even be a hundred years older than Islam itself. Even within the Islamic traditions there is a huge body of contradictory information, including a significant Christian substrate; one can derive a whole Islamic anti-history from them if one wants. The Quran claims for itself that it is "mubeen," or clear, but if you look at it, you will notice that every fifth sentence or so simply doesn't make sense. Many Muslims will tell you otherwise, of course, but the fact is that a fifth of the Quranic text is just incomprehensible. This is what has caused the traditional anxiety regarding translation. If the Quran is not comprehensible, if it can't even be understood in Arabic, then it's not translatable into any language. That is why Muslims are afraid. Since the Quran claims repeatedly to be clear but is not—there is an obvious and serious contradiction. Something else must be going on.[*]

Critics of this view say that the Sana manuscripts, from what they can tell, are not particularly revolutionary and suggest that if the manuscripts do contain textual variants, the variants are likely the result of the fact that the manuscript predates the Uthmanic codex. Adding to the controversy is the fact that Puin and his German colleagues have largely blocked access to the manuscripts. They oddly reason that if the Yemeni authorities were to know what is in them, they might well block further access to the manuscripts.[†]

[*]Quoted in Toby Lester, "What Is the Koran?" *Atlantic Monthly*, January 1999, http://www.theatlantic. com/magazine/archive/1999/01/what-is-the-koran/4024/1/.

[†]See, however, Karl-Heinz Ohlig and Gerd R. Puin, eds., *The Hidden Origins of Islam: New Research into Its Early History* (Amherst, N.Y.: Prometheus Books, 2009).

statement, however conflicts with the initial version in 4:23, which forbids marriages with "your daughter-in-laws." This verse was later changed to read: "the wives of your sons who are from your own loins."[8] This new claim, "from your own loins," meant that Muhammad could in fact marry Zayd's widow because Zayd was not his biological son. In addition to such variant verses, Powers also shows how legal and political verses from the Quran were also emended and changed over time.

Such variations may well be related to divergent traditions of Quranic recitation. According to a tradition attributed to Muhammad, the Quran was said to have been revealed according to "seven *ahruf*," which many take to mean seven different manners of reciting the text, perhaps accounting for tribal dialects.[9] Others, however, argue that the term *ahruf* might well refer to variant readings (so-called *variae lectiones*) that were around even after the Uthmanic recension.[10] There is some debate in later Muslim sources as to whether these seven *ahruf* are still in existence. Some say yes; others claim, however, that only a single tradition is dominant. Shi'is, the subject of chapter 5, also claim that the Quran for the most part was revealed in only one version; however, their tradition of recitation is today largely that of the Sunni majority.[11]

The Linguistic Matrix of the Ancient Near East

Some of the earliest nonpolemical Western scholarship on the Quran emerged in Germany in the nineteenth century. A pioneering book in this regard was written by one of the central figures in the development of Reform Judaism: Abraham Geiger (1810–1874). In his prize-winning *Was hat Mohammad aus den Judenthume aufgenommen?* (*What Did Muhammad Take from Judaism?*), Geiger argues that Muhammad or the earliest redactor of the Quran employed technical terms "borrowed" from earlier religions as a way to legitimate the new message.[12]

It would be difficult to adopt Geiger's thesis today, especially given the problems inherent in such terms as "borrowing." The preference, as mentioned, is to stress the common cultural heritage of ancient Near Eastern peoples. However, Geiger's argument is still interesting because it is not polemical and because it focuses on language common to numerous Near Eastern religious traditions. Although Geiger problematically envisages rabbinic Judaism as fixed and the Muhammad movement to be in a state of fluidity, his claim that Muhammad (or the final redactors of the Quran) employed terms that would have appealed to other monotheists in the area is not that far-fetched.

Geiger, for example, argues that Muhammad used certain biblical terms both to authenticate his own message and to differentiate it from earlier ones. He claims that the message of Islam caught on not simply because of Muhammad's genius, but because the populace of seventh-century Arabia would have been familiar with the monotheistic terms that Muhammad recast from earlier religions, such as *tabut* (ark), *tawrat* (torah), and *sakina* (divine presence).

There are certainly a number of problems with Geiger's thesis. He is unable, for example, to demonstrate that the similarities between Hebrew and Arabic were tantamount to borrowing—they may, after all, just be part of a shared vocabulary based on their common Semitic ancestry. However, Geiger's thesis is interesting because—unlike so many accounts today that wish to bypass the thorny question of Quranic or Islamic origins—it takes seriously the rich and complex social milieu in which Muhammad lived. Geiger does not work on the assumption that Islam or the Quran simply appeared, but that both existed in conversation with other religious traditions in the area.

What immediately strikes the reader of the Quran is its different relation of familiar themes found in previous scriptures. Muslims believe that this difference is proof that the Quran is a unique work, thus reinforcing the theological claims found within the Quran itself. Other scholars, however, have pointed out that the redactors of the Quran were perhaps less familiar with the Bible than with subsequent rabbinic interpretation of biblical stories. James Kugel has argued that some stories found within the Quran—for example, in 12:30–33, the story of how Potiphar's wife and her friends cut their hands when they see how beautiful Joseph is—are in fact rabbinic expansions of the biblical story. Although this motif of the friends and the cutting of their hands is nowhere to be found in the Genesis account in the Bible, such motifs emerged in subsequent Jewish texts that improvise and interpret biblical narratives and that predate the Quran.[13]

But we surely have to be aware that such an argument can cut both ways. Again, given the common Near Eastern heritage and the fluidity of terms within rabbinic Judaism and Islam in the seventh and eighth centuries there is no reason to assume that redactors of the Quran might well have "influenced" the formation of rabbinic legend as much as vice versa. For example, some the rabbinic collections detailing these extrabiblical narratives postdate the compilation of the Quran.

A more recent variation of this argument can be found in the writings of a controversial author bearing the pseudonym "Christoph Luxenberg."[14] This individual claims to have uncovered a Syrian Christian subtext within the Quran that early readers of the text, in addition to modern Western scholars of the past two hundred years, have largely failed to recognize. Despite his (some would say fatal) methodological flaws, his argument has generated a great deal of nonscholarly excitement and has been featured in many American and European newspapers and magazines.[15]

Luxenberg's argument is that we should regard Syro-Aramaic, not classical Arabic as constructed in later centuries, as the language spoken by Muhammad's tribe and the language used in the earliest compositions of the Quran. For Luxenberg, Aramaic was prevalent throughout the Middle East during the early period of Islam and was, moreover, the language of culture and Christian liturgy. If we make this adjustment in our thinking, he suggests, problematic passages that have long bothered traditional Muslim exegetes begin to make sense. He claims that Muhammad was preaching concepts that were not necessarily new to many of his Arab listeners and that Muhammad would have likely learned from his conversations with the Arabian Jews and Christians or from the Christians of Syria.

Not surprisingly, Luxenberg's thesis has received much criticism and should thus be approached with a great deal of caution.[16] Other scholars have proposed more sober and less sensational assessments of certain connections and commonalities between Eastern Christianities and the Quran.[17]

Such is the status of the debate over the origins and redactions of the Quran. To believers, the Quran is the word of God and presents a guide for life. This view, however, need not curtail further scientific and philological research into how the book came to be. Research into such questions will inevitably help us better understand and further contextualize the early Islamic polity in its immediate linguistic, social, intellectual, and religious environments.

Why Don't Muslims Have an "Old Testament"?

If the Quran admits that it relies so heavily on Jewish and Christian scriptures and claims to restore their original messages, the following question might well arise: Why doesn't the Muslim tradition append the Old Testament and New Testament to the Quran? A hint comes from a passage in sura 9:

The Jews say, "Ezra is the son of God";

The Christians say: "the Messiah is the son of God."

That is what they say with their mouths,

Conforming to what was said by those who disbelieved before them.

God confound them.

How they are embroiled in lies!

They have taken their rabbis and their monks

as lords apart from God,

as well as the Messiah, the son of Mary—

yet they were commanded to serve only one God;

there is no god but Him.

May He be glorified high above what they associate with Him. (9:30–31)

Using such verses for justification, the theological and polemical belief emerged that both Jews and Christians tampered (*tahrif*) with their scriptures. This belief would eventually lead to full-blown charges that both religions actually excised references to Muhammad from their scriptures.[18] Because of such charges, Muslims tend to regard both the Old Testament and the New Testament as corrupt: these books may well have been correct at one point in their history, these Muslims argue, but as they stand now, they are unusable. The Quran, on this claim, is the only unadulterated scripture.

Messages and Contents

Rather than spend more time on the thorny question of Quranic origins, which is impossible to answer definitively, we might find it more worthwhile to explore some of the key messages and themes within the book as it came to be understood by subsequent generations. In this respect, the message of the Quran is remarkably simple to summarize. It is worth reiterating that Muslims regard the Quran as Muhammad's primary miracle and as the overwhelming proof of his prophethood. For Muslims, the Quran represents the culmination in the Arabic language of a series of divine messages that began with the revelation to Adam and included the Torah (*tawrat*) and the New Testament (*injil*)—even though they regard these scriptures as corrupted. The Quran assumes a basic familiarity with some of the major themes and narratives recounted in both Jewish and Christian scriptures—summarizing some of these accounts, dwelling at length on others, and, in some cases, presenting alternative accounts and interpretations of events. The Quran describes itself as a book of guidance, rarely offering detailed accounts of specific historical events and often emphasizing the moral significance of an event over its narrative sequence.

In Quran 2:177, we find a list of qualities and beliefs that believers (*muminun*; sing., *mumin*) should hold:

> Piety [lies in] those who believe in God and the Last Day
> and the angels and the Scripture, and the prophets;
> those who give their possessions, for the love of Him, to kinsmen,
> orphans, the destitute, the traveler and those who ask,
> and [give them] for the freeing of slaves;
> who perform prayer and pay alms.

Although many of the themes on this list resurface in subsequent chapters, let us briefly focus on some of them here, especially those that play a prominent role throughout the Quran. A description of these themes should, in turn, allow us to understand something of the Quran's message.

THE UNITY OF GOD

Islam is predicated on absolute monotheism (**tawhid**). Implicit in the Arabic term—which literally means "to make one"—is the notion of action. The believer, in other words, must actively engage in the process of making God one in his or her life. According to 40:65–66,

> He is the Living.
> There is no god save Him.
> Call to Him, devoting your religion solely to Him.
> Praise belongs to God, Lord of created beings.
> Say, "I have been forbidden to serve those to whom you call,
> to the exclusion of God,

since the clear proofs have come to me from My Lord,
and I have been ordered to surrender to the Lord of created beings."

In this passage, we see the centrality of God to Islam and to all facets of Muslim worship. He is described as omniscient, omnipotent, merciful, and compassionate. The greatest sin is *shirk*, "associating" something else (other gods, individual persons, power, money, and so on) with God.

God's place in both the Quran and Islam more generally is summarized in the opening sura, the *fatiha*, which plays a special role in the daily prayer cycle (see chapter 8). A transcription of the Arabic transcribed in English letters, preceding the translation, allows one to get a better sense of the use of language in the original:

Bismilla-hi r-rahmani r-rahim
Al-hamdu lillahi rabbi l-alamin
Ar-rahmani r-rahim
Maliki yawmi d-din
Iyyaka nabudu wa iyyaka nastain
Ihdina s-sirat al-mustaqim
Sirat al-ladhina anamta alayhim ghayril
maghdhu bialayhim wala d-dallin

[In the name of the merciful and compassionate God.
Praise belongs to God, the Lord of all Beings,
The merciful, the Compassionate
Master of the Day of Reckoning
You we serve;
to You we turn for help.
Guide us on the straight path
the path of those You have blessed,
not of those against whom there is anger
nor of those who go astray.]

This sura, as mentioned, plays an important role in practicing Muslims' lived experiences. It is recited seventeen times in the course of the five daily prayers (see chapter 9). In fact, so important is this chapter that it is frequently referred to as the "essence of the book" (*umm al-Quran*; literally, "the mother of the Quran"), wherein the entire Quran exists as a microcosm.

THE DAY OF JUDGMENT

According to the Quranic message, all prophets essentially preach the same simple message: the coming of the Last Day or the Day of Judgment (*al-yawm al-din*). The earliest Meccan revelations describe this day in very apocalyptic and poetic terms. Here is part of chapter 82, "The Tearing," as translated by Michael Sells:

In the Name of God the Compassionate the Caring
When the sky is torn
When the stars are scattered
When the seas are poured forth
When the tombs are burst open
Then a soul will know what it has given
and what it has held back
Oh, O human being
what has deceived you about your generous Lord
who created you and shaped you and made you right
In whatever form he willed for you, set for you.
But no. Rather. You deny the reckoning
that over you they are keeping watch
ennobled beings, writing down
knowing what it is you do.
The pure of heart will be in bliss
The hard of heart will be in blazing fire
the day of reckoning, burning there—
they will not evade that day.
What can tell you of the day of reckoning
Again, what can tell you of the day of reckoning
A day no soul has a say for another
and the decision is at that time with God.[19]

Although all power ultimately resides with God, individuals must take it upon themselves to take responsibility for their own actions. In this regard, the Quran divides the world into two types of people: the faithful (*muminun*) and the unfaithful (*kuffar*; sing., *kafir*). The former, alternatively portrayed as the "friends of God,"

... will enter paradise and will not be wronged in anything
—Gardens of Eden,
which the Merciful has promised to His slaves in the Invisible.
His promise is always fulfilled
They will hear no idle chatter there, but [only] Peace;
And they will have their sustenance morning and evening. (Quran 19:60–63)

This passage is also interesting in that it reveals that salvation is not dependent on sectarian or religious affiliation. Those who disobey God, in contrast, will face a much different fate:

On the day when the enemies of God are rounded up to the Fire, driven on,
Then, when they reach it,
Their hearing and their sight and their skins
bear witness against them about what they had been doing
And they say to their skins,
"Why do you testify against us?";
they say, "We have been given speech by God,
who can give speech to everything
and who created you the first time
and to whom you will be returned." (41:19–21)

THE BOOK AND EARLIER PROPHETS

The Quran is one of the few works of scripture that refers to itself as a book or, perhaps more properly, as "the book." In this regard, it also recognizes its own ambiguities. In Quran 3:7, for example, we read:

It is He who has sent down to you the Scripture,
In which are firm signs
that are the matrix of the Scripture
While there are others that are ambiguous.
As for those in whose hearts is deviation,
They follow the ambiguous part,
seeking mischief and seeking its interpretation;
Only God knows its interpretation.

The Quran makes it clear both that its divine author is the same God who spoke with past prophets in other languages and that its message is the same as previous scriptures. Roughly twenty-eight prophets are mentioned as having been chosen by God to communicate His message to humanity. Among them, only a few were given scriptures (e.g., Moses, David, Jesus). The Quran also mentions a series of prophets who were not linked to the biblical past, but who emerged on Arabian soil prior to the advent of Muhammad. For example, Salih and Hud are mentioned, but they did not receive a book in the sense that Muhammad did.

The Quran uses a similar structure to describe most of these earlier prophets: after the prophet is commissioned by God with his message, the people to whom the prophet brings the message ultimately reject it and are as a result destroyed. God is always presented as triumphing over the unbelievers, and the divine message is always in the world in some form or manifestation.

In this regard, the Quran does not see its message as unique. On the contrary, its uniqueness resides in the fact that it is an "Arabic recital," a message no different from earlier messages but meant for the Arab tribes of the Arabian Peninsula. As noted earlier, however, the Quran presents novel "twists" on familiar Near Eastern myths. One example is the case of Jesus's crucifixion. According to the Quran, Jesus is a prophet of God, but not God himself. Negating the accounts in the New Testament and perhaps reminiscent of various heterodox Christian movements in the Arabian Peninsula, Jesus is not described as dying on the cross. According to Quran 4:157–158, the Jews

> ... did not kill [Jesus] or crucify him,
> but it was made to seem so to them.
> Those who disagree about him are in doubt about it.
> They have no knowledge of it
> and only follow conjecture.
> No. God raised him to Himself.
> God is mighty and wise.[20]

Such a fragment is typical of the Quran, which truncates much larger biblical stories into just a few lines.

The Inimitability of the Quran

If the most important evidence of Muhammad's prophecy is the Quran, the most important miracle of the Quran is its inimitability (*ijaz al-quran*). Perhaps owing to the highly literary milieu in which the Quran was compiled or redacted, there arose the notion that it could compete with the best of literature but at the same time must not be confused with such literature. The Quran itself challenges those who deny its claim of divine origin to produce a text like it (e.g., 10:38). This challenge did not stop some later poets—for instance, Abu al-Tayyib al-Mutanabbi (915–965)—from trying to outdo the Quranic narrative on a literary level.

There exist many variations on this theme of the Quran's inimitability in later Islamic literature. For instance, a recent largely apologetical argument can be found among certain contemporary Muslims who claim that the Quran predicts modern scientific discoveries in medicine, geology, physics, and climatology.

PROBLEMATIC VERSES

Perhaps one of the biggest mistakes when it comes to dealing with non-Christian religious scriptures is to invoke the Protestant assumption that what the scripture literally says necessarily equates to how the subsequent religious tradition interprets it. Although many Muslim literalists would indeed like this to be the case (see chapter 9), the fact remains that a literal understanding of the Quran ignores or negates the lengthy historical interpretive traditions—traditions that define Islam as much as, if not more so, than the Quran itself does. These interpretations, often codified as part of the tradition, mediate scripture—reinforcing parts of it, negating other parts, and generally providing more nuance than the original offers.

In recent years, many people critical of Islam have selected particular verses that they hold up as proof to demonstrate Islam's inability to conform to the modern world. Such verses invariably highlight the tradition's misogyny or violence against non-Muslims. They point, for example, to verses such as the following:

Men are the overseers of women
because God has granted some of them bounty in preference to others
and because of the possessions that they spend.
Righteous women are obedient,
guarding the invisible
because God has guarded [them].
Admonish those women whose rebelliousness you fear;
Shun them in [their] resting-places
And hit them
If they then obey you, do not seek a [further] way against them.
God is Exalted and Great. (Quran 4:34)

Or they point to this passage:

And kill [unbelievers] wherever you come upon them,
and drive them out of the places
from which they drove you out.
Persecution is worse than killing.
Do not fight them at the Sacred Mosque until they fight you there.
If they fight you, kill them.
Such is the reward of the unbelievers. (2:191)

Such verses certainly bother modern sensibilities (both Muslim and
non-Muslim). Some Muslim commentators, both in the past and in the
present, have tried to interpret them so that they are not as abrasive.
Yet other Muslims see nothing wrong with such statements. A categorical mistake, however, is to assume that *all* Muslims read such verses
in the same way. Perhaps the modern force of such verses is that they
tend to say less about the Quran, whose ethos derives from much different social and cultural contexts (not unlike the Hebrew and Christian
Bibles), than they do about the subsequent formation of Muslim identities. Liberal Muslims decry such verses and seek to allegorize them,
whereas more extreme interpretations take such verses literally as an
excuse to subjugate women and as a call to struggle violently against
the West. At stake is not the validity or invalidity of the Quran or of
Islam, but the struggle among Muslims for what gets to count as a proper interpretation.

The Quran in Muslim Life

The Quran plays a major role in Muslim religious. One does not read it silently but rather recites it aloud as a form of active participation in divine speech. One ideally handles a copy of the Quran only in a state of ritual purity (see chapter 7). Before one recites from it, one must utter the formulaic phrase "a'udhu b'illahi min al-shaytan al-rajim" (I take refuge in God from the accursed Satan), lest one mispronounce any of the words. When one finishes reciting, one is supposed to utter the phrase "sadaqa Allahu al-azim" (God the Mighty has spoken), again showing that the Quran is regarded as the word of God spoken to humans.

As mentioned, memorization of the entire Quran is seen as a virtuous activity. After lengthy study, those who master the art of recitation—known in Arabic as *ilm al-tajwid* (science of elocution)—enter a greatly respected profession, with the more famous ones making tapes and discs of their recordings for sale and gaining followers across the Muslim world.

Verses from the Quran, especially *al-fatiha*, the opening sura, are recited in the fixed cycle of Muslim prayer known as **raka**. Each *raka* involves uttering Quranic phrases in addition to performing the prescribed bodily movements of standing, bowing, kneeling, and prostrating. The Quran also plays an important role in popular piety, such as being used as a physical object to ward off evil spirits. Quranic verses are sometimes written down and enclosed in a pendant to be worn around the neck for protection.

Tafsir: *Commentary on the Quran*

Because Islam is a religion that is focused on a book, and because this book is often obscure, the role of interpretation is central to the religion. Commentary keeps religious scripture alive: updating it, nuancing it, expanding on it as need arises. Although there are certainly rules as to what gets to count as a "valid" or "good" interpretation, the point here is that the Quran, despite what some modern interpreters might claim, does not stand alone. As a result, the Quran has initiated a large body of commentary (*tafsir*) that seeks to explain or uncover the meanings of words, verses, or entire passages. Muhammad was the first person who engaged in this activity when he described the meanings of verses for his followers. In the earliest period, such commentary was largely confined to the explanation of literary aspects of verses, the context of its revelation, and occasionally the interpretation of one verse with the help of another. It was also not uncommon to invoke hadith to help clarify meaning.

Some of the most important *tafsir* collections include those by Muhammad ibn Jarir al-Tabari (838–923) and Isma'il Ibn Kathir (1301–1373). The following example comes from another important commentator, Abdullah Ibn Abbas (d. ca. 687) on the first sura of the Quran, *surat al-fatiha*. In this selection, Ibn Abbas seeks to unpack and explain the Quran's language so as to make it more familiar to his readers:

This is a Medinan sura, although some say it is Meccan. . . .

"Lord of the worlds": [This means] Lord of all possessors of spirit moving on the face of the earth and of all the inhabitants of heaven. It is also said that it means: Master of the jinn and of humanity. It is also said that it means: Creator of the created beings for whom He provides the subsistence and whom He takes from one condition to another. . . .

"Lord of the Day of judgment": [This means] the Judge on the day of religion [*din*], which is the day of reckoning and destiny on which He shall divide up His creatures. That is, the day on which people will be repaid for their deeds. There is no judge other than Him. . . .

"Guide us on the straight path": [This means that He] directs us to the steadfast religion which please You, which is Islam. It is also said that this means strengthen us in it. It is also said that it means it is the book of God such that He is saying: "Guide us in its categories of permitted and forbidden and in explication of what is in the book."[21]

Tafsir continues to preoccupy Muslim theologians to this day, and how one uncovers what one considers to be the "true" meaning of the Quran is often dependent on what one's preconceived notion of Islam is. A conservative commentator's *tafsir* will not surprisingly be highly conservative; a liberal theologian's *tafsir* will tend to be liberal.

Ta'wil: *Esoteric Interpretation of the Quran*

Related to the concept and genre of *tafsir* is **ta'wil**, a genre that attempts to discover mystical or esoteric meanings in the Quran. Although it is based on the same principle as *tafsir*, it is less interested in philological clarification and more in discovering secret messages below the literal level. Such interpretations *usually* do not contradict the conventional meaning. This type of interpretation was and continues to be very important to both Shiʿis and Sufis (discussed in chapters 4 and 6, respectively). For example, in his mystical commentary to the *miraj* briefly recounted in sura 53 of Muhammad, the ninth-century mystical commentator Sahl al-Tustari writes: " 'By the star when it plunges' (53:1) refers to Muhammad when he returned from heaven. 'Your comrade is not astray neither errs' (53:2) means, in no case was he astray from the reality of the professions of God's oneness, neither did he in any event follow Satan. 'Nor speaks he out of caprice' (53:3): by no means did he utter falsehood. . . . 'His heart lies not what he saw' (53:11): namely what [Muhammad] saw at the mystical vision of his Lord, as he face to face encountered him with the sight of his heart."[22]

The fact that so much interpretative commentary emerges from the Quran reveals just how central this text is to Muslim life and belief. All types of Islamic identity formations, described in parts II and III—Sunni, Shiʿi, Sufi, liberal, conservative, humanist, fundamentalist—draw their energy and momentum from the Quran. Like all religious scriptures, it can be interpreted and manipulated to reveal any number of often competing claims. This is why it is a mistake to ask, as so many wish to, "What does the Quran have to say about topic X?" The Quran, like the Hebrew Bible, takes on meaning only once it is connected to trajectories of interpretation supplied by various notions of what communities believe Islam should be.

NOTES

1. Michael Sells, trans., *Approaching the Qurʾan: The Early Revelations*, 2nd ed. (Ashland, Ore.: White Cloud Press, 2007), 190.

2. According to a theory proposed by Uri Rubin, the Arabic word *ummi* is an abbreviated form of the Hebrew term *ummot ha-olam* (nations of the world), which can refer either to the nations other than Israel or, metaphorically, to Jews who are ignorant of the Torah and the religious obligations derived from it. In which case, Muhammad could be conceived either as a non-Israelite prophet or as an Israelite prophet ignorant of Judaism. See Uri Rubin, *The Eye of the Beholder: The Life of Muhammad as Viewed by the Early Muslims* (Princeton, N.J.: Darwin Press, 1995), 21–30.

3. Norman O. Brown, "The Apocalypse of Islam," *Social Text* 8 (1983–1984): 155–171.

4. John Wansbrough, *Quranic Studies: Sources and Methods of Scriptural Interpretation* (Oxford: Oxford University Press, 1977).

5. Michael Cook, *The Koran: A Very Short Introduction* (Oxford: Oxford University Press, 2000), 118–119.

6. Quoted in ibid.

7. David S. Powers, *Muhammad Is Not the Father of Any of Your Men: The Making of the Last Prophet* (Philadelphia: University of Pennsylvania Press, 2009), 228, 66.

8. Ibid., 228.

9. See, for example, Claude Gilliot, "Creation of a Fixed Text," in Jane Dammen McAuliffe, ed., *The Cambridge Companion to the Qur'an* (Cambridge: Cambridge University Press, 2006), 48–51.

10. See the comments in John Burton, *The Collection of the Qur'an* (Cambridge: Cambridge University Press, 1977), 148–156.

11. Meir M. Bar-Asher, "Variant Readings and Additions of the Imami-Shi'a to the Qur'an," *Israel Oriental Studies* 13 (1993): 39–74.

12. Abraham Geiger, *Was hat Mohammad aus den Judenthume aufgenommen?* (Bonn: Baaden, 1833; repr., Berlin: Parega, 2005), translated as *Judaism and Islam*, trans. F. M. Young (Madras: MDCSPK Press, 1835; repr., New York: Ktav, 1970), 21.

13. James L. Kugel, *In Potiphar's House: The Interpretive Life of Biblical Texts* (Cambridge, Mass.: Harvard University Press, 1994).

14. Christoph Luxenberg, *The Syro-Aramaic Reading of the Koran: A Contribution to the Decoding of the Koran* (Berlin: Schiler, 2007).

15. For example, Alexander Stille, "Scholars Scrutinize the Koran's Origins: The Promise of Moist Virgins or Dried Fruit?" *New York Times*, March 4, 2002; and Stefan Theil, "Challenging the Qur'an," *Newsweek*, July 28, 2003.

16. See, for example, Walid A. Saleh, "The Etymological Fallacy and Qur'anic Studies: Muhammad, Paradise, and Late Antiquity," in Angelika Neuwirth, Nicolai Sinai, and Michael Marx, eds., *The Qur'an in Context: Historical and Literary Investigations into the Qur'anic Milieu* (Leiden: Brill, 2010), 649–699.

17. See, for example, Sidney Griffith, *Arabic Christianity in the Monasteries of Ninth-Century Palestine* (Ashgate, Eng.: Variorum, 1992); and Gabriel Said Reynolds, "Introduction: Qur'anic Studies and Its Controversies," in Gabriel Said Reynolds, ed., *The Quran in Its Historical Context* (London: Routledge, 2009), 1–25.

18. See the comments in Camille Adang, *Muslim Writers on Judaism and the Hebrew Bible: From Ibn Rabban to Ibn Hazm* (Leiden: Brill, 1996).

19. Sells, *Approaching the Qur'an*, 180–181.

20. The meaning of this verse, including its translation, has been the subject of tremendous debate over the centuries. See the comments in Todd Lawson, *The Crucifixion and the Qur'an: A Study in the History of Islamic Thought* (Oxford: Oneworld, 2009).

21. "Three Commentaries on Surat al-Fatiha, the Opening," trans. Andrew Rippin, in John Renard, ed., *Windows on the House of Islam: Muslim Sources on Spirituality and Religious Life* (Berkeley: University of California Press, 1998), 31–32.

22. Quoted, with some modification, from Gerhard Böwering, *The Mystical Vision of Existence in Classical Islam: The Qur'anic Hermeneutics of the Sufi Sahl at-Tustari* (Berlin: de Gruyter, 1980), 213.

SUGGESTIONS FOR FURTHER READING

Ayoub, Mahmoud. *The Quran and Its Interpreters.* 2 vols. 2nd ed. Albany: State University of New York Press, 1992.

Bell, Richard. *Introduction to the Quran.* Revised by W. Montgomery Watt. Edinburgh: Edinburgh University Press, 1970.

Burton, John. *The Collection of the Qur'an.* Cambridge: Cambridge University Press, 1977.

Cook, Michael. *The Koran: A Very Short Introduction.* Oxford: Oxford University Press, 2000.

Geiger, Abraham. *Judaism and Islam.* Translated by F. M. Young. 1835. New York: Ktav, 1970.

Griffith, Sidney. *Arabic Christianity in the Monasteries of Ninth-Century Palestine.* Ashgate, Eng.: Variorum, 1992.

Kugel, James L. *In Potiphar's House: The Interpretive Life of Biblical Texts.* Cambridge, Mass.: Harvard University Press, 1994.

Lawson, Todd. *The Crucifixion and the Qur'an: A Study in the History of Islamic Thought.* Oxford: Oneworld, 2009.

Luxenberg, Christoph. *The Syro-Aramaic Reading of the Koran: A Contribution to the Decoding of the Koran.* Berlin: Schiler, 2007.

Madigan, Daniel. *The Quran's Self-Image: Writing and Authority in Islam's Scripture.* Princeton, N.J.: Princeton University Press, 2001.

McAuliffe, Jane Dammen, ed. *The Cambridge Companion to the Qur'an.* Cambridge: Cambridge University Press, 2006.

Ohlig, Karl-Heinz, and Gerd Puin. *The Hidden Origins of Islam: New Research into Its Early History.* Amherst, N.Y.: Prometheus Books, 2009.

Powers, David S. *Muhammad Is Not the Father of Any of Your Men: The Making of the Last Prophet.* Philadelphia: University of Pennsylvania Press, 2009.

Rahman, Fazlur. *Major Themes of the Quran.* 2nd ed. Chicago: University of Chicago Press, 2009.

Reynolds, Gabriel Said, ed. *The Quran in Its Historical Context.* London: Routledge, 2009.

Rippin, Andrew, ed. *The Blackwell Companion to the Quran.* Oxford: Blackwell, 2006.

Rubin, Uri. *The Eye of the Beholder: The Life of Muhammad as Viewed by the Early Muslims.* Princeton, N.J.: Darwin Press, 1995.

Sells, Michael A., trans. *Approaching the Qur'an: The Early Revelations.* 2nd ed. Ashland, Ore.: White Cloud Press, 2007.

PART II

IDENTITY FORMATIONS

4

ISLAM BEYOND THE ARABIAN PENINSULA

A Historical Overview

A S WE saw in part I, the first two hundred years of Islam are mired in obscurity, and although we possess a great deal of material documenting these centuries, the fact is that much of that material comes from a later period. In the years after Muhammad's death in 632, the veil slowly begins to lift, and we eventually can see more clearly as Muhammad's message gradually becomes the cornerstone of what will emerge as a major social movement from Morocco in the West to as far as India in the East (and gradually beyond that). Nevertheless, the problem of later sources' claiming to be eyewitness accounts remains omnipresent in these early centuries. Sorting through this material—reading it selectively and contextually—will ideally shed some light on how the Muhammad movement transformed into Islam, one of the "world religions."[1]

One of the major themes of the previous chapters, worth reiterating here, is that we should beware of assuming that Islam appeared fully formed in the early seventh century and that, on Muhammad's death in 632 C.E., its religious teachings spread simply and easily throughout the Mediterranean basin and beyond. A slower growth should not surprise us: all the world's religions took time to develop in response to any number of political, legal, and social needs of early communities. In the case of Islam, it took centuries to work out the theological, intellectual, social, and legal ramifications of Muhammad's message: what its teachings were, how they were to be interpreted, and by whom. It is also a mistake to assume that non-Arab populations simply converted to this message en masse and overnight. On the contrary, it took centuries for these populations to convert.[2] What we now recognize as Islam took time to develop and often did so in response to numerous theological and legal controversies that with hindsight would be labeled as heterodox.

This chapter provides the general historical and social backdrop for the remaining chapters in part II, all of which concern themselves with both the formation and the development of sectarian differences and the doctrines associated with these differences. It examines, in broad stokes, the historical spread of Islam, taking stock of the dramatic changes that it underwent as it moved beyond the Arabian Peninsula and encountered a range of new political, religious, and cultural challenges. The question of how or even whether to incorporate non-Arabs in the movement was an important feature in the early geographic spread and religious development of Muhammad's message. Questions that need to be addressed are: Where did all the Muslims come from? The majority of new Muslims consisted of non-Arabs who had no genealogical or ethnic connection to the Arabian Peninsula, so how did they know or learn what it meant to be a Muslim? What, other than a political label (e.g., "Islam"), held the movement together and how?

The shape of what became Islam was greatly affected by the needs and questions of non-Arab converts who lived in places far removed from Mecca and Medina, the faith's two epicenters. Individuals could not become Muslim, in other words, if they did not know what Islam was. The spread of Muhammad's message beyond the confines of the Arabian Peninsula meant that Islam, as a religion with a set of doctrines and practices, had to be developed in response to non-Arabs' needs. The message had to be articulated and refined, which meant that there arose individuals and eventually classes responsible for carrying out these tasks. It was, in other words, no longer enough simply to act like Muhammad acted or act like Arabs who knew how Muhammad acted. We should not underestimate the importance of the new converts, who probably did more than anyone to influence the emerging shape of Muslim society, including the reception of the Quran, the collection of hadiths and other biographical materials, and developments in the spheres of law, theology, and philosophy. Such an influence is often overlooked in narratives that focus primarily on the elites and the political institutions they developed in places such as Damascus and Baghdad.[3] The fact of the matter is that for the first five centuries of Islam's existence, despite the theoretical inclusion of all Muslims within something imagined as the *umma*, it is perhaps more accurate to think of numerous Islams, with much doctrinal and ritualistic differentiation contingent on numerous geographical and cultural factors.

But before we explore this view of Islam "from the edge"—that is, on the margins of the growing empire as opposed to at its center—we need to return to our narrative and pick up with the events immediately surrounding Muhammad's death and the need to find a successor.

The Death of Muhammad and the Seeds of Division

It seems that, first and foremost, Muhammad regarded himself as a messenger of God and that his career as statesman was intimately connected to his prophetic message. If he were simply state building or, as later Christian polemicists would put it, power hungry, then surely he would have put firmly in place a mechanism to determine his successor. Contrary to later hadith reports marshaled by rival claimants, it is not at all clear that Muhammad designated his successor. By the same token, however, it is also not at all clear that he did *not* designate such a successor. The issue of Muhammad's succession, in other words, cannot be decided on the basis of the historical record. And despite what later theological dogma claimed, it is uncertain whether Muhammad saw himself as the *last* prophet and messenger to humanity. Although the Quran (33:40) speaks of Muhammad as the "seal of the prophets," the original intent or meaning of this phrase is by no means obvious.[4] Given the Quran's highly apocalyptical and eschatological nature, Muhammad might well have had no idea what God's plans for the future would be.

It should not be a surprise to us that Muhammad's death created numerous sectarian movements within his *umma*, most of which can be reduced to the question of establishing legitimate authority in the light of his absence. On one level, this sectarianism is again unsurprising given the fact that the *umma* was at the time of his death the most highly complex and extensive social unit that the Arabian Peninsula had ever witnessed. Within this unit, there existed at least four primary groups: (1) the *muhajirun* (immigrants), those individuals who first converted to Islam and who had made the *hijra* with Muhammad; (2) the *ansar* (helpers), those persons in Medina who first helped the immigrants in their new home; (3) other Arabs (especially in Iraq) who were gradually being assimilated into the emerging polity; and (4) those subjugated non-Arabs who were increasingly becoming part of the community and who in order to be absorbed into the existing social system had to become clients of Arab clans and tribes. These groups reveal both the diversity and the potential for social and political division within the early hierarchical community. One of the biggest potentials for such division existed between the earliest converts and the Meccan elites associated with the Quraysh tribe who converted to Muhammad's message relatively late. The latter had been initially responsible for the persecution of his earliest followers, many of whom were from lower socioeconomic strata.

These groups gave momentum to what most likely emerged as one of the earliest sectarian or ideological divisions in the nascent Islamic polity: What set of actors possessed legitimacy to guide the community? Although the end of this legitimacy process witnessed the formation of Shiʿism and Sunnism (discussed in chapters 5 and 6), it is worth noting that neither of these sects existed at the time of Muhammad's death. Rather, both took decades, if not centuries, to develop and form, and they did so largely in response to each other. We should also avoid assuming that Sunni Islam was normative and that Shiʿism somehow broke away as a heterodox movement, as certain later sources would like to have us believe.

The Events at the Portico of the Banu Saʿida

In the immediate aftermath of Muhammad's death, the leaders among the *ansar* apparently assembled at the Portico (*saqifa* [entranceway]) of the Banu Saʿida clan in Medina to elect a man to lead the community.[5] Their choice appears to have been Saʿd ibn Ubada, one of the clan's main chieftains. The *ansar*'s claim was predicated upon their role as protectors of the early immigrants to Medina, the *muhajirun*, and the fact that they had played a key role in Muhammad's earliest battles against the Quraysh. The *muhajirun*, however, heard of these political developments at the Portico, and one of their main tribesmen, Abu Bakr—Muhammad's father-in-law, Aisha's father, and, according to later (Sunni) tradition, the first male to accept Muhammad's message—headed there to confront the *ansar*. Again according to later accounts, Abu Bakr informed the *ansar* that the Arabs would accept a leader only from the Quraysh, so the Quraysh should be the leaders, and the *ansar* their ministers. Abu Bakr seems to have been successful because he emerged from the Portico as the first successor (*khalifa* or **caliph**) of Muhammad.[6]

The Four Rashidun

The first four caliphs (successors) to Muhammad are referred to as the "four rightly guided ones" (*al-rashidun*).[7] Many later Muslims look to this period as a "golden age" in terms of both its purity and its righteousness, presumably on account of its close proximity to the source of Islam's message. It is a common theme in the history of religions that the farther one moves from the originary source responsible for a religion's or movement's formation, the greater the likelihood that corruption enters into the original message, thereby tainting it. It is for this reason that various reform movements arise to try and restore what they perceive to be the original message. Many so-called Muslim fundamentalists (see chapter 9) look to this period of Muhammad and his early followers with such fondness that they reject *certain* features of modernity in their desire to re-create that period. For historical purposes, however, and given the sectarian milieu and internecine strife associated with this period, it is perhaps not insignificant to note that three of the four *rashidun* were assassinated. Beyond the sectarianism, however, this period was also one of the rapid expansion of Islam beyond the Arabian Peninsula.

ABU BAKR

After Abu Bakr emerged from the Portico of the Banu Saʿida as the first caliph, much of his reign (632–634) was spent fighting the so-called Ridda (Apostasy) Wars, which threatened the new community's unity and stability. According to pre-Islamic custom, the death of a tribal leader often signaled that the alliances agreed to by that leader's tribe had ended. Alliances, in other words, were valid for only as long as the tribal leader was alive. As a result, when Muhammad died, many Arab tribes claimed that they had submitted to Muhammad only, that their allegiance was thus no longer in effect, and that they accordingly refused to pay taxes to the new leader. In fact, some of these tribes now claimed to have prophets of their own that they looked to for guidance. The leader of one such tribe, Musaylima from the tribe Banu Hanifa, located to the east of Mecca, is reported to have sent Muhammad the following letter: "From Musaylima the apostle of God to Muhammad the apostle of God. Peace upon you. I have been made partner with you in authority. To us belongs half the land and the Quraysh half, but Quraysh are a hostile people."[8] After Muhammad's death, Musaylima apparently started a rebellion against the new caliph, Abu Bakr, but Abu Bakr's army eventually killed Musaylima during one of the Ridda Wars.

It seems that as long as Muhammad was alive, many of these tribes were content to be nominally followers of the new message, but after his death they renounced this religious aspect of their allegiance as well. Abu Bakr, however, seems to have insisted that these tribes had not just submitted to a simple human leader but had joined a religious community under God, of which he was the new head. So, in contrast to pre-Islamic times and the usual treaty practices created therein, their allegiance was not seen as having ended. To protect the new community and prevent it from imploding, Abu Bakr attempted to stem the tide of apostasy and seems to have been largely successful in doing so. Thus, the main accomplishment of his short two-year tenure was the reestablishment of the Arabian Peninsula under the central authority of the caliph based in Medina.

UMAR IBN AL-KHATTAB

Umar ibn al-Khattab (ca. 586–644, r. 634–644), eventually Muhammad's father-in-law, was originally hostile to Muhammad's message and was part of the Meccan elite that persecuted the earliest followers of that message. Converted just before the *hijra*, Umar became a powerful believer in the new message. As caliph, he greatly pushed expansion of the message beyond the Arabian Peninsula. The Fertile Crescent, Jerusalem, Egypt, and most of Iran now became part of the burgeoning Islamic Empire. A subsequent section in this chapter addresses the logistics by which a region became at least nominally "Muslim," but the point to emphasize now is the geographic extent of what was for all intents and purposes a new transregional empire in the area.

Umar seems to have been a quite astute and successful administrator. He divided this new empire into provinces and had them run by provincial governors that he personally chose. Tradition also attributes to Umar the beginning of the Islamic lunar calendar that he argued should begin with Muhammad's *hijra* to Medina as year 1. This lunar calendar is also appropriately called the *"hijri* calendar." Umar was assassinated in 644 by a Persian slave believed to have been upset with the conquest of the Sassanian Empire in Iran.

Umar's replacement was secured through a *shura* (electoral council) that consisted of six elders—all of whom were companions (*sahaba*) of Muhammad—who would choose one of their number to succeed. This council elected Uthman ibn Affan to become the third caliph to Muhammad.

UTHMAN IBN AFFAN

Uthman ibn Affan (r. 644–656) was a member of the Umayya family in Mecca, a family that represented the old Meccan aristocracy and whose members held out the longest against Muhammad. Uthman was an early convert despite his family's opposition. Some of the earliest immigrants to Medina treated these conversions with suspicion and as a matter of convenience. The fact that many of these later converts rose to power again under Uthman seemed to violate the principle of *sabiqa*, or precedence, an unwritten rule that held that those who had converted first to the new message had more prestige than those who converted at a later date.

Later Muslims have considered Uthman, as noted in chapter 3, to be the one responsible for the final redaction of the Quran. Many of his enemies, however, criticized him for putting his tribesmen into major positions of power throughout the still growing empire, power that his enemies no doubt sought for themselves. Uthman was assassinated in 656, presumably by disaffected tribesmen from Egypt.

ALI IBN ABI TALIB

After the death of Uthman, Ali ibn Abi Talib (r. 656–661), Muhammad's cousin and son-in-law, was appointed as caliph. Ali's position was immediately criticized from several sides. Uthman's kinsman Mu'awiya, who was the governor in Syria, revolted. And Muhammad's widow Aisha started a rebellion with two other Companions, Talha and Zubayr. Tradition records this rebellion as the first *fitna* (civil war).

It is unclear why Aisha was so opposed to Ali; regardless of her reasons, the tensions between them culminated in the Battle of the Camel, in which Talha and Zubayr were killed and Aisha's political aspirations, whatever they may have been, were all but quashed. Dealing with Mu'awiya would prove to be more difficult, however. Ali's and Mu'awiya's forces soon met in what is known as the Battle of Siffin. After some indecisive skirmishes, they agreed to arbitration, which focused on the issue of whether the murder of Uthman was justified. That Ali would agree to this arbitration upset many of his supporters and in their opinion served to undermine his right to be caliph. At this point, Ali's supporters split: some remained with him, and this group is often referred to as the *shi'at* Ali (Party of Ali); others opposed Ali for his willingness to arbitrate and referred to themselves as "Kharijites," or "those who had gone out" from the community.

In 661, Ali was assassinated by a Kharijite, at which point Mu'awiya seized power. His reign was to last for some twenty years, and even later sources that are quite critical of the way he seized power speak grudgingly of the prosperity of his rule.[9] However, later sources say, he seems to have engaged in very little state building, nor did he use the Muhammadan message as the legitimizing ideology of his rule, preferring instead to rely on his sway with the tribal chiefs in the Arabian Peninsula. "When Mu'awiya died," states one scholar, "his polity died with him."[10] Mu'awiya, however, is credited with establishing a hereditary dynasty of caliphs, known as the Umayyad Caliphate or Umayyad dynasty (661–750).

Abd al-Malik and the Creation of an Islamic Empire

The decades after Muhammad's death witnessed the transformation of his largely inchoate message into a global movement, with a bureaucratic infrastructure to support it. One of the key figures in this development was Abd al-Malik (b. ca. 645, r. 685–705), one of the first caliphs who had no direct experience of Muhammad's time. Surrounded by second-generation Muslims, many of whom were undoubtedly non-Arab converts, Abd al-Malik drew liberally on the imperial tradition that Muslim rulers had inherited from the larger empires they had conquered (e.g., the Sassanian and Byzantine empires). Among his innovations were the professionalization of the army, the replacement of fickle chieftains with paid commanders, and the transformation of warrior tribesman into a standing army loyal to the state. Abd al-Malik is also credited with centralizing the administration of the caliphate and establishing Arabic as its official language. He introduced a uniquely Muslim coinage, marked by its aniconism (i.e., absence of human images), which supplanted the Byzantine and Sassanian coins that had previously been in use. Some modern scholars even credit him rather than Uthman with the final canonization of the Quran.[11]

Perhaps most important, Abd al-Malik seems to have been instrumental in making Muhammad's religious message the major ideological pillar of his burgeoning empire. According to the evidence marshaled by Patricia Crone and Martin Hinds,[12] he and subsequent Umayyad caliphs styled themselves as God's representatives on earth, interestingly a category that the later spiritual heads of Shi'ism would adopt. Moreover, the caliphs did this in opposition to the concept of "representatives of the Prophet of God," which would eventually become normative Sunni belief under later dynasties. Again, this stylization attests to the fluidity of ideas, terms, and concepts at this still very early stage of Islam's theological development. Umayyad religious language, monuments, and understanding of Muhammad's message thus spoke to a particular understanding of the message of Islam that would be contested by later dynasties.

Abd al-Malik's reign also witnessed the construction of the Dome of the Rock mosque in Jerusalem (figure 5). Although the chronology remains uncertain owing to the removal of Abd al-Malik's name from an inscription and the addition of a later caliph's name, the building seems to have been completed in 692, making it one of the earliest surviving Islamic architectural structures. Some have argued that the Dome of the Rock was built to rival the Ka'ba, which, at the time of the Dome's construction, was under the control of a rival caliph in Mecca.

A more likely explanation for the construction of the mosque in Jerusalem, however, is that the nascent Muslim community was articulating a set of religious beliefs and practices for itself in ways that sought to make it distinct from the Near Eastern religious (including pilgrimage) heritage that it had inherited.[13] That the Ka'ba eventually won out as the main site of Islamic faith is probably the result of later rulers in the eighth century. Both sanctuaries, it should be noted, revolve around a

FIGURE 5 Dome of the Rock, Jerusalem. (Photograph by David Baum;
courtesy of Wikimedia Commons)

rock and its circumambulation, have connections to earlier prophets, and form the focal point for prayer and pilgrimage in Islam practice.

However, centralized authority and a nascent political message can tell us only part of the story. In this regard, it is also important to keep in mind that at this very early date the new Umayyad soldiers brought with them no monolithic Islamic message, contents, or practice. Many different Islamic societies began to develop in these early years, all of which grew up around a combination of local social and cultural customs, previous (i.e., non-Muslim) religious beliefs and practices, and still fluid ideas of who Muhammad was and what his message consisted of. Each of these societies, in turn, had its own particular history and set of traditions to which Muhammad and his message could be adopted and adapted. So even though the Umayyad Empire was nominally Muslim, what this actually meant on the ground is not so easy to determine.

As later caliphs sought to impose a uniform message on such a diverse populace, many groups of "Muslims" from various regions and with various understandings of Islam's message increasingly struggled to establish their own views as orthodox. Manifold and nascent Sunnisms, Shiʿisms, Sufisms—with all sorts of local variation and color—undoubtedly existed and interacted with one another in both the caliphal court and at the so-called edges of the empire. A certain degree of orthopraxy and uniformity would eventually emerge in the twelfth and thirteenth centuries, most likely as a response to these various political, religious, and cultural challenges.

Conversion to Islam in the Medieval Period

How did this rapidly growing empire become Muslim? The expansion of territory under Muslim rule certainly occurred very rapidly, but the

---

DID ISLAM SPREAD BY THE SWORD?

It is sometimes said that Islam spread by the sword, which presumably means that attacking Muslim armies gave towns, cities, and the individuals within them the choice of either converting to Islam or being killed. Although there might well have been rare instances of such threats, it is impossible that Islam could have spread so quickly and so violently. We possess very few sources that describe such bloodshed, nor would Islam have caught on in the way it did if people were forced to become Muslims on the threat of death.

As shown in this chapter and previous ones, the message of Islam was still in a state of flux, being worked out and developed as need arose, in its early period. It would accordingly be rather difficult to impose a still largely inchoate message on others. Rather, modern scholars who have studied conversion rates argue that the "Islamicization" of regions would have taken centuries to occur and that those responsible for its spread most likely would have been Sufi holy men (see chapter 5) as opposed to murderous marauders.[*] The former would have been more tolerant of local custom and would, at least in theory, have been more familiar with what was developing as orthodoxy. There probably would have been many reasons for conversion: social (e.g., the new religion offered social mobility), religious (e.g., the belief that a religion that spread so quickly must be guided by God), financial, and so on.

Moreover, just because a local ruler or the elite classes of a particular area converted to Islam did not necessarily mean that the entire region quickly followed suit. Or, if they did, they might well have been "Muslim" in name only and gone about their daily lives, including their religious lives, as they always had. This mixture of practices undoubtedly created numerous syncretistic beliefs and practices as many tried to fuse local custom with the new religion.

Finally, many Muslim rulers might well have preferred that locals keep their own religion because this ensured that they would pay the *jizya* (poll tax) that non-Muslim minorities had to pay. These minorities, referred to as **dhimmis**, were often Christians, Jews, and Zoroastrians. They received many legal rights, depending on the time and place, and often went about their business, both religious and secular, with little or no discrimination. The poll tax that these minorities paid was frequently an important revenue for the Muslim authorities.

[*]See, for example, Richard Bulliet, *Conversion to Islam in the Medieval Period: An Essay in Quantitative History* (Cambridge, Mass.: Harvard University Press, 1979).

spread of Islam itself in those territories was a much slower process. Popular legend regards the spread of Islam to be the result of the sword. A much more probable paradigm is one that recognizes that conversion was a process that occurred over many centuries and that the Islamic society that arose from this process included many of the cultural, social, religious, and intellectual traits of the areas into which Islam spread.

In his quantitative history of conversion, Richard W. Bulliet argues that in Egypt by the tenth century, for example—three hundred years after the initial arrival of Muslims there—roughly 50 percent of the population had converted to Islam. By the thirteenth century, he surmises, more than 90 percent of the population was Muslim.[14] This process of conversion most likely occurred in other regions of the empire, albeit at different rates and at different times.

If one question is *when* the diverse regions of the empire became Muslim, an equally important one is *how* they became so. Merchants, mystics, storytellers, poets, and garrison towns undoubtedly did much to spread various interpretations of what they considered to be the authentic contents of Muhammad's message in various regions. Yet, as mentioned earlier in this chapter, the religious, theological, and legal articulation of Islam arose largely in response to the needs of non-Arabs who otherwise had no idea what the message consisted of. We should not assume that ready-made articulations were simply brought to these regions; rather, they most likely developed there and oftentimes went from there back to the center (as opposed to vice versa).[15]

The Abbasid Caliphate

There soon arose a group that sought to depose the Umayyads. It seems to have been based in Khurasan, northeastern Iran, and comprised those who claimed descent from al-Abbas, one of Muhammad's paternal uncles. They attacked the Umayyads' moral character, administration, and ability to understand Muhammad's message. The Abbasids seem to have drawn much of their logistical support from non-Arab Muslims, known as *mawali*, who remained outside the kinship-based society of the Arabs and who were perceived as occupying a lower class within the Umayyad Empire. They also drew their ideological support from their claims of connection to Muhammad's family.[16] One of their slogans was that only a descendent from Muhammad's immediate household had the authority to lead the community. Such a position, not surprisingly, granted them the support of the followers of Ali, the Prophet's son-in-law, many of whom felt disaffected by the ascension of the Umayyads and who were centered in and around Kufa, about 125 miles (200 kilometers) south of Baghdad.

In 750, the Abbasids overthrew the Umayyad dynasty and transferred the administrative center of the new empire from Damascus eastward to Baghdad. One of the Umayyad princes, sometimes identified as Abd al-Rahman, left Syria as a youth and subsequently installed himself as a rival leader on the Iberian Peninsula (including modern-day Spain).

The Abbasids, however, quickly turned on those supporters and ideas that had invoked connections to Ali and his descendents to get to power. Perhaps fearful of their symbolic power, Abbasid authorities over time essentially put many of the spiritual leaders of the Alid (later to be called Shi'i) movement under house arrest. Once their usefulness was over, the followers of Ali were thus largely pushed aside, and the caliphs began to take on new trappings of power and recycled terminology loaded with religious significance, such as "Amir al-Muminin" (Commander of the Faithful). To say that they simply rejected Shi'ism and adopted Sunni Islam is too anachronistic because neither of these movements had fully developed or extricated itself from the other at this early period in Islamic history.

The early Abbasid Empire was responsible for facilitating many important cultural and intellectual contributions to Islamic and world civilization. Baghdad quickly became the intellectual and artistic center of the empire, the place where many Islamic and nonreligious sciences (e.g., philosophy, science) were developed and studied. Muslim scholars encountered the sciences, mathematics, and medicine of antiquity through the works of Aristotle, Plato, Galen, Ptolemy, Euclid, and others. These works, translated into Arabic, and the important commentaries written on them were the wellspring of Arab science during the medieval period.

This period also saw a great florescence of literature. We fortunately get a window to this period from a late-ninth-century bookseller from Baghdad, Abu'l-Faraj Muhammad Ibn al-Nadim. He wrote *Kitab al-fihrist*, a catalog of all the books available for sale in Baghdad at this time, thereby giving us an overview of the state and popular genres of literature.[17] He tells us, for example, that one of the most common forms of literature was the compilation: collections of facts, ideas, instructive stories, and poems on a single topic, such as the garden, women, emotions, and so on.

This period also included the belletristic traditions associated with the charming tales of *Arabian Nights*, often called *A Thousand and One Nights*. Interestingly, although these tales were set in the Baghdad under the early Abbasids, they seem to have been written at a much later date. This period also witnessed important advancements in philology and grammar, which were developed in large part to help contextualize the Quran and its language, which was regarded as pristine, within its original Arab context.

Al-Andalus, or Muslim Spain

At the Battle of Guadalete in July 711, most of the Iberian Peninsula (modern-day Spain and Portugal) came under Muslim rule. Armies of Muslims (often given the generic name "Moors") later crossed the Pyrenees to continue their conquest but were defeated in October 732 at the Battle of Tours by Charles Martel. The Iberian Peninsula, now part of the Umayyad Empire, was given the name "al-Andalus" and ruled by a series of governors appointed by the caliph based in Damascus. In 750, as noted earlier, the Abbasids defeated the Umayyads, but an exiled Umayyad prince escaped to al-Andalus and established himself there as the emir of Córdoba. Refusing to submit to the Abbasid caliph, he established a tenuous rule over much of al-Andalus.

In 929, Abd al-Rahman III assumed the emirate and established control over much of the peninsula, including parts of North Africa. He switched his title to caliph, thereby establishing al-Andalus and its capital, Córdoba, as the rival to Abbasid Empire in Baghdad.

The period of Abd al-Rahman III's caliphate is often regarded as the so-called Golden Age of al-Andalus. (The "Golden Age" epithet may say more about the memory of later generations than about the actual period in question.) Some estimates put the population of Córdoba and environs at as much as 500,000, which would mean that it was larger than Constantinople, then the largest city in Europe. Within the Islamic world, Córdoba became one of the leading cultural and cosmopolitan centers, with numerous libraries to which scholars (including Christian and Jewish) from all over Europe and the Near East came to study and examine manuscripts. More generally, al-Andalus was also the home of several important philosophers, the most famous of whom were Ibn Bajja (d. 1139), Ibn Tufayl

---

TRANSLATION, PHILOSOPHY, AND POLITICAL
LEGITIMACY THROUGH THE DAR AL-HIKMA

The translation movement in the ninth and eleventh centuries centered at the Dar al-Hikma (House of Wisdom) in Baghdad was no fleeting phenomenon: it last for more than two hundred years and included the support (intellectual, institutional, and financial) of the elite classes of the Abbasid caliphate. Attempts to account for the rise of this translation project usually involve crediting a few Syriac-speaking Christians for the movement or claiming that it was the result of an enlightened ruler.

Dimitri Gutas has argued more recently, however, that the depth and vision of the translation project transcend such traditional romantic or superficial accounts. He instead argues that the project was intimately connected to the political and ideological aspirations of the nascent Islamic Empire.* Engaging in this translation, he argues, was similar to creating other genres of Islamic literature (e.g., Quranic commentaries, hadith literature). The early Abbasids' translation project was, it seems, based on the attempt to legitimate the caliph's right to rule and to ensure that others perceived the new dynasty to have inherited its political legitimacy from its Muslim and non-Muslim predecessors.

*Dimitri Gutas, *Greek Thought, Arabic Culture* (London: Routledge, 1998), 2.

(d. 1185), and Ibn Rushd (d. 1198), the last known in the West as Averroes (see chapter 8).

The Córdoba Caliphate collapsed through civil war between 1009 and 1013 and was finally abolished in 1031. Political rule in al-Andalus then broke up into a number of mostly independent states called *tawa'if* (sing., *ta'ifa*), often translated as "petty kingdoms" or, perhaps more accurately, "independently ruled principalities."[18] These kingdoms often fought among themselves, which meant that they were too weak to defend themselves from those Christian armies that sought to retake the peninsula. In 1085, for example, these Reconquista (Reconquering) armies took control of Toledo. The *tawa'if* kingdoms looked to the south, to the empires in North Africa (e.g., the Almoravids and the Almohads), for help, and although they received it momentarily, the North African empires ultimately conquered and absorbed al-Andalus.

Although this period should not be romanticized as an "interfaith utopia" (as in the "Golden Age of Muslim Spain"),[19] many of the minor kingdoms, following the Córdoba Caliphate, were extremely tolerant of non-Muslim minorities. In Granada, for example, a Jew by the name of Shmuel Hanagid (d. ca. 1056) served as the equivalent of its prime minister. It was in al-Andalus, for example, that the Jews were first attracted to and began to compose Arabic poetry, philosophy, and belles lettres. Famous Jewish thinkers emerged from this environment (e.g., Abraham ibn Ezra, Judah Halevi, Moses Maimonides). Many of these individuals, however, migrated to the northern and Christian parts of the peninsula or left it altogether when the independent kingdoms were taken over by the larger and less tolerant dynasties from North Africa.

Al-Andalus came to an end in 1491, when the Christian Reconquista was all but complete. The Treaty of Granada ended Muslim rule, and in 1492 all the Jews and Muslims who refused to convert to Christianity were forced to leave Spain.

Independent Emirates

Although the Abbasid Empire would carry on nominally for centuries, as early as the late ninth century its massive empire and the bureaucracy needed to administer it began to fragment, giving way to various regional independent movements in places such as North Africa, Spain, and the eastern provinces. The rise of such independent and semi-independent kingdoms did much to circumscribe the power and influence of the Abbasid caliph still based in Baghdad. Although some argue that this period marked the end of Muslim unity, it is unlikely that such unity ever existed because the empire, even at the height of its power, could do little to unify and systematize the many different interpretations of Muhammad's message.

Outside Iraq, virtually all the autonomous provinces that composed the Abbasid Empire gradually began to take on the characteristics of mini-empires, complete with hereditary rulers, armies, and revenues. By as early as 820, for example, the Samanid dynasty exercised independent authority in eastern Iran and Central Asia. In 890, the Hamdanid dynasty, influenced by the emerging teachings of Shʿism, ruled in northern Iraq and Syria before they were conquered by another Shiʿi-inspired dynasty, the Fatimids, in 1003.

By the early tenth century, the Abbasids risked losing control of Iraq, their power base, to various emirates. In 945, for example, one of these regional dynasties, the Buyids, took over Baghdad and made the caliph into a puppet ruler for those with actual military power. In the eleventh century, the loss of respect for the caliphs continued; some of the provincial rulers no longer mentioned the caliph's name in the Friday religious sermons and struck it off their coinage. Although the Abbasids gradually regained some of their old strength in the late twelfth century, they were no match for the Mongols, who on February 10, 1258, destroyed the city of Baghdad.

The Abbasid dynasty was, however, eventually resurrected as a way to legitimize the power of the Mamluk dynasty centered in Cairo. *Mamluk* is the word for the Turkish "slaves" that the Abbasids had imported earlier to serve as the army for their caliphate. Although the Mamluks used the mantle of the Abbasids, they certainly had no pretenses regarding the universal government of all Muslims. They did, however, hold out against the Mongol attacks. In 1519, though, the Ottomans from Anatolia (Turkey) conquered the Mamluk dynasty, and the capital was moved from Cairo to Constantinople.

The View from the Edge

In an important study, historian Richard W. Bulliet correctly cautions against assuming that all the important theological and intellectual developments in the gradual emergence of Islam took place in caliphal courts among Arab elites. Islam, in other words, was not invented there and then sent out to the provinces for its various inhabitants to assent to. On the contrary, numerous Islams—with all sorts of local colors and teachings— were scattered throughout the vast Islamic Empire. The Islam of Córdoba, for example, would not necessarily be the Islam of Cairo or the Islam of Baghdad. Local religious authority, Bulliet argues, was based on local hadiths and in local systems of interpretation by locally prominent families of religious scholars.[20] Although many hadiths and the traditions associated with them would ultimately take on a supralocal legitimacy, this unification did not take place until roughly the thirteenth century.

Local diversity eventually gave way to a more uniform set of teachings and practices. Some local hadith, which were probably more responsible than the Quran for defining the religion to many devout believers, never traveled beyond villages or cities or, if they did, were ultimately rejected as weak. The uniformity that Islam invented for itself in the eleventh and twelfth centuries was largely the product of communal religious institutions brought about by the migration of scholars and what Bulliet calls the need "to feel at one with other members of the universal umma in the dark period before and after the Mongol destruction of the caliphate."[21]

The Ottoman Empire

The Ottoman Empire was a massive power that lasted from 1299 to 1923 and at the height of its power in the sixteenth and seventeenth centuries spanned three continents: southeastern Europe, western Asia, and northern Africa.[22] The empire also controlled distant overseas lands through declarations of allegiance, such as that by the sultan of Aceh (Indonesia) in 1565.

Given its broad geographic extension, the Ottoman Empire functioned at the cross-section of the Eastern and Western worlds for more than six centuries. The Ottomans conquered Constantinople in 1453, at which point it entered a long period of conquest and expansion, making its way into Europe and North Africa. Its conquests were enabled by its army's technical superiority and its navy's ability to contest and protect key seagoing trade routes in competition with the Italian city-states in the Black, Aegean, and Mediterranean seas and with the Portuguese in the Indian Ocean.

One of the Ottoman Empire's more famous rulers, Suleiman the Magnificent (r. 1520–1566), captured Belgrade in 1521, and he and his armies subsequently conquered the southern and central parts of Hungary. In 1529, he laid siege to Vienna but failed to take the city after the onset of winter forced his retreat. In 1532, he attacked Vienna again but was repulsed just south of the city.

In the seventeenth and eighteenth centuries, the empire entered a period of increasing stagnation. During this period, much territory in the Balkans was surrendered to Austria. Other parts of the once gigantic empire, such as Egypt and Algeria, became largely independent. By the eighteenth century, centralized authority gave way to varying degrees of provincial autonomy enjoyed by local governors and leaders.

The dissolution of the Ottoman Empire was brought about in part by the reform-minded and pro-secular Young Turk Revolution of the early twentieth century, which sought to establish a constitutional state, and in part by the outcome of World War I (1914–1918) and the victorious factions' subsequent partitioning of the empire. The Republic of Turkey succeeded the Ottoman Empire on October 29, 1923, and European countries such as France and Britain controlled major portions of the former empire.

The historical and sociological complexity of Islam witnessed in this chapter provides an important antidote to essentialism—the notion that there exists a unified Islamic or Muslim essence that has moved effortlessly through time. The broad historical time frame presented in this chapter is meant as a general backdrop against which numerous doctrinal developments took place. These developments, associated with manifold interpretations of Islam, are the subject of the remaining chapters in part II. These chapters reveal that there were often highly contentious debates about how to interpret the teachings, the authority, and the very figure of Muhammad. These debates played a formative role in shaping various Islamic identities, each one of which claimed to be the authentic vehicle to channel Muhammad's message.

NOTES

1. For an illuminating discussion of the creation of a "world religions" discourse and how Islam fits into it, see Tomoko Masuzawa, *The Invention of World Religions, or, How European Universalism Was Preserved in the Language of Pluralism* (Chicago: University of Chicago Press, 2005), 179–206.

2. Nehama Levtzion, ed., *Conversion to Islam* (New York: Holmes & Meier, 1979); Richard W. Bulliet, *Conversion to Islam in the Medieval Period: An Essay in Quantitative History* (Cambridge, Mass.: Harvard University Press, 1979).

3. On this point, I am greatly influenced by Richard W. Bulliet, *Islam: The View from the Edge* (New York: Columbia University Press, 1994).

4. Here, again, I refer to Yohanan Friedmann, *Prophecy Continuous: Aspects of Ahmadi Religious Thought and Its Medieval Background*, new ed. (New Delhi: Oxford University Press, 2003).

5. Accounts of this election emerge from the history of al-Tabari and the *Ansab al-ashraf (Lineage of the Nobles)* of al-Baladhuri (fl. ninth century). A discussion of these figures can be found in Husain M. Jafri, *Origins and Development of Shiʿa Islam* (London: Longman, 1979), 27–57. Al-Yaqubi (d. 897) offers a pro-Shiʿi account of these events.

6. Jafri, *Origins and Development of Shiʿa Islam*, 57–65.

7. On the use of the term *khalifa* (caliph) in early Islam, see Patricia Crone and Martin Hinds, *God's Caliph: Religious Authority in the First Centuries of Islam* (Cambridge: Cambridge University Press, 1986), esp. chap. 1.

8. Muhammad Ibn Ishaq, *The Life of Muhammad: A Translation of Ibn Ishaq's "Sirat Rasul Allah,"* trans. Alfred Guillaume (1955; repr., Oxford: Oxford University Press, 2009), 649.

9. See the comments in Chase Robinson, *Abd al-Malik* (Oxford: Oneworld, 2005), 24–25.

10. Ibid., 25.

11. See, for example, Alfred-Louis de Premare, *Aux origines de Coran* (Paris: Broché, 2004).

12. Crone and Hinds, *God's Caliph.*

13. Robinson, *Abd al-Malik*, 100.

14. Bulliet, *Conversion to Islam*, 92–113.

15. Bulliet, *Islam*, 10–12.

16. Moshe Sharon, *Black Banners from the East: The Establishment of the Abbasid State* (Jerusalem: Magnes Press; Leiden: Brill, 1983), 21–37.

17. An English translation is given in Bayard Dodge, ed. and trans., *The Fihrist of al-Nadim: A Tenth-Century Survey of Muslim Culture* (New York: Columbia University Press, 1970).

18. David Wasserstein, *The Rise and Fall of the Party-Kings: Politics and Society in Islamic Spain, 1002-1086* (Princeton, N.J.: Princeton University Press, 1985), 1–22.

19. As is done, for example, in Maria Rosa Menocal, *The Ornament of the World: How Muslims, Jews, and Christians Created a Culture of Tolerance in Medieval Spain* (Boston: Beacon Press, 2002).

20. Bulliet, *Islam*, 114.

21. Ibid., 204.

22. Giancarlo Casale, *The Ottoman Age of Exploration* (Oxford: Oxford University Press, 2010).

SUGGESTIONS FOR FURTHER READING

Bulliet, Richard W. *Conversion to Islam in the Medieval Period: An Essay in Quantitative History*. Cambridge, Mass.: Harvard University Press, 1979.

——. *Islam: The View from the Edge*. New York: Columbia University Press, 1994.

Casale, Giancarlo. *The Ottoman Age of Exploration*. Oxford: Oxford University Press, 2010.

Crone, Patricia, and Martin Hinds. *God's Caliph: Religious Authority in the First Centuries of Islam*. Cambridge: Cambridge University Press, 1986.

Dodge, Bayard, ed. and trans. *The Fihrist of al-Nadim: A Tenth-Century Survey of Muslim Culture*. New York: Columbia University Press, 1970.

Donner, Fred McGraw. *The Early Islamic Conquests*. Princeton, N.J.: Princeton University Press, 1981.

Friedmann, Yohanan. *Prophecy Continuous: Aspects of Ahmadi Religious Thought and Its Medieval Background*. New ed. New Delhi: Oxford University Press, 2003.

Levtzion, Nehama, ed. *Conversion to Islam*. New York: Holmes & Meier, 1979.

Robinson, Chase. *Abd al-Malik*. Oxford: Oneworld, 2005.

Sharon, Moshe. *Black Banners from the East: The Establishment of the Abbasid State*. Jerusalem: Magnes Press; Leiden: Brill, 1983.

Wasserstein, David J. *The Caliphate in the West: An Islamic Political Institution in the Iberian Peninsula*. Oxford: Clarendon, 1993.

——. *The Rise and Fall of the Party-Kings: Politics and Society in Islamic Spain, 1002-1086*. Princeton, N.J.: Princeton University Press, 1985.

5

EARLY SECTARIANISM AND THE
FORMATION OF SHIʿISM

B ASED ON the broad historical survey presented in chapter 4, we can now explore some of the major doctrinal developments that emerged from the spread of Islam beyond the Arabian Peninsula. This chapter and chapters 6 and 7 shift from a synthetic narration of political, cultural, and religious history to a more narrow focus on the emergence of theological, legal, and religious difference. They accordingly present the rise and development of the major sectarian movements in Islam: Shiʿism, Sunnism, and Sufism. It is a mistake to assume, as is frequently done, that Sunni Islam emerged as normative from the chaotic period following Muhammad's death and that the other two movements simply developed out of it. This assumption is based in part on the problem that we have confronted frequently in these early chapters—the taking of later and often highly ideological sources as accurate historical portrayals—and in part on the fact that the overwhelming majority of Muslims throughout the world follows now what emerged as Sunni Islam in the early period. The result of these two claims, the former problematic and the latter a fact, is that Sunni Islam is often mistakenly regarded as synonymous with Islam.

This view is not surprisingly far from accurate. Islam, whether of the Shiʿi variety or the Sunni variety (leaving aside Sufism until chapter 7), represents the end product of several centuries of compromise and contestation between competing ideologies and interpretations of Muhammad's message. Rather than posit separate tracks of development for these movements, a history of Islam should regard them as intertwined at an early stage, deriving their potency from various historical and sociological forces alluded to in the previous chapter. Each of these sectarian movements—and again it is important not to assume that there simply exists one Shiʿism or one version of Sunni Islam—used the other to define itself more clearly and in the process to articulate better its doctrinal contents and rituals.

Before proceeding, we should reflect more generally on the problems that emerge for any community after the death of a leader. Questions that arise in this situation include: How might the leader have wished the community to carry on in his absence? Who has the authority to rule in his absence? Will he return at some later date? Such questions are by no means unique to the early followers of Muhammad, and perhaps an informative parallel might be drawn to those early followers of Jesus who also struggled to understand his message in the light of his death. The early Jesus movement eventually, after several centuries, gave way to Christianity as the early Catholic Church, which sought to harness Jesus's charisma, developed numerous theological positions that would become normative in response to a variety of controversies (e.g., Gnosticism, Arianism).

The history of religions, in other words, abounds in creative solutions to these most human of concerns. The solutions put forth to answer these human concerns eventually become crystallized as dogma for later generations, the stuff of faith and presumably of history. This process results once again in the complex intersection of faith and history, objectivity and subjectivity, from which it is very difficult to pry one apart from the other.

Wilferd Madelung's The Succession to Muhammad

In 1997, Wilferd Madelung published a scholarly study wherein he sought to reassess the nature of the conflicts that arose among the early successors to Muhammad. He works on the assumption that much of the basic Western research carried out and published in the early nineteenth century on the topic of Muhammad's succession, scholarship that modern historians subsequently accepted, largely bought into what later ascendant Sunni accounts say. He therefore rejects the position of indiscriminately dismissing everything not included in the earliest (pro-Sunni) sources and instead tries to use other (pro-Shiʿi) narrations compiled in later periods. He argues that the "wholesale rejection [of such sources] as late fiction is unjustified and that with judicious use of them a much more reliable and accurate portrait of that period can be drawn than has so far been realized."[1]

In order to distinguish his approach from both the academic and the theological status quo, Madelung returns to the sources—the Quran, hadith reports, later accounts—in order to reassess them. Calling most of the earliest Islamic historiography—the record on which even secular Western scholars have traditionally relied—"tendentious," Madelung contends that the Shiʿi claims may well be more normative than that of the Sunnis. Without choosing a side in this debate, we can follow his lead and be cautious about simply repeating as true the accounts that we find in the earliest Islamic sources. This chapter provides both insider and outside accounts. Although this brief presentation is not the venue to rewrite the history of Islam from the perspective of Shiʿism, it does break with convention in that it follows Madelung's hypothesis and presents an account of Shiʿism before going on to examine Sunni Islam in chapter 6.

The Events at the Portico of the Banu Saʿida: A Pro-Shiʿi View

Before proceeding, we would do well to return to the events at the Portico of the Banu Saʿida, where some of Muhammad's followers congregated following his death. There, Abu Bakr, who, as later pro-Shiʿi historians note, came from a relatively insignificant clan within the Quraysh tribe, emerged as the first caliph. Ali, who came from Muhammad's own clan, the Banu Hashim, was—again according to these later sources—largely overlooked in the process. These sources say that Ali was the first male to embrace Muhammad's message. Ali was part of Muhammad's clan and as such, especially given the unwritten rules in a heavily tribal culture, had the right to emerge as the true successor.

Thus began the first of what would later be perceived as a series of slights to deprive the most capable and deserving person of the caliphate. Ali, the first male convert to Islam and Muhammad's cousin and son-in-law, was very close to Muhammad and formed an intimate part of his family. Both Shiʿi and Sunni sources agree that after the events at the Portico, a crowd of men marched to Ali's house and demanded that he swear allegiance to Abu Bakr, the new caliph. The situation would have turned violent if not for the intercession of Fatima, Ali's wife and Muhammad's daughter, who later pro-Shi'i sources say was injured and miscarried in the process. These sources also agree that some of Ali's immediate kinsmen encouraged him to set himself up as a rival to Abu Bakr. Despite these events, Ali did not advance his claim to the caliphate—perhaps thus becoming a symbol for what would later emerge as Shi'i helplessness and resignation in mundane political affairs.

Supporters of Ali to this day draw on numerous hadiths, albeit ones collected in the early ninth century, to attest to his position as Muhammad's successor. For example:

> We were with the Apostle of God in his journey and we stopped at Ghadir Khumm. We performed the obligatory prayer together and a place was swept for the Apostle under two trees and he performed the mid-day prayer. And then he took Ali by the hand and said to the people: "Do you not acknowledge that I have a greater claim on each of the believers than they have on themselves?" And they replied "Yes!" And he took Ali's hand and said, "Of whomsoever I am lord [mawla], then Ali is also his lord. Be Thou the supporter of whoever supports Ali and the enemy of whoever opposes him." And Umar [the second caliph] said to him: "Congratulations, O son of Abu Talib! Now morning and evening [i.e., forever] you are the master of every believing man and woman."[2]

Ali's supporters also point to the following story, which is regarded as sound (sahih) even by the ninth-century Sunni collector al-Tirmidhi. In this story, when Muhammad arrived in Medina, he assigned to each of the muhajirun—that is, those who had made the hijra with him—except Ali a "brother" from Medina to ease the transition and smooth over potential social tensions. "The Apostle of God made brothers between his companions, and Ali came to him with tears in his eyes crying: 'O Apostle of God! You have made brethren among your companions but you have not made anyone my brother.' And the Apostle of God said to him, 'You are my brother in this world and in the next.'"[3]

Despite the apparent authority of such hadiths, which seem to designate Ali clearly as Muhammad's self-appointed successor, the fact of the matter is that they were written much later and likely date to the origins of the early Abbasid dynasty. This dynasty, it will be recalled, sought to legitimate itself through its claim of descent from the Hashim clan—the clan of Muhammad and Ali—as opposed to the clan of Abd Shams (the clan of Uthman and Muʿawiya, from which the Umayyad dynasty sprang). Like many of the earliest sources of Islam, hadiths extolling Ali's claim to the caliphate are not necessarily historical documents, but rather attempts to make the past meaningful in the context of the present and in anticipation of the future.

Moreover, Ali was not the only one with a familial relationship to Muhammad. Both Abu Bakr and Umar, the first and second caliphs, respectively, were Muhammad's fathers-in-law. And Uthman, the third caliph, was, like Ali, Muhammad's son-in-law. Based on their level of intimacy to Muhammad, then, it is unclear why Ali should have a larger claim to leadership than these individuals—unless, of course, this claim was based on the level of clan affiliation, which, as we saw in the part I, played a crucial role in ascertaining loyalty and, despite the universality of Muhammad's message, did not seem to go away in the period immediately following his death. Once again, the events and their later interpretations return us to uncertain historical ground owing to the paucity of eyewitness accounts of the events in question.

Shiʿat Ali

It is a mistake to label Abu Bakr, Umar, Uthman, and the subsequent Umayyad dynasty as "Sunnis." As noted in chapter 4, this dynasty essentially invented an identity for itself using Muhammad's still inchoate message and the bureaucratic and legal infrastructures inherited from earlier empires in the region. Just as we cannot call the Umayyads "Sunnis," it would be equally incorrect to call supporters of Ali and his claim to the caliphate "Shiʿis." Certainly, we witness the catalyst for both movements at places such as the Portico and in the events immediately following the election of Abu Bakr to the caliphate. Although both groups began to coalesce slowly as *political* ideologies at this point, one cannot yet say that they represented or crystallized into two distinct *theological* sets of doctrines and practices, something that will only occur in the eighth century.

With the death of Ali, many of his partisans looked to his two sons (and hence Muhammad's biological grandsons), Hasan and Husayn, for political leadership. Hasan, perhaps striking some sort of a deal with Muʿawiya, declared that he was not interested in claiming the caliphate. (Later Shiʿi propaganda will assert that Hasan was murdered, presumably by agents of Muʿawiya, just as he was about to make a claim.) Much of the nascent support for Ali was in Kufa, in modern-day Iraq just south of Baghdad. There, following the death of Muʿawiya, the Kufans pledged support to Husayn and encouraged him to come there to start a rebellion against the rise to power of Yazid, Muʿawiya's son. Despite the Kufans' enthusiasm, Husayn was warned by several people close to him that the Kufans' support had been fickle for both his father and brother. Despite reservations, he departed Mecca for Kufa in the company of about fifty armed men and a number of women and children.

The Events at Karbala

Upon taking the throne, Yazid was faced with a number of local rebellions throughout the empire, and one of his first tasks was to put an end to them and reestablish the order maintained in his father's time. One of the largest of these disturbances came from Kufa, with the result that Yazid instructed one of his most energetic generals to take control of the town and suppress the rebellion. Although Husayn had received word of the state of affairs in Kufa, he pressed on, declining other proposals that might have secured his safety. As he made his way to Kufa, he was set upon on the tenth day of the Muslim month of Muharram in 680 by Yazid's forces on the plains of Karbala and murdered.[4]

Although this event put an ostensible end to the Kufans' immediate political aspirations, it proved to be a watershed moment in the later formation and self-identity of what would subsequently emerge as Shiʿism (figure 6). The murder of Husayn functioned as an important catalyst for transforming the Kufans' political grievance and Ali's followers into a largely religious movement—although we must also be aware of the categorical problems of neatly separating the "political" from the "religious" in eighth-century Iraq or Arabia. To this day, the commemoration of the suffering and murder of Husayn—a practice referred to as "Ashura"—is the most fervently celebrated ritual in the Shiʿi religious calendar (see chapter 9).[5]

Certain sectarian groups formed around the figure of Husayn in the immediate aftermath of his murder. The Tawwabun, for example, felt guilty

FIGURE 6   Shrine of Husayn, Karbala, Iraq. (Photograph by Toushiro; courtesy of Wikimedia Commons)

that they had not done more to support Husayn and his companions as they made their way to Kufa. So in 684 the Tawwabun marched toward Syria to challenge Umayyad rule.[6] However, they were no match for the Umayyad troops and were easily slaughtered on the battlefield.

Although Husayn was murdered on the plains of Karbala, the movement did not terminate with his death. Ali's partisans thereafter located religious and political legitimacy in Husayn's son and, by extension, Ali's grandson and Muhammad's great-grandson. This individual, Abu Muhammad Ali ibn Husayn, also known as Zayn al-Abidin (Ornament of the Worshippers), was the only son of Husayn to survive the massacre at Karbala. The Umayyad forces that captured him sent him to Yazid in Damascus, and he was then allowed to retire to Medina, presumably in return for some sort of agreement that he would remain politically quiescent.

With respect to all these political machinations, it is important not to lose sight of the fact that in the aftermath of Muhammad's death two distinct leadership paradigms were slowly emerging and developing within the early community. On the one hand, the early community seems to have agreed, at least implicitly, that consensus should determine the right to rule the growing *umma*—a paradigm that would be presented as the majority opinion in subsequent generations. The partisans of Ali, on the other hand, located the right to rule not in consensus, but in the special qualities inherent to Muhammad, his immediate family (*ahl al-bayt*; literally, "people of the house" in the sense of family), and their descendants. This biological proximity legitimated their authority and right to rule.

The male descendents of Ali, whom his followers or partisans regard as the legitimate successors of Muhammad, are known as **Imams**. After the murder of Husayn, many of these Imams tended to maintain a sense of quietism, functioning largely as private scholars within the larger context of the Umayyad and Abbasid empires. The institution of the Imamate underwent various developments as the centuries went on, and it is important to understand that the term "Imam" was understood by someone such as Zayn al-Abidin and his followers much differently than it would have been understood by the followers of the later Imams.

What emerged as mainstream Shi'i doctrine is contingent on the existence of a set of twelve Imams, all of which claim biological descent to Muhammad through Ali. We have so far encountered the first four: Ali, Hasan, Husayn, and Zayn al-Abidin.

These Imams played a crucial role in the development of Shi'i religious identity. Although rarely, if ever, having any sort of political power, they derived their right to rule through their lineage to Muhammad and the fact that each Imam personally chose his own successor based on divinely inspired designation, although, perhaps not surprisingly and as the list in "The Twelve Imams" clearly shows, the succession tended to be from father to son. Whether under house arrest or in hiding, these figures functioned as the spiritual leaders of the followers of Ali and eventually as the fully developed theological and legal movement known as Shi'ism.

THE TWELVE IMAMS

1. Ali ibn Abi Talib (d. 661)
2. Hasan, Ali's son (d. 669)
3. Husayn, Ali's second son (d. 680)
4. Ali, Zayn al-Abidin, Husayn's son (d. 712 or 713)
5. Muhammad al-Baqir, Zayn al-Abidin's son (d. ca. 735)
6. Ja'far al-Sadiq, Muhammad al-Baqir's son (d. 765)
7. Musa al-Kazim, Ja'far's son (d. 799)
8. Ali al-Rida, Musa's son (d. 818)
9. Muhammad al-Taqi, Ali's son (d. 835)
10. Ali al-Hadi, Muhammad's son (d. 868)
11. Hasan al-Askari, Ali al-Hadi's son (d. 873 or 874)
12. Muhammad al-Mahdi (b. 868)

The Ghulat

The speculation that grew up around the Imams and their connection to the family of Muhammad through Ali inevitably led some individuals and groups to ascribe divine characteristics to them. Several groups tended to adopt Ali's family as the embodiment of their religious speculation. Such groups were labeled *ghulat* (those who exaggerate) because they attributed divinity to beings other than God and prophecy to persons other than Muhammad. And although the concept of *ghuluww* (exaggeration) would eventually come to be labeled as immoderate and heterodox, in the first two centuries after the death of Muhammad it was quite commonplace, especially with respect to figures such as Ali and Husayn. We would do well to remember that views later considered heterodox were often in this early period seen as legitimate and that what emerged as orthodox did so in response to such views.

Many of the early followers of the Imams (it is still too early to call them "Shi'i") possessed the view that would later be classified as *ghuluww*. This view was undoubtedly enhanced by the martyrdom of Husayn on the Karbala battlefield, which gave Ali's family a quasi-cultic significance and thereby took the movement out of the realm of politics and placed it in the realm of religious pathos. It is important not to underestimate the importance of such *ghulat* groups in the formation of what would eventually emerge as mainstream Shi'ism and to understand that views later deemed "extremist," including divine incarnation in humans, most likely circulated widely in earlier periods.

The Importance of Ja'far al-Sadiq

The sixth Imam, Ja'far al-Sadiq (d. 765), is generally considered to be the one most responsible for the formation of what would emerge as distinctly Shi'i religious teaching and doctrine. Many later traditions, for example, ascribe to him anti-*ghulat* views. Prior to him, it is likely that only largely inchoate groups existed that located in certain individuals the right to rule based on their descent through Ali.

According to some accounts, the leaders of the Abbasid revolution asked Ja'far al-Sadiq if he wanted to be the new caliph, but he refused on quietist grounds so as to lead a life devoted to religious scholarship.

Whether this story is accurate or not is, of course, impossible to determine. However, it seems likely that Ja'far al-Sadiq would have wanted to avoid the many competing interests at work in the revolution. His choice led to a view among the partisans of Ali that true leadership cannot be found in those who govern.

Here, as in earlier discussions, it is important to be aware of the fact that later sources project their understanding onto an earlier period. Indeed, it is only in the period after the Twelfth Imam, in the ninth and tenth centuries, that we begin to have sources that tell us anything about what exactly Shi'i belief consists of.

Many of these later sources, however, do point to Ja'far al-Sadiq as the figure most responsible for working out the theological doctrine of what constituted an Imam, especially the features by which he should be recognized. According to Ja'far and as elaborated in later Shi'i doctrine, the Imam possesses several key features, including *ilm*, or "knowledge" (of the truths of the universe, including those of the Quran). This feature is illustrated in the following anecdote recorded by the seventeenth-century Shi'i thinker Muhammad Baqir Majlisi:

> I was with Abu'l-Hasan in Mecca when a man said to him: "You are commenting from the Book of God some matters that you did not hear."
>
> And he replied: "It was revealed to us before it was revealed to the people and we commented upon it before it was commented upon by others. We know what is permitted and what is forbidden in it, we know which verses abrogate and which verses are abrogated in it, and how many verses were revealed on which night, and concerning what and to whom they were revealed. We are the judges of God on His earth and His witnesses for His creation."[7]

Another feature of the Imam is *isma* (infallibility and sinlessness). According to a hadith by Ja'far al-Sadiq, "The one who is sinless is the one who is prevented by God from doing anything that God has forbidden. For God has said: 'He who cleaves to God is guided to the Straight Path.'"[8]

Another feature that defines the Imam is **nass**, his ability to explicitly designate his successor. This principle might well have developed as a way to protect what was slowly coalescing as a clear line of Imams who the majority of supporters of Ali agreed on were the true Imams distinguished from, sources tell us, other claimants to the office. For example, Ja'far al-Sadiq relates the following about Ali:

The Apostle of God said, "God does not cause a prophet to die until he has ordered him to appoint a successor, someone from his close family." God ordered me to appoint a successor. And so I asked Him, "Who, O Lord?"

And God replied, "Appoint your cousin Ali, the son of Abu Talib, as your successor, O Muhammad! For I have established this in the former books and have written that he is your successor and have made a covenant with all created things and with My prophets and apostles. I have made covenants with them all concerning My Lordship and your prophethood, O Muhammad, and the succession of Ali, the son of Abu Talib."[9]

The importance of Ja'far al-Sadiq undoubtedly stems from the fact that he was the Imam at the time of the ascendency of the Abbasid caliphate, from whom he may well have received some sort of official patronage. The Abbasids, it will be recalled from the previous chapter, rose to power using the claims and symbols of Ali's partisans, but, the sources say, Ja'far al-Sadiq eventually was harassed by the caliphs and even held in a Kufan prison. Sources also speak of his academic gifts, and it is said that many renowned scholars and jurists were his disciples, including Abu Hanifa and Malik ibn Anas, two of the founding fathers of Sunni law schools that bear their name. According to Shi'is, he met the same fate as the majority of the Imams: poisoning under the orders of the reigning caliph, who undoubtedly recognized and feared his power to lead.

The Role of the Imam

The main function of the Imam, again largely according to later sources, is to provide his followers with the proper direction in the law and to guide them toward a spiritual understanding of religious truths. The Imams were and still are regarded as God's gift to creation; they possess a cosmic significance, and miraculous powers are often attributed to them.

The position of what would eventually crystallize as Sunni Islam contends that with the death of Muhammad, both the prophetic function and specific individuals' sense of guidance toward God largely ended. In contrast, what would eventually emerge as official Shi'i doctrine is the notion that although the prophetic function may well have ended, the need to guide humans and to explain the contents of the divine teaching continued through the line of the Imams.

DIFFERENCES BETWEEN SHI'I IMAM AND SUNNI IMAM

There is sometimes confusion among non-Muslims over the term "imam." In Shi'i Islam, it is used to refer explicitly to one of the Twelve Imams, who are believed to be direct descendents of Muhammad. There currently exists no Imam on earth because he is in occultation, abiding in such a state until the time arises when he will return as the Mahdi (Guide).

In Sunni Islam, however, there are plenty of imams. The word *imam* in Arabic is a preposition that means "in front of" and traditionally refers to the person who leads the daily prayers. The religious leaders of local mosques and Muslim communities are also increasingly referred to as imams, especially in North America.

The Imams accordingly take on a quasi-mystical significance for Shi'is. They are referred to as the "proof of God" (*hujjat Allah*) to humans and the "sign of God" (*ayat Allah*, or **ayatollah**) on earth. The Imam, then, is essentially the living successor to the Prophet, the person who embodies, in theory if not in actual practice, all political authority and sovereignty. According to the sixth Imam, Ja'far al-Sadiq, for example, "We are the ones to whom God has made obedience obligatory. The people will not prosper unless they recognize us, and the people will not be excused if they are ignorant of us. He who has recognized us is a believer [*mumin*] and he who has denied us is an unbeliever [*kafir*]. He who neither recognizes nor denies us is in error unless he returns to the right guidance which God has made obligatory for him. And if he dies in a state of error, God will do with him what he wishes."[10]

According to later tradition, the Imams possess a body of literature that no one else has, such as a book said to have been revealed by Jibril (the angel Gabriel) to Fatima to console her on the death of her father and a copy of the Quran personally transcribed by Ali that includes his commentary. The special powers and unique literary tradition that are perceived to be part and parcel of the Imamate enable those who hold its office to have a special gnosis, or knowledge, of one of Islam's great mysteries: the Name of God. In words attributed to Ali, "Our Lord has given to us knowledge of the Greatest Name, through which, were we to want to, we would render asunder the heavens and the earth and paradise and hell; through it we ascend to heaven and descend to earth and we travel to the East and to the West until we reach the Throne [of God] and sit upon it before God and He gives us all things, even the heavens, the earth, the sun, the moon and stars, the mountains, the trees, the paths, the seas, heaven and hell."[11]

The Twelfth Imam

The Twelfth Imam has a date of birth but not of death and also, not coincidentally, has the same name as the Prophet: Abu al-Qasim Muhammad. According to Shi'i tradition, the Twelfth Imam is said to have gone into occultation or hiding (*ghayba*) and will return at the end of time. The lesser *ghayba* is the time the Imam lived a human life, after which he entered the greater *ghayba*, which will last until the arrival of the messianic age.

According to later tradition, the Twelfth Imam made only one public appearance, at the death of his predecessor, and none of the notables knew of his birth. When the eleventh Imam's brother was about to assume the mantle of the Imamate, he entered his brother's house to lead the funeral prayers, but a young boy suddenly appeared and said, "Uncle, stand back! For it is more fitting for me to lead the prayers for my father than you."[12] The boy was never seen again, and from this point the occultation is marked.

Much mythical speculation would grow around the identity of the Twelfth Imam. According to various later Shi'i accounts, he was the son of the eleventh Imam and a Christian slave girl or the daughter of the Byzantine emperor or a descendent of Peter. Such stories undoubtedly tried to connect evolving Shi'i apocalypticism to the figure of Jesus, who figures highly in Islamic eschatological speculation.[13] The Twelfth Imam is the **Mahdi** (Guide) who will reveal himself in the messianic era. According to some texts, when the Mahdi arises, "he will experience as a result of the ignorance of the people worse than what the Apostle of God experienced at the hands of the ignorant people of the Time of Ignorance because the Apostle of God came to a people who worshipped stones and wood but the [Mahdi] will come to a people who will interpret the Book of God against him and will bring forward proofs against him. When the flag of the [Mahdi] is raised, the people of both East and West will curse it." Or, "When the [Mahdi] arises, he will rule with justice and will remove injustice in his days. The roads will be safe and the earth will show forth its bounties. Everything due will be returned to its rightful owner. And no people of religion will remain who do not show forth submission and acknowledge belief. . . . And he will judge among the people with the judgment of David and Muhammad. . . . At that time men will not find anywhere to give their alms or to be generous because riches will encompass all."[14]

Historically speaking, it is most likely that the concept of a hidden Imam became a safer alternative for the partisans of Ali to develop as a group. As long as there was a living Imam, he continually posed a threat to the ruling authorities, who were increasingly identifying themselves with the emerging Sunni legal schools (see chapter 6). The occultation became a convenient way for Shiʿis to remain loyal to the idea of an Imam and thereby define their own identity as distinct from other Muslims and at the same time to partake of the larger Muslim state. In this regard, another common feature of Shiʿism is the notion of *taqiyya* (pious dissimulation), a concept that sanctions the concealing of one's true religious identity or convictions in the face of adversity.

Shiʿi Dynasties

Although the Abbasids would quickly renounce their sympathies with the followers of Ali, there would soon arise other dynasties with real commitments to Shiʿi ideology. Indeed, in the eleventh century, many of the dynasties in the splintered Abbasid Empire were, at least in name, Shiʿite. For instance, the rulers of the Fatimid dynasty (909–1171) in Egypt and the Buyid dynasty (tenth and eleventh centuries) in Iran and Iraq were Shiʿite, although it is highly unlikely that the majority of inhabitants in those areas was.

Twelver Shiʿism

The major "denomination" of Shiʿism that exists today is the Ithna Ashariyya (Twelvers), although they refer to themselves as "Imamis." This moniker refers to a certain cross-section of the partisans of Ali that eventually coalesced into a cohesive group who acknowledged the Twelve Imams and their authority and who held that the Twelfth Imam was hidden and was the Mahdi. Other partisans of Ali had identified some of the earlier Imams with the Mahdi, and for this reason it is important not to ascribe Twelver doctrine to the period before the last Imam's occultation.

Twelvers really built a new paradigm of leadership within Islam by concentrating authority on a particular individual. As we have seen, this authority began to develop under Jaʿfar al-Sadiq in the mid-eighth cen-

tury and was taken to its logical conclusions by Shiʿi jurists and legal theorists after the occultation of the Twelfth Imam in the ninth century. As
the Imam became less and less active in Muslim society, more and more
Shiʿites had to become involved in leading the community. This process
led to an intricate system of agents (*wikala*) who represented the authority
of the Imam within various Shiʿi communities. Many of these agents were
scholars and were responsible for collecting taxes and for developing and
interpreting the law.[15]

Although the Imams had always had around them a set of agents, by the
time of the Twelfth Imam there was in place a large system of such agents
who probably represented many competing factions. After the occultation, these agents were responsible for the community's legal, religious,
and fiscal sustenance.[16] In many ways, today's ayatollahs are the modern
incarnation of these medieval agents because they are responsible for the
maintenance of the tradition during the greater occultation. The title ayatollah (literally, "sign of God") is an explicitly Shiʿi designation. Contrary
to popular belief, there are no ayatollahs in Sunni Islam.

According to some estimates, roughly 15 percent of today's Muslims
are Shiʿites. Of this group, roughly 90 percent are Twelvers. The largest
populations may be found in Iran, Iraq, and Lebanon. A general rule of
thumb to remember is that Shiʿis in general and Twelvers in particular
have for most of their history been largely politically quiescent, awaiting
the return of the last Imam.

Other Shiʿi Denominations

Not all Shiʿis are Twelvers. There exist other denominations, and their existence is based on tracing their lineage through a different line of authority. Ismaʿil, the eldest son of Jaʿfar al-Sadiq, was appointed by his father
to be the next Imam, but he died before his father did, which created a
problem: How could Jaʿfar al-Sadiq be wrong in his choice of successor?
And why wasn't one of Ismaʿil's sons chosen to be Imam instead of Musa
al-Kazim? Although the majority of those who would later be designated
"Shiʿis" would settle on Musa, a significant group argued that Ismaʿil and
his offspring were the legitimate descendents of Jaʿfar al-Sadiq. This gave
rise to the Ismaʿilis, sometimes also referred to as "Seveners" because Ismail was seventh in line.

The main doctrines of the Isma'ilis—sometimes also referred to in later Muslims sources by the pejorative name "Batiniyya" (Esotericists)—is to get humans to move from the exoteric or obvious (*zahir*) expression of religious truth to the hidden or esoteric (*batin*) expression. This movement corresponds to a movement from law (sharia) to its eternal core (*haqiqa*). An elaborate cosmology also arose around this movement.

Today, the best-known of the Isma'ilis are the Nizaris. They are an ethnically and culturally diverse community that lives in many countries, and they are united in their allegiance to the *aga khan*, who claims descent from Isma'il ibn Ja'far al-Sadiq.

The Zaydis, another such group, rest authority in Zayd ibn Ali rather than in the person who would become the more normative choice, Muhammad al-Baqir, who was murdered in an uprising in Kufa in 740. Because the Zaydis broke off so early, they maintain that any descendent of Ali can be elected as Imam, that this individual need be neither sinless nor infallible, and that he has a duty to claim political power from the illegitimate rulers. Zaydis are today found largely in parts of Lebanon and especially in Yemen, where they held political power until 1962.

Distinctive Doctrines

As mentioned at the beginning of this chapter, it is important not to think of Shi'ism as a heterodox movement that departed from a normative and thus orthodox Sunnism. It should by now be clear that Sunnism and Shi'ism represent two distinct ideological positions on key issues such as legitimacy, authority, and succession. But neither ideology, despite practitioners' claims to the contrary, was there at the death of Muhammad. Although we get a glimpse of both positions at the Portico of the Banu Sa'ida, what would emerge as Sunnism and Shi'ism did so at roughly the same time, and, perhaps not surprisingly because the very nature of legitimate authority was at stake, each developed its positions in response to the other.

As we have seen, the most distinctive aspect of Shi'ism is its emphasis on Muhammad's line of descent and its location of this line in the institution of the Imamate. As it would take shape, especially in the aftermath of the formation of Twelver Shi'ism, the Imam became a cosmic individual, existent from the beginning of time. At work here is the notion that the world, even before the emergence of Shiʿism as a historical movement, needs the Imam for guidance. There has never been, according to Shiʿis, a time without an Imam. Even after the Imam became "hidden in the books," as it were, he is believed to watch over his community still. This symbology was heavily exploited in the Iranian Revolution in 1979 (see chapter 9).

Despite the sectarian milieu within the early *umma*, partisans of Ali never really (for the most part) argued that the Quran had been tampered with. Remember that later tradition put the codification of the Quran in the hands of Uthman, who, in later Shiʿi tradition, represents one of the earliest to take the caliphate from its rightful claimants. This tradition further corroborates the point, however, that Sunnism and Shiʿism parted ways—at least on theological grounds—at a time when the text of the Quran was readily established and agreed upon.

Where Shiʿis do differ from other Muslims, however, is in the existence of a distinct body of hadith literature. As we saw in chapter 2, hadiths are written reports that recount some activity or saying of Muhammad. Whether we consider hadiths valid historical sources or not, Shiʿis possess a large body of hadiths that they trace back to or through the various Imams. Again, however, much of this literature does not have a provenance before the ninth century.

As worked out in later Shiʿi legal theory of the fifteenth and sixteenth centuries, scholars took over all the duties of the occulted Imam. Ayatollahs largely interpret what they perceive to be the will of the Twelfth Imam through legal reasoning as a largely theological or textual construct. As becomes clear in chapter 6, however, much of Shiʿi legal thought parallels that of the various Sunni schools.

NOTES

1. Wilferd Madelung, *The Succession to Muhammad: A Study of the Early Caliphate* (Cambridge: Cambridge University Press, 1997), xi.

2. Quoted in Moojan Momen, *An Introduction to Shiʿi Islam: The History and Doctrines of Twelver Shiʿism* (Oxford: Ronald, 1985), 15.

3. Quoted in ibid., 13.

4. Ibid., 28–34.

5. Mahmoud Ayoub, *Redemptive Suffering in Islam: A Study of the Devotional Aspects of Ashura in Twelver Shiʿism* (The Hague: Mouton, 1978).

6. Momen, *Introduction to Shiʿism Islam*, 35.

7. Majlisi, *Bihar al-anwar*, 110 vols. (Tehran: Matbaʿa al-Islamiyya, 1956–1972), 23:196.

8. Quoted in Momen, *Introduction to Shiʿi Islam*, 155.

9. Quoted in Muhammad Karim Khan Kirmani, *Kitab al-Mubin*, 2 vols. (Kirman, Iran: Chapkhana Saʿadat, 1970), 1:308.

10. Quoted in Muhammad ibn Yaqub Kulayni, *Al-Kafi*, ed. Ali Akbar Ghaffari (Tehran: Kaktabat al-Saduq, 1961), 1:187.

11. Majlisi, *Bihar al-anwar*, 26:7.

12. Quoted in Momen, *Introduction to Shiʿi Islam*, 161.

13. Abdulaziz Sachedina, *Islamic Messianism: The Idea of Mahdi in Twelver Shiʿism* (Albany: State University of New York Press, 1981).

14. Quoted in Momen, *Introduction to Shiʿi Islam*, 169.

15. Norman Calder, "Judicial Authority in Imami Shiʿi Jurisprudence," *British Society for Middle Eastern Studies Bulletin* 6 (1979): 104–108.

16. Wilferd Madelung, "Authority in Twelver Shiism in the Absence of the Imam," in *Religious Schools and Sects in Medieval Islam* (London: Variorum, 1985), 163–173.

SUGGESTIONS FOR FURTHER READING

Arjomand, Said Amir. *The Shadow of God and the Hidden Imam: Religion, Political Order, and Social Change in Shiʿite Iran from the Beginning to 1890*. Chicago: University of Chicago Press, 1984.

Daftary, Farhad. *The Ismailis: Their History and Doctrines*. Cambridge: Cambridge University Press, 1990.

Dakake, Maria Massi. *The Charismatic Community: Shiʿite Identity in Early Islam*. Albany: State University of New York Press, 2007.

Halm, Heinz. *The Fatimids and Their Traditions of Learning*. London: Tauris, in association with the Institute of Ismaili Studies, 1997.

——. *Shiʿism*. 2nd ed. New York: Columbia University Press, 2004.

Jafri, Husain M. *Origins and Development of Shiʿa Islam*. London: Longman, 1979.

Madelung, Wilferd. *The Succession to Muhammad: A Study of the Early Caliphate*. Cambridge: Cambridge University Press, 1997.

Momen, Moojan. *An Introduction to Shiʿi Islam: The History and Doctrines of Twelver Shiʿism*. Oxford: Ronald, 1985.

Mottahedeh, Roy P. *Loyalty and Leadership in an Early Islamic Society*. Princeton, N.J.: Princeton University Press, 1980.

——. *The Mantle of the Prophet: Religion and Politics in Iran*. Oxford: Oneworld, 2000.

Sharon, Moshe. *Black Banners from the East: The Establishment of the Abbasid State*. Jerusalem: Magnes Press; Leiden: Brill, 1983.

Walbridge, Linda S. *Without Forgetting the Imam: Lebanese Shiʿism in an American Community*. Detroit: Wayne State University Press, 1997.

6

LEGAL DEVELOPMENTS AND THE RISE OF SUNNI ISLAM

A s MUHAMMAD's message spread into various areas, each in possession of its own set of local religious, legal, and cultural traditions, subsequent generations—unlike earlier generations, for whom "being Arab" went a long way to defining "Islam" and who relied largely on prevailing custom and human reason—needed some form of systematic law to deal with pressing issues such as expansion and conversion, and to define what exactly constituted Islamic belief and practice. As a result, courts and their legal rulings (fatwas), perhaps more than any other institution, began to shape various Muslim worldviews. This chapter focuses on the legal developments that made this possible, showing how the rise of Islamic law was intimately connected to the gradual emergence of "Sunnism."

Muhammad was regarded by his immediate followers as a politician, a military leader, a judge, a prophet, and a religious guide. He most decidedly was not a legal jurist who put in place a system of law governing every aspect of a Muslim's life. It is also highly unlikely that such a system developed either in his lifetime or in the period immediately thereafter. Too little is known about his life or even from the final redaction of the Quran to make such claims. What we can say with some degree of certainty is that customs of understanding Muhammad's evolving message most likely subsequently crystallized into distinct theories of legal reasoning, which in turn led to the gradual formation of a systematic legal code.

Moreover, it is important not to assume that the formation of Islamic law occurred in a vacuum; it most likely was also influenced by and responsive to earlier legal codes, especially Jewish and Roman.[1]

The name "Sunni" derives from a technical term that we have already encountered: "Sunna." In chapter 2, we saw how the latter term was used to refer to the customs and precedent established by an authoritative individual that ideally functioned as a model or paradigm of emulation for others.[2] When the term "Sunna" appears in Islamic legal theory, it is used in a more restrictive sense to refer to the normative life of Muhammad that was constructed and imagined as authoritative by later generations. (It should be noted, though, that Shiʿis also employ it to refer to the Sunna of their Imams.) This construction was certainly connected to the collection of hadith reports, wherein Muhammad's Sunna is both established and encountered.

The name "Sunni" abbreviates a phrase that better clarifies the Sunni movement's ideological parameters: "ahl al-sunna waʾl-jamaʿa" (the People of the Tradition [of Muhammad] and the Community). As with Shiʿism, however, it is imperative that we not regard this tradition as emerging fully formed at the time of Muhammad. On the contrary, it took time to develop, often in relationship to a series of legal and theological disputes, certain answers to which would emerge as "orthodox." Although many of these answers would at a later date be taken to have existed at the time of Muhammad, there is no clear evidence that they did.

Sunni Islam is defined not by its allegiance to a particular individual (e.g., Ali and the *ahl al-bayt*) or institution (e.g., the Imamate), as Shiʿism is, but by following one of the four authentic schools of law that are envisaged as representing the true elaboration of Muhammad's Sunna. These schools took generations to develop and were done so largely by means of a group of legal scholars (*ulama*; sing., *alim*), whose main concern was to determine what obedience to God should mean in a daily context.[3] The product of their collective efforts is the sharia, literally the "path" or "way" that Muslims should follow.

According to Muslim belief as it developed in these circles, God is the sole author of the law. Humans articulate this law by means of the science of jurisprudence (*fiqh*). Although this law is ultimately considered to be an eternal and ideal system, human intelligence and experience are required to elucidate its parameters. So even though legal rulings may change over time, the law itself is considered to remain eternal. The rules of jurisprudence were elaborated by distinct methods and techniques developed in the centuries after the death of Muhammad. Because jurisprudence is considered a science (*ilm*), it is overseen by specialists or "doctors of the law" (*fuquha*; sing., *faqih*) who are responsible for working through its legal and ethical ramifications.[4] These *fuquha*, it should be noted, did not simply pronounce the law but disagreed and debated over its formulation and application. And these disagreements and debates played a major role in the formulation of manifold Islamic identities.

The Origins of Islamic Law: Two Approaches

As is the case with regard to so much in the formative period of Islam, there is considerable debate in the secondary literature concerning the origins of Islamic law. The major paradigm, supplied by the German Orientalist Joseph Schacht (1902–1969),[5] contends that Islamic law, as we recognize it today, did not exist during the first one hundred years after Muhammad's death. Based on a close analysis of legal hadiths, Schacht argued that most if not all the legal texts were fabricated by scholars writing centuries after Muhammad's death and that they reflect those jurists' opinions. The origins of the Islamic legal tradition, according to Schacht, derived from unacknowledged borrowings from various Near Eastern (e.g., Persian, Jewish, Roman) legal codes. In the eighth century, roughly two hundred years after Muhammad's death, circles of legal scholars arose in Mecca, Medina, Egypt, Kufa, Basra, and Yemen. These geographic schools of law were subsequently "personalized" around eponymous founders. The key figure in the history and crystallization of Islamic jurisprudence was Muhammad ibn Idris al-Shafiʿi (d. 820), who was largely responsible for creating the methodology for ascertaining legal principles, known as **usul al-fiqh** (roots of jurisprudence). Within a century of al-Shafiʿi's death, however, independent legal reasoning largely ceased, with the result that, according to Schacht, Islamic legal thinking became increasingly rigid.

Highly critical of Schacht's methodology, Wael Hallaq disputes everything from Schacht's chronology to the existence of distinct "geographical schools."[6] He argues, for example, that in the eighth century schools associated with individual doctrines transformed into schools oriented around the doctrines of groups of like-minded scholars. Although Hallaq does not dispute al-Shafiʿi's significance, he argues that the *usul al-fiqh* did not arise until the century after al-Shafiʿi. He maintains that Islamic law, rather than becoming rigid after al-Shafiʿi's death, actually became more dynamic and creative.[7]

Understanding the Concept of Law in Islam

Despite debates in the secondary literature concerning the origins of the Islamic legal tradition, it is important to be aware that the concept of "law" in the Muslim sense is much broader than our modern and non-Muslim understanding of it. Although words such as "religious" and "secular" derive their potency from a much later date, Islamic law, broadly speaking, pertains to both of these domains. It deals with subjects that we consider both religious (e.g., prayer, ritual purity) and secular (e.g., murder, adultery), thereby calling into question the utility of such terms within a religious studies context. One's allegiance to this all-encompassing system of law is in theory the defining element of a Sunni Muslim's identity. And although this concept of law also functions highly in Shiʿism, it is also connected to other concepts there, such as the role of the Imamate.

Determining the law is based on certain ways of reading, elucidating, and commenting on the Quran and Muhammad's Sunna, as encountered in the hadith literature, which is believed to have been faithfully and accurately transmitted from Muhammad's Companions to later times. Because of Muhammad's purity as the vehicle of revelation, his life had to be constructed as perfect (hence, the use of adjectives such as "illiterate" and "sinless" to describe him). His Sunna accordingly represents the perfect embodiment of the individual before God, and his life becomes the ideal for every Muslim. However, what determines Muhammad's Sunna, especially how this Sunna is meant to correspond to every feature of a Muslim's life, is not always clear. For this reason, scholars arose to work out the legal precedents and other such minutiae to establish the law.

In its most general terms, the Muslim conception of the law is primarily ideal and theoretical in the sense that it did not emerge from a series of precedents. Rather, it developed at the hands of legal theorists in response to what they considered to be a set of concerns involving what the ideal Muslim response to various phenomena and instances should be. This process created a tension between the theoretical nature of the law and its more practical aspects. Much like the concept of the law in rabbinic Judaism, Muslim law is primarily "religious" in the sense that the threat of punishment comes primarily from God. For instance, one who does not fast during the month of Ramadan or who does not pray on a daily basis does not receive any sort of punishment in this world (although the issue of enforcement, as indicated in later chapters, is not always left to God). In the modern world, the place of sharia—or, as it is often called, "sharia law"—has been a topic of great interest and concern to secular European and North American nations (see chapter 12).

Sharia is customarily divided into two domains: *ibadat* (ritual actions) and *muʿamalat* (social transactions). The majority of *ibadat* deals with the various ritual obligations and acts of worship (e.g., prayer, fasting) that comprise Muslim life. *Muʿamalat*, on the contrary, concern the more mundane and social aspects of a Muslim's life (e.g., marriage, divorce, inheritance).[8]

The ultimate goal of sharia is to enable believers to secure a place in the world to come. The definition of this goal led to a five-fold taxonomy of human actions. Although all actions require correct intention (*niyya*), such actions are classified as obligatory (*wajib*); recommended (*mandub*); permissible (*mubah*); disapproved (*makruh*); and forbidden (*haram*). Without getting into all the subtle distinctions between these five groups, suffice it to say that these distinctions show the intersection of the legal, the ritualistic (i.e., the religious), and the moral. Obligatory actions are those that bring reward when performed and punishment when avoided. Forbidden actions are the opposite: they bring reward when avoided and punishment when performed. The majority of actions, however, fall into the "permissible" category and thus have little effect on one's status in the hereafter.

"Hadith Folk" and the Emergence of Sunni Islam

What would emerge as both Shiʿism and Sunni Islam created systems of law in response to developing need. Although these two denominations had radically different conceptions of what constituted authority and the structures perceived to surround it, they often developed comparable or even identical answers to similar legal questions and issues, which again presents evidence of the fluidity between the two denominations at an earlier stage before crystallization. It is for this reason that, despite real historical tensions between the two, they largely tend to regard each other as "Muslims" in the sense that they did not become separate religions. Where they differ legally, not surprisingly, is on matters relevant to their own particular concerns, especially as they relate to their specific "religious" and authoritative systems.

Powering the emergence of what would become full-blown Sunni Islam was a group of people known as *ahl al-hadith*, whom Marshall Hodgson felicitously calls "Hadith folk."[9] This group coalesced around the hadith reports attributed to Muhammad, which seemed to have functioned largely as one of their primary sources of religious authority. The hadith folk were interested in preserving the religious and moral authority of what they considered to be an ideal past (i.e., the time of Muhammad). They also tended, at least initially, to deprecate Ali and to elevate Muʿawiya—Ali's successor and founder of the Umayyad dynasty—as an associate of Muhammad.

Whereas the pathos emerging from the martyrdom of Husayn seems to have played a key role in the eventual development of Shiʿism, hadith folk were engaged in a process of self-definition based on a sense of community consciousness and personal devotion stemming from loyalty to this developing legal system. The rest of this chapter seeks to describe this legal system in greater detail.

It is important to realize that one of the earliest debates in the emerging Sunni movement—one that would have important consequences for subsequent legal and theological speculation—was between those who held that all legal matters could be derived solely from the hadiths and those who argued that there was also room for the deployment of common sense (*raʾy*).[10]

In addition, the system of "law," as it would emerge at the end of this process, functions in Sunni Islam as the perceived locus wherein the believer encounters God. In the period in which the law was being developed, this perception undoubtedly contributed to the formation of the idea—now omnipresent but still being worked out in the earlier period—that the Quran represents God's eternal speech, the bedrock for legal formulation. This sentiment undoubtedly contributed to the elevation of the Quran and the Sunna as the constitutive elements of both communal and personal piety.

It quickly became apparent, however, that these two sources could not function as the sole arbiters of all legal, religious, social, or political concerns for the simple reason that they did not address all such concerns. There soon arose, then, the notion that they needed to be interpreted and supplemented. The result was the gradual formation and encoding of other principles to interpret the Quran and the Sunna so as to make them relevant to all possible features of a Muslim's life. Taken together, all these sources succeeded in establishing the sharia as a universal and universalist code of law.

The Importance of Muhammad al-Shafi'i

Muhammad ibn Idris al-Shafi'i (767–820) is regarded as a towering figure in the development of Islamic legal practice. Although it is important to note that some scholars, most notably Norman Calder, date al-Shafi'i's main works, including the so-called *Risala* (*Treatise*), to a period about a century later than has generally been assumed,[11] very little is known about al-Shafi'i's life—the earliest biography dates to the tenth century and provides little more than a series of anecdotes. He seems, however, to have been largely responsible for both establishing and clarifying Muhammad's Sunna as an authoritative basis of law. Tradition furthermore ascribes to al-Shafi'i the formation of a series of principles known as the *usul al-fiqh*, the four "roots of jurisprudence" responsible for ascertaining all legal decisions in Islam.[12] As Joseph Lowry has recently argued, al-Shafi'i's originality may not reside so much in the theoretical development of these "roots," which appear only in passing in the *Risala*, but in an increasingly and more narrowly defined relationship between the Quran and the Sunna.[13]

Against traditionalists who maintained that jurists could produce legal verdicts based only on authentic hadith, al-Shafi'i argued that legists could in fact engage in *ijtihad* (independent reasoning), but without engaging in arbitrary or personal deductions.[14] He attempted to standardize the procedure of legal reasoning. He argued that the only authoritative Sunna was that of Muhammad as passed down from Muhammad himself in contrast to those traditions passed on by the Companions. Al-Shafi'i also reasoned that the Sunna could not contradict the Quran and that the Sunna could be used only to explain the Quran. Furthermore, he claimed that if a practice was widely accepted throughout the Muslim community, it could not be in contradiction to the Sunna. This claim is further evidence for the notion that Quranic commentary, the development of legal reasoning, and hadith criticism were interconnected "disciplines" in the formation of Islam.

A SELECTION FROM SHAFIʿI'S *RISALA*

On the importance of Sunna:

God has sent down to you the Book and the Wisdom, and has taught you what you did not know before; the bounty of God towards you is ever great (Q 4:113). So God mentioned His Book—which is the Quran—and Wisdom, and I have heard that those who are learned in the Quran—whom I approve—hold that Wisdom [referred to in this verse] is the sunna of the Apostle of God. This is what God Himself has said and God knows best! For the Quran is mentioned [first], followed by Wisdom; then God mentioned His favor to mankind by teaching them the Quran and Wisdom. So it is not permissible for Wisdom to be called here [anything] save the sunna of the Apostle of God. For [Wisdom] is closely linked to the Book of God, and God has imposed the duty of obedience to His Apostle, and imposed on men the obligation to obey His orders. So it is not permissible to regard anything as a duty save that set forth in the Quran and the sunna of His Apostle. For [God], as we have just stated, prescribed that the belief in His apostle shall be associated with belief in Him.

The sunna of the Apostle makes evident what God meant [in the text of His Book], indicating His general and particular [commands]. He associated the Wisdom [embodied] in the sunna with his Book, but made it subordinate [to the Book]. Never has God done this for any of His creatures save His Apostle.[*]

On *usul al-fiqh*:

We make decisions on the basis of the [text of the] Book and the generally accepted sunna, concerning which there is no disagreement, and we maintain that therefore such decisions are right according to both the explicit and implicit [meaning of the sources]. We also make decisions on the basis of a single-individual tradition on which there is no general agreement, and we hold that we have made the decision correctly according to its explicit meaning, since it is possible that he who related the tradition may have made an error in it.

We also acknowledge on the basis of consensus and analogy, although the latter is the weaker of the two instruments. Analogy is used only in the case of necessity, since it is not lawful if a tradition exists, just as performing the ritual ablution with sand renders one pure when one is travelling and there is no water; but it does not render one pure if water is available. It produces a state of purity only if water is not at hand. Similarly, a source other than the sunna can be used as the basis for a decision if there is no sunna.[†]

[*]Muhammad ibn Idris al-Shafiʿi, *Islamic Jurisprudence: Shafiʿi's "Risala,"* trans. Majid Khadduri (Baltimore: Johns Hopkins University Press, 1961), 111–112.

[†]Ibid., 350–351.

Given his role in the elevation and systematization of the Sunna as recorded in the hadith, al-Shafiʿi was also a crucial figure in the development of "*isnad* criticism," the goal of which was to guarantee the authenticity of those who passed on Muhammad's sayings (see chapter 2).

Guardians of the Law:
The Rise and Function of the Ulama

In order to protect the law—by interpreting it "faithfully," thereby maintaining correct procedure in its application—there arose a class of scholars, the so-called learned ones (ulama), those whose domain of expertise was knowledge (ilm), broadly conceived. It is from their ranks, for instance, that the legists (fuquha) emerged. These individuals were responsible for interpreting and elaborating on the legal program for both private and public life. The term ulama is in many respects an omnibus one. Although well versed in legal theory as the main class of Islamic lawyers, many ulama also specialized in other fields, such as Quranic interpretation, theology, and even philosophy, and in many instances all these fields were seen to overlap with one another.

The origin of the ulama is not easily adducible. One account sees them emerge as a group that defined itself largely in terms of its adherence to and interpretation of Muhammad's Sunna. In the second quarter of the ninth century, they began to challenge the caliph's religious function as the sole arbiter of orthodoxy. This challenge was exacerbated by the mihna (inquisition) imposed by the caliph al-Mamun (d. 833) to establish religious orthodoxy and requiring religious scholars to swear that they believed the Quran to be created (as opposed to eternal). Some scholars, however, contend that we should conceive of the relationship between the caliph and the ulama as more complex and dynamic and not simply and necessarily antagonistic.[15]

As a social category, the ulama are those Muslim scholars who have completed several years of specialized training and study of Islamic sciences (Quran, hadith, and the like). They were and indeed still are trained at institutions of Islamic higher education referred to as **madrasas**. As legal scholars, ulama tend to work within a preexistent tradition associated with one of the four legal schools (see the section "The Four Madhahib").

The modern period has witnessed a considerable loss of the ulama's authority and influence, a loss that has largely occurred on two fronts. First, many secular Arab governments attempted to control the madrasas' influence by nationalizing them. In 1961, for example, the Egyptian president Gamal Abd al-Nasser put the ulama at al-Azhar University, one of the oldest institutions of Islamic learning, under the state's direct control. Second, the rise of more militant varieties of Islam has stemmed the influence of the *ulama* today. Later chapters discuss this topic more fully, but suffice it to say here that such militant individuals and groups are highly critical of the traditional authority associated with the *ulama*. They contend that the *ulama*, as an institution, are often complicit with the interests of the secular and by definition corrupt states, for whom they are little more than state employees.

Naskh

One of the earliest set of legal concerns in the emerging Islamic tradition was the concept of **naskh** (abrogation), a principle used in Islamic legal exegesis to account for apparent contradictions within the Quran itself or between the Quran and the Sunna. It eventually would become a full-blown issue—complete with its own hermeneutic—in ascertaining the law. *Naskh* is based largely on the principle of chronology and progressive revelation, with the assumption that Muhammad lived for more than twenty years as a prophet and that the Muslim community's social, political, and thus legal situation changed as it grew. To account for these changes, it was acknowledged that certain verses might have been only temporary and then replaced as new situations demanded. Earlier verses might have been replaced by later verses for several reasons:

SPECIFICATION

Later verses made the concepts expressed in earlier verses more specific. In Quran 2:175, we have a fairly open-ended proscription: "Prescribed for you, when any of you is visited by death, and he leaves behind some goods, is to make testament in favor of his parents and next of kin honorably—an obligation on the God-fearing." This verse is abrogated—made more specific—by another verse:

> God charges you as regards your Children: to the male, a portion equal to that
> of two females: if only daughters, two or more, their share is two-thirds of the
> inheritance; if only one, her share is a half. For parents, a sixth share of the
> inheritance to each, if the deceased left children; if no children, and the par-

ents are the heirs, the mother has a third; if the deceased has brothers, the mother has a sixth. The distribution in all cases after the payment of legacies and debts. Ye know not whether your fathers or your sons are nearest to you in benefit. These are settled portions ordained by God. And God is All-knowing, All-wise. (4:11)

INTENSITY

Later verses also intensified earlier verses. A verse that seems to tell the believer to avoid being drunk during prayer is intensified by the banning of alcohol (in addition to other practices) altogether. "O ye who believe! Approach not prayers when you are drunken, until you know what you are saying" (4:46) is abrogated by "O believers, wine and arrow-shuffling idols, and divining arrows are an abomination, some of Satan's work; so avoid it; haply you may prosper" (5:92).

Abrogation applies to both the Quran and the Sunna. A Quranic verse may abrogate another Quranic verse, and a prophetic Sunna may likewise abrogate another prophetic Sunna. The possibility of abrogation between these two sources, though, is a much more contentious issue.

Sources of Ascertaining the Sharia

As should now be apparent, the two major sources of the law in Sunni Islam are the Quran and the Sunna of Muhammad; in Shi'ism, they are Muhammad and the Imams. Both the Quran and the Sunna, it must be remembered, took years to develop and be codified as a collection of texts. As Islam spread and encroached into larger and more cosmopolitan centers, however, it had to develop an expanded and more complex legal system. To apply these two sources to every legal situation proved both impossible and untenable. Even though the Quran is regarded as the most important text in Islam, it provides no clear or consistent method of jurisprudence. In like manner, it does not deal with many aspects of human life that fall under the broad category of "law." On a practical level, then, the Quran and the Sunna had to be understood as legal documents. However, neither provides strict legal guidance for all aspects of Muslim life precisely because neither was composed as a legal document in a strict sense. As a result, subsequent scholars would play a formative role in the creation of Islamic legal theory that they perceived to emerge from these two sources. Several hermeneutical principles developed that could be employed to derive the law from these two sources. Taken together, these principles are the four "roots of jurisprudence" (*usul al-fiqh*): the Quran, the Sunna, *qiyas*, and *ijma*. The first two have already been discussed in some detail, so let us move on to the latter two.

QIYAS

Whenever a legal problem arose for which the Quran and the Sunna could not provide an answer, legists would search for an analogous situation (*qiyas*) for which a clear ruling had already been made. The result is that most laws in the Islamic legal tradition derive from this principle owing to the paucity of legal rulings in the Quran and the Sunna.

For example, wine drinking is forbidden in Islam because of its intoxicative properties. Intoxication is considered bad because it removes Muslims from their duties, including mindfulness of God. Although there is no ruling in the Quran or Sunna on the use of cocaine or other "hard" drugs, legal scholars can rule that they, too, are forbidden because their effects are analogous to the effects of wine.

One of the biggest fears in Islam is that one can be charged with **bida** (innovation)—a concept often regarded as heretical from an orthodox legal or doctrinal perspective—so the employment of *qiyas* is not without criticism. However, most law schools gradually accepted analogy as a principle in various forms. Perhaps not coincidentally, there exists a hadith that dates the principle of analogy to the time of Muhammad. According to this report, when Muhammad sent a Companion to Yemen, he asked him the following question:

> "How will you decide when a [legal] question arises?" [The Companion] replied, "According to the Book of God." [Muhammad then said]: "If you do not find the answer in the Book of God?" [The Companion replied]: "Then according to the *Sunna* of the messenger of God." [Muhammad then said]: "What if you do not find it in either the *Sunna* or the Book?" [The Companion replied]: "Then I will come to a decision according to my own opinion without hesitation." Then the Messenger

of God slapped him on the back with his hand, saying, "Praise be to God who has led the messenger of the Messenger of God to an answer that pleased him."[16]

It should not come as a surprise that many of the same scholars responsible for the transmission of the hadith were also responsible for the formation of the various legal schools and the principles associated with them.

IJMA

The principle of *ijma* ideally refers to the consensual agreement of those responsible for the formation of legal rulings. Its justification also comes from a hadith attributed to Muhammad: "My community will never agree on an error." Consensus is often regarded as the most important source after the Quran and the Sunna because it is the principle by which the legal scholars agree on subsequent principles. In other words, if consensus had not accepted *qiyas* as authoritative, it would not be a valid source of Islamic law.

The principle of *ijma* would subsequently become the most important principle in the Islamic legal tradition. It is also the principle by which the Sunna and the Quran are confirmed as authoritative. Yet consensus paradoxically derives from precisely these two sources. *Ijma* works on the notion that if there are no dissenting voices from the next generation in which a law has to be developed, then the law is subsequently deemed confirmed. It is thus not necessary for every generation to reach consensus on laws that have already been formulated according to this principle.

Some have argued in the modern period that the principle of *ijma* makes Islam compatible with democracy.[17] It is worth pointing out, without getting into the issue of the compatibility between Islam and democracy here, that the term *ijma* in its classical usage refers solely to the consensus of male scholars. Some reformers, however, have claimed that this concept should be expanded so as to include not just legal scholars, but the entire Islamic community.[18]

The Closing of the Gates of Ijtihad

Ijtihad (independent reasoning) was employed in the period of the formation of Islamic jurisprudence as a way to create legal rulings independently of the other two main principles, consensus (*ijma*) and analogical reasoning (*qiyas*). It is intimately related to the latter owing to the fact that one derives rulings analogically owing to the free exercise of one's intellect. In the century or so after al-Shafiʿi, at least according to Schacht, Muslims increasingly tended to accept on authority the legal rulings of their predecessors without relying on original reasoning. Implicit in such a claim is that al-Shafiʿi represents the zenith of jurisprudential thought in Islam up until the present. The opposite of *ijtihad* is *taqlid* (imitation), when one simply imitates the legal rulings of one's predecessors. It is customarily said that the "gates of *ijtihad* closed" in the tenth century. Others, however, most notably Wael Hallaq, have argued that the gates of *ijtihad* never closed and that much creative legal thought occurred in the centuries after al-Shafiʿi up to the present.[19]

The Four Madhahib

After Muhammad's death, many local customs arose for interpreting and understanding the Quran and the emerging Sunna in relationship to new situations. In the ninth century, older regional schools were redefined largely as personal schools.[20] Sharing common interpretations of the ways in which the law should be deduced and interpreted, these schools (**madhahib**; sing., *madhhab*) began to coalesce around the teachings and names of well-known teachers. It is unlikely that these eponymous individuals intended to form schools in their names; but certain schools, even though originally inchoate, began to share a common interest in a body of legal interpretation that seems to have originated with a particular founder and that was expounded on and developed by his subsequent followers.

Islamic legal theory seems to have had its origins in different regional centers under the early dynasties. The most important center, perhaps not surprisingly, was apparently Medina, but Iraq (Basra and Kufa) and Syria (Damascus) also witnessed important traditions of interpretation. Each center developed its own ways of understanding and interpreting the law that were undoubtedly connected to the local traditions found therein. Although many different schools of legal thought emerged in these centers, over time they consolidated into only four main schools, which survive today. One of these schools is associated with Kufa and Abu Hanifa (d. 767), and the other three are associated with Medina and three individuals: Malik ibn Anas (d. 795), Muhammad ibn Idris al-Shafi'i (d. 822), and Ahmad ibn Hanbal (d. 855).

By the end of the tenth century, the four schools associated with these four individuals had so crystallized their legal positions that no further legal schools emerged thereafter. This certainly does not mean that no further legal speculation occurred, only that such speculation largely took place within the parameters established by these particular schools.

The differences between these schools should not be exaggerated. Each recognizes the others as orthodox, and although they may differ slightly on certain minor points (e.g., certain points of taxation), they all agree on the four *usul al-fiqh* (principles of jurisprudence): the Quran, the Sunna, consensus, and analogy. However, the legal rulings produced by the various courts associated with these schools did more than anything to shape Muslim life.

THE HANAFI *MADHHAB*

The Hanafi school, like the other three Sunni schools, was the product of a process that went on for centuries. This process most likely involved the gradual recognition of the authority of a school's eponym, acceptance of the school's legal views as valid, a sense of affiliation to the school, the application of the school's legal teachings and rulings by *qadis* (judges) in court, and so on. It is now widely believed that the four schools' formative period ended as late as the tenth century, by which point they had acquired all their central elements and reached maturity.[21] The spread of these schools was contingent on government support in particular regions as well as on individual jurists' community and tribal connections.[22]

Of the four schools, the Hanafi school is the largest and generally considered to be the most liberal in terms of its use of reason and interpretation of the law. Early on it stressed the importance of *ra'y* (personal opinion) in deriving legal rulings; however, with time, this principle largely fell out of use in favor of a reliance on past authority. Its founder, Abu Hanifa, is often credited with perfecting the principle of *qiyas*, analogical reasoning, in Islam. Today this school is the dominant *madhhab* among Muslims in Central and western Asia (Afghanistan to Turkey), Lower Egypt (including Cairo), and the Indian subcontinent.

THE MALIKI *MADHHAB*

The second oldest legal school is associated closely with Malik ibn Anas, who played an important role in the transmission of many hadith. The Maliki school had its origins in Medina, but it spread in the generations following him. It seems to have been an attempt to follow a more traditionalist form of jurisprudence compared to the Hanafi school, but without the rigid dogmatism and avoidance of power of the more conservative Hanbali school.[23] This *madhhab* is today prominent in Upper Egypt and throughout North Africa.

THE SHAFIʿI *MADHHAB*

We have already encountered the importance of al-Shafiʿi in the development and systematization of *fiqh*. He is largely responsible for the standardization encountered in all the schools. He was also responsible for replacing the more independent legal reasoning associated with *ijtihad* with the more conservative notion of *ijma*, consensus. The *madhhab* associated with his name is found today mostly among Muslim communities in Southeast Asia, southern Arabia, southern Egypt, and the Indian Ocean.

THE HANBALI *MADHHAB*

The most conservative of the four schools in terms of its reliance on tradition, the Hanbali *madhhab*, is associated with Ahmad ibn Hanbal, a poor individual who spent time in jail for defying the caliphal decree to assent to the notion of the Quran's createdness.[24] His refusal and time in jail, where he was reportedly tortured, captivated the imagination of many and seems to have been the impetus for the eventual overthrow of a legal status quo that stressed reason and personal opinion in favor of a perceived strict adherence to scripture and hadith. This school would play a large role in the formation of more conservative or fundamentalist movements in later centuries—such as the Wahhabis/Salafis (see part IV). It is the dominant legal school in the Arabian Peninsula and Persian Gulf states.

The existence of these various schools further reveals the diversity in the Islamic world. Yet, despite this diversity, many commentators, both non-Muslim and Muslim, insist on referring to sharia law as if it were a monolith.

Shi'i Legal Schools

Like their Sunni counterparts, Shi'i legal scholars acknowledge the Quran and the Sunna as authoritative sources. They expand the concept of Sunna, however, to include not just Muhammad, but also the Twelve Imams. The Shi'i law schools tend to differ from one another based on their particular denomination. So, for example, Twelvers, who believe that the Twelfth Imam is in occultation, have their own *madhhab*, and the Isma'ilis, who believe that there is an uninterrupted succession of living Imams, have their own. The most prominent Shi'i *madhhab* is the Ja'fari—a Twelver legal school named after the sixth Imam, Ja'far al-Sadiq (702–765). In Twelver Shi'ism, the concept of *ijtihad* has remained open; legal scholars are largely responsible for interpreting the Twelfth Imam's will until he returns in the messianic era.[25]

Al-Azhar: The Center of Sunni Learning Today

Al-Azhar, founded in 970, represents the oldest and most venerable institution of learning and jurisprudence in the Sunni world. Its mission includes the propagation of Islam throughout the world, including appointing and training individuals in the proselytization (*dawa*) of non-Muslims. Its *ulama* render legal opinions (fatwas) on disputes submitted to them from all over the Sunni Islamic world regarding proper conduct, whether for individuals or for society at large (recent examples include the illegality of suicide bombing and the prohibition against female circumcision).

In 1961, Nasser established al-Azhar as a university and introduced a wide range of secular faculties, such as economics, medicine, and engineering. An Islamic women's faculty was also added. In 1959, the rector of

---

THE EMERGENCE OF THE MEDIEVAL
ISLAMIC UNIVERSITY

Institutions of learning (madrasas) did not exist when Islam was born. Their early formation is most likely traceable to the early Islamic custom of meeting in places—for example, mosques—to discuss any number of religious issues. Those seeking guidance tended to gather around those more knowledgeable than themselves, and these informal teachers later became known as *shaykhs*, an honorific title meaning "elder." These shaykhs began to hold regular religious education sessions, which gradually formed into the institution of the madrasa.

The oldest such madrasa was the Jami'at al-Qarawiyyin established in 859 in the Fez, Morocco. In 970, the famous al-Azhar was founded in Cairo. During the late Abbasid period, Nizam al-Mulk, the Seljuk vizier, established the *madrasa nizamiyya* (named after himself), which formed the basis of the system of state madrasas in various Abbasid cities.

During the twelfth to fourteenth centuries, many of the madrasas taught what we would consider to be both religious subjects (e.g., *fiqh* [jurisprudence]) and secular subjects (e.g., logic, philosophy). It is significant to note, however, that madrasas were not centers of advanced scientific study, something that was usually carried out by scholars working under the patronage of a royal court. The madrasa curriculum varied widely and was often contingent on the wishes of either the founder or the patron.

Some scholars have noted parallels between madrasas and medieval European universities, inferring that the latter might well have been influenced by the former.[*] Many, however, argue that they merely developed at the same time, but that one did not necessarily influence the another.

[*]See, for example, George Makdisi, *The Rise of Colleges: Institutions of Learning in Islam and the West* (Edinburgh: Edinburgh University Press, 1981).

---

al-Azhar, Mahmud Shaltut (1897–1963), issued a fatwa to establish a *taqrib* (rapprochement) between Sunni and Twelver Shi'ism. Shaltut, generally considered to be a modernist and a reformer, argued that the legal school of Twelver Shi'ism—the Ja'fari *madhhab*—should be recognized as one of five acceptable traditions of interpreting the law (in addition to the Sunni Hanafi, Maliki, Shafi'i, and Hanbali schools). Needless to say, many on both sides have disagreed with Shaltut, especially on topics such as marriage, divorce, and inheritance.

This chapter has presented a survey of Sunni Islam as it emerged out of the legal tradition of the early period. Although the authoritative and ideological impetuses for both Sunnism and Shi'ism were most likely present at the death of Muhammad, it is imperative to remember that what would eventually emerge as the two main branches of Islam did not exist at the beginning. On the contrary, both took centuries to crystallize, at times overlapping with each other, at other times defining themselves in explicit opposition to each other. Chapter 5 charted the rise of Shiʿism in the sectarian battles surrounding the successorship of Muhammad, and this chapter has charted the role of law and legalism in the formation of Sunni Islam. Chapter 7 describes yet another possible paradigm of early Muslim religiosity, which, like the Shiʿi and the Sunni, would emerge in the aftermath of Muhammad's death and eventually form as a full-blown movement.

NOTES

1. See the comments in Patricia Crone, *Roman, Provincial, and Islamic Law: The Origins of the Islamic Patronate* (Cambridge: Cambridge University Press, 1987).

2. Joseph Schacht, *An Introduction to Islamic Law* (Oxford: Oxford University Press, 1964), 17–20.

3. Michael Cook, *Commanding Right and Forbidding Wrong in Islamic Thought* (Cambridge: Cambridge University Press, 2000), 32–45.

4. See the helpful comments in A. Kevin Reinhart, "Islamic Law as Islamic Ethics," *Journal of Religious Ethics* 11 (1983): 186–203.

5. Schacht, *Introduction to Islamic Law.*

6. For example, Wael Hallaq, "From Regional to Personal Schools of Law? A Reevaluation," *Islamic Law and Society* 8 (2001): 1026.

7. Wael Hallaq, "Was al-Shafiʿi the Master Architect of Islamic Jurisprudence?" *International Journal of Middle Eastern Studies* 25, no. 4 (1993): 587–605. For a critical overview of Hallaq's work that attempts to contextualize it within the larger field of Islamic legal studies, see David S. Powers, "Wael B. Hallaq on the Origins of Islamic Law: A Review Essay," *Islamic Law and Society* 17, no. 1 (2010): 126–157.

8. On these two types of sharia more broadly, see Noel J. Coulson, *A History of Islamic Law* (Edinburgh: Edinburgh University Press, 1964), 75–85.

9. Marshall G. S. Hodgson, *The Venture of Islam: Conscience and History in a World Civilization*, 3 vols. (Chicago: University of Chicago Press, 1974), 1:386.

10. See the discussion in Christopher Melchert, *The Formation of the Sunni Schools of Law, 9th–10th Centuries C.E.* (Leiden: Brill, 1997), 1–31.

11. Norman Calder, *Studies in Early Muslim Jurisprudence* (Oxford: Oxford University Press, 1993), 223–243.

12. Joseph Schacht, *The Origins of Muhammedan Jurisprudence* (Oxford: Oxford University Press, 1950), 11–20.

13. Joseph E. Lowry, *Early Islamic Legal Theory: The "Risala" of Muhammad Ibn Idris al-Shafiʿi* (Leiden: Brill, 2007), 23–59.

14. Schacht, *Origins of Muhammedan Jurisprudence*, 98–132.

15. See, for example, Muhammad Qasim Zaman, *Religion and Politics Under the Early Abbasids: The Emergence of the Proto-Sunni Elite* (Leiden: Brill, 1997), 70–118.

16. Quoted in "Kiyas," in H. A. R. Gibb and J. H. Kramers, eds., *Shorter Encyclopedia of Islam* (Ithaca, N.Y.: Cornell University Press, 1953), 267 (my modifications).

17. Abdulaziz Abdulhussein Sachedina, *The Islamic Roots of Democratic Pluralism* (Oxford: Oxford University Press, 2001).

18. This claim, indeed, is part of Sachedina's argument, in ibid.

19. Wael Hallaq, "Was the Gate of *Ijtihad* Closed?" *International Journal of Middle East Studies* 16, no. 1 (1984): 3–41. See also Coulson, *History of Islamic Law*, 202–217.

20. Melchert, *Formation of the Sunni Schools of Law*, 32–47.

21. See, for example, Wael Hallaq, *Authority, Continuity, and Change in Islamic Law* (Cambridge: Cambridge University Press, 2001), 1–10; and Melchert, *Formation of the Sunni Schools of Law*, 198–203.

22. See, for example, Nurit Tsafrir, *The History of an Islamic School of Law: The Early Spread of Hanafism* (Cambridge, Mass.: Harvard University Press, 2004), 116–120.

23. Melchert, *Formation of the Sunni Schools of Law*, 174–176.

24. Nimrod Hurvitz, *The Formation of Hanbalism: Piety into Power* (London: Routledge, 2002).

25. For a comparison of Sunni and Shiʿi legal systems, see Devin J. Stewart, *Islamic Legal Theory: Twelver Shiite Responses to the Sunni Legal System* (Salt Lake City: University of Utah Press, 1998).

SUGGESTIONS FOR FURTHER READING

Burton, John. *The Sources of Islamic Law: Islamic Theories of Abrogation.* Edinburgh: Edinburgh University Press, 1990.

Calder, Norman. *Studies in Early Muslim Jurisprudence.* Oxford: Oxford University Press, 1993.

Cook, Michael. *Commanding Right and Forbidding Wrong in Islamic Thought.* Cambridge: Cambridge University Press, 2000.

Coulson, Noel J. *A History of Islamic Law.* Edinburgh: Edinburgh University Press, 1964.

Crone, Patricia. *Roman, Provincial, and Islamic Law: The Origins of the Islamic Patronate.* Cambridge: Cambridge University Press, 1987.

Hallaq, Wael. *A History of Islamic Legal Theories: An Introduction to Sunni Usūl al-Fiqh.* Cambridge: Cambridge University Press, 1997.

——. "Was the Gate of *Ijtihad* Closed?" *International Journal of Middle East Studies* 16, no. 1 (1984): 3–41.

Hurvitz, Nimrod. *The Formation of the Hanbalism: Piety into Power.* London: Routledge, 2002.

Lowry, Joseph E. *Early Islamic Legal Theory: The "Risala" of Muhammad Ibn Idris al- Shafiʿi.* Leiden: Brill, 2007.

Makdisi, George. *The Rise of Colleges: Institutions of Learning in Islam and the West.* Edinburgh: Edinburgh University Press, 1981.

Melchert, Christopher. *The Formation of the Sunni Schools of Law, 9th–10th Centuries C.E.* Leiden: Brill, 1997.

Motzki, Harald. *The Origins of Islamic Jurisprudence: Meccan Fiqh Before the Classical Schools.* Translated by Marion H. Katz. Leiden: Brill, 2002.

Powers, David S. *Law, Society, and Culture in the Maghrib, 1300–1500.* Cambridge: Cambridge University Press, 2002.

——. "Wael B. Hallaq on the Origins of Islamic Law: A Review Essay." *Islamic Law and Society* 17, no. 1 (2010): 126–157.

Powers, Paul R. *Intent in Islamic Law: Motive and Meaning in Medieval Sunni Fiqh.* Leiden: Brill, 2006.

Sachedina, Abdulaziz Abdulhussein. *The Just Ruler in Shiʿite Islam: The Comprehensive Authority of the Jurist in Imamite Jurisprudence.* New York: Oxford University Press, 1988.

Schacht, Joseph. *An Introduction to Islamic Law.* Oxford: Oxford University Press, 1964.

Al-Shafiʿi, Muhammad ibn Idris. *Islamic Jurisprudence: Shafiʿi's "Risala."* Translated by Majid Khadduri. Baltimore: Johns Hopkins University Press, 1961.

Stewart, Devin J. *Islamic Legal Orthodoxy: Twelver Shiite Responses to the Sunni Legal System.* Salt Lake City: University of Utah Press, 1998.

Tsafrir, Nurit. *The History of an Islamic School of Law: The Early Spread of Hanafism.* Cambridge, Mass.: Harvard University Press, 2004.

Weiss, Bernard, ed. *Studies in Islamic Legal Theory.* Leiden: Brill, 2002.

Zaman, Muhammad Qasim. *Religion and Politics Under the Early Abbasids: The Emergence of the Proto-Sunni Elite.* Leiden: Brill, 1997.

——. *The Ulama in Contemporary Islam: Custodians of Change.* Princeton, N.J.: Princeton University Press, 2002.

Zebiri, Kate. *Mahmud Shaltut and Islamic Modernism.* Oxford: Clarendon Press, 1993.

7

SUFISM

MUSLIM IDENTITY is a potentially fluid concept that is contingent on the perceived correct or normative interpretation of Muhammad's message. Such interpretations are based on various groups' ability to marshal sources that they construct as authoritative to legitimate a particular perspective on diverse matters that include everything from the political to the religious. Previous chapters focused largely on the institutions that developed over the issue of prophetic succession and the various legal, political, and institutional developments that emerge from it; the present chapter again returns us to Muhammad and offers yet another window onto the manifold ways that both his personality and his teaching have been interpreted. Sufism, or Islamic mysticism, further displays the dynamic use of Muhammad in the development of Muslim identity after his death.

The word "mysticism," narrowly defined, refers to a religious experience that involves a paranormal state of consciousness wherein the individual claims to encounter or unite with some form of what is considered to be ultimate reality. The individual subsequently claims a special knowledge or gnosis that derives from his or her illumination, which is usually characterized by a loss of self-identity and intense joy and bliss.

Scholars formerly assumed that mysticism exists in all the world's religions. Recent scholarship, however, has tended to argue that mysticism cannot be easily removed from its cultural contexts,[1] and, as a result, it is very difficult to speak of mysticism outside of specific religions. Linguistic and cultural vocabularies both color the mystic's interpretation of any given experience and thereby shape the very contents of the experience. Although mystical traditions certainly share common features, each one's cultural specificity demands that it be studied in its appropriate historical, social, and cultural context.

Mystical traditions consist of speculative doctrines, ethical values, literary texts, rituals, and social institutions. The relationship between mysticism and the religious tradition in which it functions is certainly a complex one. Some mystical movements express a religion's basic values; others challenge and conflict with certain aspects of the tradition; and yet others offer creative and elaborate ways to reinterpret the religion. The mystical elements associated with any religion are certainly not monolithic and, as such, display a rich diversity over time and geography. Finally, it is necessary to be aware that what has emerged as mysticism in any religious tradition is often contingent on the establishment of a discourse with a distinctive vocabulary, concerns, canonical texts, and authoritative interpretations.

Locating Sufism

Although scholars of the nineteenth century were largely critical of what they considered to be the aridity of orthodox Islamic doctrine, they were greatly impressed by the spiritual teachings and exercises of Sufism. Some even referred to Sufism as the "rose in the desert of Islam." Because they doubted that Islam could have fostered such a movement, they imagined all sorts of extra-Islamic origins for the existence of a mystical strain in Islam, from Neoplatonism to Christian monasticism to some sort of generic "Oriental" spiritualism.

It is sometimes said that there exist three "denominations" in Islam: Sunni, Shi'i, and Sufi. Although it is certainly true that Sufism possesses its own teachings and structures of authority based largely on the relationship that develops between the shaykh (master) and the *faqir* (disciple, sometimes referred to as a *murid*), a Muslim's commitment to Sufi doctrine and practice usually occurs over and above his or her commitment to Sunnism or Shi'ism. But even this distinction may be drawing a line where none in fact exists. Millions of Muslims—from Morocco in the West to Indonesia in the East—know only of an Islam that includes saints, amulets, pilgrimages to the tombs of "holy men," and other such practices that are often and perhaps misleadingly referred to as "Sufic." This Islam is sometimes referred to pejoratively as "popular Islam," is roundly criticized by theologians, and until relatively recently has been largely ignored in academic treatments, which have tended to focus on the so-called great men of Sufism, such as Ibn Arabi or Rumi.

The difficulty in defining Sufism may well stem from the fact that dating when exactly it emerged is itself a problem. Although later Sufis would claim that Muhammad was the first Sufi and the progenitor of all later mystics, the situation is not surprisingly more complex. At some later point in the historical development of the movement, people with certain mystical or renunciatory tendencies began to be recognized as "Sufis." However, it would be incorrect to assume that Sufism emerged as a unified movement at a specific point in time.[2] Rather than claim, as many want to, that there exists an unchanging core to all Sufi phenomena, it is more appropriate to imagine disparate and heterogeneous groups of renunciants that by the ninth century—especially in Baghdad, the center of the Abbasid dynasty—began to be part of a mode of piety regarded as distinct from the slowly emerging movements we now know as Sunnism and Shi'ism.

There certainly existed groups of renunciants in other areas of the enormous empire, particularly in Persia and Central Asia. Possessing their own ideas and practices, these groups were not originally identified as "Sufis," but they gradually became identified as such as "Sufism" spread beyond Baghdad in the following centuries. It is thus important to be aware of the great variety inherent to the generic term "Islamic mysticism"—a variety that combines the teachings of key mystical figures with various local teachings and practices.

Another problem in trying to locate Sufism is that there has always existed firm opposition to Sufi teaching, belief, and practices within certain quarters of conservative interpretations of what Islam should be. Such critics deem Sufism heretical and contrary to the "real" teachings of Islam, and they juxtapose Sufi teaching with the austere and radical monotheistic Islam that they have constructed in their reading of the Quran and related sources. Despite this opposition, Sufism exists in all sorts of local variations and is integral to the way that millions of Muslims go about their daily lives. Far removed from the theological formula-

AN EARLY ORIENTALIST ENCOUNTER WITH SUFISM

In 1815, Sir John Malcolm published *The History of Persia*. An ambassador of the British East India Company to the Persian court, Malcolm had the following to say of Sufism: "It is in India, beyond all other climes, that this delusive and visionary doctrine has most flourished. There is, in the habits of that nation, and in the character of the Hindoo religion, what peculiarly cherishes the mysterious spirit of holy abstraction in which it is founded; and we may grant our belief to the conjecture which assumes that India is the source from which other nations have derived this mystic worship of the divinity."*

Malcolm fairly typically saw in Sufism an Indian or a Hindu origin. Writing four years later, in 1819, Lieutenant James William Graham published an article in the *Transactions of the Literary Society of Bombay*, "A Treatise on Sufiism, or Mahomedan Mysticism," in which he praises "Sufiism" for its spiritual refinement and unwillingness to be bogged down by the law:

> With regard to the religion (if it can be so termed in the general acceptance of that word) or rather doctrine and tenets of the sect of Sufis, it is requisite to observe, first, that any person, or a person of any religion or sect, may be a *Sufi*: the mystery lies in this;—a total disengagement of the mind from all temporal concerns and worldly pursuits; an entire throwing off not only of every superstition, doubt, or the like, but of the practical mode of worship, ceremonies, &c. laid down in every religion, which the Mahomedans term *Sheryat*, being the law, or canonical law; and entertaining solely mental abstraction, and contemplation of the soul and Deity, their affinity, and the correlative situation in which they stand; in fine, it is that spiritual intercourse of the soul with its Maker, that disregards and disclaims all ordinances and outward forms, of what sect or religion soever; such as observance of feasts, fasts, stated periods of prayer, particular kinds of meat to be eaten, ablutions, pilgrimages, and such like other rites and ceremonies which come under the head of practical worship (*Jismani amul*), being the deeds of the law, in contradistinction to mental or spiritual worship (*Roohani amul*), that is, as I take it to be, grace or faith.†

*John Malcolm, *The History of Persia, from the Most Early Period to the Present Time: Containing an Account of the Religion, Government, Usage, and Character of the Inhabitants of that Kingdom*, 2 vols. (London: John Murray, 1815), 2:384.

†Quoted in Carl Ernst, *The Shambhala Guide to Sufism* (Boston: Shambhala, 1997), 13–14.

tions produced at places such as al-Azhar University and from the customary "five pillars of faith" traditionally used to teach about Muslim life and practice, Sufism remains a vibrant religious and political force throughout the Islamic world.

Even the names "Sufi" and "Sufism" are modern translations that turn on the Arabic term *suf* (wool), in reference to the woolen garments that Sufis wore to indicate their poverty and asceticism. The Arabic phrase that mystics in Islam used to refer to themselves is **ahl al-tasawwuf**, perhaps best translated into English as "People of the Woolen Way." Although the "mystical trend" seems to have existed only among individuals very early in the development of Islam—later Sufis claiming, perhaps not surprisingly, that Muhammad was the first to engage in such practices—those individuals eventually collected themselves into orders or brotherhoods, some of which were actively involved in political affairs throughout the centuries.

Like other aspects of Islam that we have encountered in previous chapters, we should not assume that the term *ahl al-tasawwuf* or the category "Sufism" existed from the beginning. However, we can say fairly confidently that very early on there existed individuals involved in the "renunciation" (*zuhd*) of material comforts and the constant "remembrance" (*dhikr*) of God and that they were the catalyst for what would eventually emerge as what is called "Sufism." Because this movement had roots in the apocalypticism associated with the earliest Meccan suras (e.g., suras 56 and 81), the early renunciants derived legitimacy from the Quran's imperative to remember the name of God (76:25) and to sleep little at night (51:15). Although Sufis may well have been inspired later by the woolen cloaks of Christian monks, the ascetic impulse within the Quran apparently negates the thesis that a mystical impulse is somehow foreign to Islam.

Like all Muslims, Sufis claim that their interpretation of the tradition is the one that most closely coincides with the life of Muhammad. Like other Muslims, they also seek to legitimate their identity by looking to the sources that the community as a whole has signified as authoritative (Quran, Sunna). Of particular interest to Sufis is Muhammad's asceticism, which, they contend, led to his initial moments of revelation atop the mountains surrounding Mecca and which culminated in the "mystical" experiences associated with his *isra* and *miraj* (often referred to as his "night journey" [see chapter 2]). The emphasis on these aspects, however, often comes at the expense of hadith and other sources that show a Muhammad who is critical of asceticism. Indeed, as discussed more fully later, Sufi claims and methods would eventually come under harsh criticism from conservative thinkers and reformers, and many later mystics were accused of **kufr** (unbelief).

The Expansion-Asceticism Theory

We know very little about the historical emergence of Islamic mysticism. We possess many records, but they date from a later period even though they claim to offer information on the period in question. These sources tell us the names of certain figures that were involved in the formation and subsequent development of the tradition; however, many of these sources represent often idealized constructions by later authors from later centuries.

The main Islamic account for the rise of Sufism is referred to as the "expansion–asceticism theory." It contends that when Muhammad was alive, especially before the *hijra* to Medina, there existed a purity and a pristineness to his message. These qualities can be witnessed in the relatively short, highly poetic, and rhythmic Quranic passages that date to this time and that can be contrasted with the longer, more legalistic ones from the Medinan period. As the religion expanded and became increasingly caught up in the mundane affairs of state and administration, the original purity and pristineness were gradually lost. After Muhammad's death, in other words, it became increasingly difficult to be a Muslim in the way that Muhammad had originally configured the category. This difficulty gradually led to various factional ways to be a good Muslim (Sunni, Shiʿi, and so on). Early Muslim asceticism, according to this theory, presented itself as an "authentic" response to the Muslim community's rapid expansion. Sufism was accordingly constructed as the other-worldly response to the this-worldliness of the new empire.

The renunciatory trend may well have developed *in part* as a reaction to a certain warrior ethic practiced during the empire's "conquest" phase, but this theory is potentially reductive and simplistic. It seems to take the words of ascetics—words often mediated by later generations—at face value. These later sources tend to speak of a group of men (and women) who turned their backs on the empire's luxury and power to move toward an ascetic lifestyle. This theory also tends to ignore the malleability of the "holy man" in late antiquity. As others have argued—especially in the context of Christianity (e.g., Peter Brown)[3]—this social type was much more complex than we tend to think and often played a role in very mundane affairs, such as expanding the Catholic Church's sphere of influence. In terms of Islam, as Richard Bulliet's studies have well argued,[4] Sufis were apparently involved at a relatively early period in converting entire villages and regions to Islam. A complicated relationship existed between political authority and ascetics, a relationship that we should not always assume was high-minded, but that might well have included political and ideological components. We should therefore not assume that Sufi sources offer adequate historical descriptions of the advent of Sufism.

Sources of the Ascetic Impulse

Asceticism was the earliest phase of a movement that would eventually grow into various Sufi circles. Historians of Sufism tend to call it "asceticism" more for convenience because many of the classical "mystical" elements developed gradually over time. In other words, the early ascetics—especially when compared to the florescence of Sufism in the ninth and tenth centuries—had only an undeveloped "mystical" component to their beliefs and practices. For this reason, these early individuals are referred to as "ascetics" rather than "mystics."

Although the earliest mystics were ascetics, it is important to be aware that there are many different reasons behind the adoption of an ascetic lifestyle. In medieval Islam, to be an ascetic was in many ways to have an occupation. One might have chosen to be an ascetic for religious reasons (e.g., the renunciation of wealth and the development of the power to remember God). However, the life of the ascetic was probably easier to live if one was poor. Moreover, one's social status might well have improved by becoming an ascetic. In early Islam, for example, a scholar who was an ascetic was perceived to be closer to God (and thus the truth) than a nonascetic.

There were, in short, many motives for becoming an ascetic. Some people were ascetics as we see them today, unattached individuals living apart from others in a life of renunciation and meditation, yet we also know that many Muslim "ascetics" had families and continued to support them. Much of early Islamic mystical writings are, perhaps not surprisingly, interested in ascertaining that one have the proper motive or intention (niyya) for choosing a life of asceticism. A common and critical motif from the earliest mystical writings is of the ascetic who loves stroking his well-groomed and bushy beard more than he does getting close to God. Such stories seem to bear witness to the fact that there existed many types of ascetics in early Islam, only some of whom were the precursors to the Sufis of later generations.

Geographic Diversity

The Sufi mode of piety that gradually emerged in Baghdad, one of the most cosmopolitan centers within the Islamic Empire, during the ninth century proved to be very adaptable as it moved into the hinterlands. During subsequent centuries, this interpretation of Muhammad's message spread to all the major cultural regions within the empire and blended there with what one scholar calls local "indigenous interiorizing trends."[5] Foundational figures' teachings and the stories of these individuals' lives most likely spread into other areas as students from these areas traveled to Baghdad and then returned to their homes to teach locals. And we should not underestimate the traveling holy men who moved throughout the empire spreading their teachings of a mystically inspired Islam.

This geographical diversity should alert us to the fact that there existed other "interiorizing" or, for lack of a better term, "spiritualist" groups within early Islam. Such groups—for example, the Karramiyya, based in the eastern empire (Khorasan and Transoxania) in the ninth century—seem to have been critical of Sufi teaching. We unfortunately know little about groups such as the Karramiyya because most of the sources we possess about them were written by their enemies as a way to discredit them. It is worth noting, however, that Sufism had to contend not only with conservative critics, but also with the spiritualists of other movements. It was only later that Sufism won out as *the* "spiritual way" within Islam.

Many of these diverse other interiorizing trends eventually died out, were persecuted into extinction, or became folded into Sufism, which, by the tenth and eleventh centuries, had become the established pietistic tradition. This does not mean, however, that Sufism simply leveled local traditions and replaced them with its own monolithic teachings. On the contrary, as already mentioned, Sufi teaching seems to have connected and merged fairly easily with local traditions that had existed in far-flung areas for centuries, including before the arrival of Islam. Once again, this regional diversity should prevent us from speaking of "Sufism" as if it were a teaching that was always and everywhere the same.

Key Terms and Concepts

The set of terms and concepts offered here is certainly not meant to be an exhaustive list of all the technical vocabulary associated with Sufism. Rather, it provides an introductory overview of terms that run throughout much of the lengthy history of the movement, from its beginnings in the renunciant tradition to the emergence of Sufism to its practice today. It is important, however, not to think that these terms somehow define the essence of the tradition.

THE *ZAHIR–BATIN* DICHOTOMY

One of the central themes and interpretive strategies in Islamic mystical writings is the dichotomy between the **zahir** (external or exoteric) and the **batin** (internal or esoteric). This dichotomy is essential to the notion that there exists some thing or teaching hidden deep within the Quranic message that only those with the proper understanding can attain. If the *zahir* is that to which all Muslims aspire, the *batin* is that which only very few can attain. If every Muslim performs the "pillars" of faith (see chapter 9) to ensure reward in the next life, the Sufi sees his or her goal as being to use these pillars as a segue into a life spent basking in their meditative performance. One of the main ways to ascertain the Quran's mystical secrets is through *ta'wil* (esoteric and mystical interpretation).

Sufis often took this dichotomy to the next level and contended that all of reality possessed a *zahir* and a *batin*. If the former refers to the material world, the world of apparent meaning, the latter refers to that which exists beyond this world and that which gives it existence. It is the movement from the *zahir* to the *batin* that symbolizes the Sufi message, hermeneutic, and worldview.

TARIQA

We can see the dichotomous relationship between the *zahir* and the *batin* at work in the concept of **tariqa** (pl., *turuq*), which has several meanings in Arabic. Much like the word "sharia," this term refers to the concept of "way" or "path" and came to denote a particular path—that is, the mystical path of Islam. The term *tariqa*, then, is in many ways symbolic of the inner dimension of the Sufi quest. Whereas the sharia came to denote Islam's outer path, the system of obligations and prohibitions of which every Muslim must be aware, the *tariqa* came to be the religion's inner dimension meant only for a select few. This distinction need not be as antinomian or opposed to the traditional understanding of the law as it first appears (although for some "drunken" Sufis it is) because one of the main teachings of Sufism is that one can enter into the *tariqa* only after one has mastered the life of sharia. In later Sufism, the term *tariqa* came to denote a specific type of Sufi order or brotherhood.

NAFS

The Quran employs the term **nafs** to refer to the self or the individual's soul. Sufis refer to it pejoratively as that which gets in the way of the individual's true realization of God. In Sufi parlance, *nafs* refers to the individual in his or her unrefined state, his or her animal nature that must be refined through renunciation and remembrance. According to the eleventh-century mystic Abu 'l-Qasim al-Qushayri, the *nafs* consists of "the defective attributes of the servant, his blameworthy character traits and actions. . . . The strongest determination of the *nafs* and the most difficult to overcome is the delusion that it contains something good or that it deserves some status."[6]

The greatest obstacle to a proper relationship with God, according to Sufism, is the individual's *nafs*. One must move beyond the carrot of reward and the stick of punishment so as to cultivate a *batin*-based relationship with God, which necessarily involves a negation of the self.

DHIKR

Dhikr, as mentioned earlier, is the Quranic word for "remembrance" or "mentioning." It is frequently applied to the concept of prayer. In Sufism, however, it has taken on the broader notion of invoking the divine presence and subsequently worshipping God. It can be both joyous and contemplative. How one engages in this remembrance is based on the Sufi order to which one belongs. Although any Muslim can and should engage in the remembrance of God, Sufis have developed *dhikr* into elaborate forms of meditation. It can take the form of reciting incantations—for example, the phrase customarily referred to as the **shahada:** "There is no god but God, and Muhammad is the messenger of God" (in Arabic, "la ilaha illa Allah wa-Muhammad rasul Allah")—or whirling in a circle, as the famous Mevlevi dervishes of Turkey do. The goal of *dhikr* is to purify the *nafs* and thereby to bring the worshipper closer to God. This process sometimes involves music and occasionally even the ingestion of alcohol or other narcotics.

As Sufism developed into different orders over time, differing *dhikr* practices connected to those specific orders arose. These practices would function as one of the main features used to define particular orders and differentiate them from one another. It was not uncommon for one order to criticize the *dhikr* practices of another order.

The Stations of Progression

Early in the development of Islamic mysticism, theories arose concerning the spiritual progression of the adept that explained, for example, the movement from fasting to the fear of God to the love of God. These theories and the manuals explaining them eventually led to the development of an elaborate and highly detailed mystical cartography that charted the experiential quest for the spiritual traveler. The journey detailed, of course, is not an external one, but something that takes place on an internal plain within each adept's soul. Central to this journey is the existence of "states of being" (*maqamat*; sing., *maqam*)—a series of discrete psychological and ethical qualities that the mystic must attain and progress through on his or her journey.[7] These stations are neither static nor agreed on by all mystical theorists. Al-Qushayri, for example, included fifty such stations that culminate in yearning for God, whereas Ansari included one hundred that culminate in the unity of the individual with God. These stations are sometimes perceived as a chronological progression; according to other perceptions, they are helixlike, with the adept moving back and forth between them. Each station is also often associated with particular meditative practices and techniques.

TAWAKKUL

Tawakkul is the "absolute trust" that the Sufi puts in God. If one believes that God is the great provider, then, according to Sufi teaching, one must put all of one's trust in him. Farid al-Din Attar (1145–1221), who wrote a hagiography of the early Sufi saints called *Memorial of God's Friends*, recounts a story that nicely illustrates this concept of radical trust:

It was related on the night [Rabia] was born, there was no lamp in her father's house, not a drop of oil to anoint her navel, nor so much as a piece of cloth to swaddle her in. Her father had three daughters, and Rabia was the fourth. And so they called her Rabia, meaning "the fourth one."

His wife said to him, "Go the neighbors and ask for a lamp's worth of oil."

Rabia's father had sworn not to ask any creature for anything. He got up, went to the neighbor's door, and returned. "They were asleep." He said.[8]

Although the story goes on to recount how Rabia's father sees Muhammad in a dream and is told that his daughter will grow up to be a great intercessor for pious Muslims, the passage related here reveals how God is seen to provide for those who trust in him. Rabia's father, for example, refuses to ask his neighbor for oil because he believes that such an action would mean violating his radical trust in God to provide for him at the particular moment. If God wanted him to have oil, according to the tenor of the anecdote, then God certainly would have provided it for him.

The notion of variety is as germane to Sufism as it is to Sunnism and Shi'ism. Related terms that also define the Sufi's quest include but are not limited to *dhawq* (taste), *sukr* (drunkenness), and *baqa* (abiding). And, as mentioned, al-Qushayri lists fifty possible stations in the practitioner's spiritual journey, and other Sufi thinkers recount even more.

FANA

Near the end of his mystical allegory *The Conference of the Birds*, Attar writes of a group of moths before a flame, a passage that is worth quoting at length:

Moths gathered in a fluttering throng one night
To learn the truth about the candle light,
And they decided one of them should go
To gather news of the elusive glow.
One flew till in the distance he discerned
A palace window where a candle burned—
And went no nearer: back again he flew
To tell the others what he thought he knew.
The mentor of the moths dismissed his claim,

Remarking: "He knows nothing of the flame."
A moth more eager than the one before
Set out and passed beyond the palace door.
He hovered in the aura of the fire,
A trembling blur of timorous desire,
Then headed back to say how far he'd been,
And how much he had undergone and seen.
The mentor said: "You do not bear the signs
Of one who's fathomed how the candle shines."
Another moth flew out—his dizzy flight
Turned to an ardent wooing of the light;
He dipped and soared, and in his frenzied trance
Both self and fire were mingled by his dance—
The flame engulfed his wing-tips, body, head,
His being glowed a fierce translucent red;
And when the mentor saw that sudden blaze,
The moth's form lost within the glowing rays,
He said: "He knows, he knows the truth we seek,
That hidden truth of which we cannot speak."
To go beyond all knowledge is to find
That comprehension which eludes the mind,
And you can never gain the longed-for goal
Until you first outsoar both flesh and soul;
But should one part remain, a single hair
Will drag you back and plunge you in despair—
No creature's self can be admitted here,
Where all identity must disappear.[9]

According to this story, some form of death or extinction represents the final goal of the Sufi's quest. The complete obliteration of the *nafs*, a state referred to as **fana**, presumably allows the Sufi to abide in God. This notion of *fana* led to a body of literature in Sufism telling of mystics who engage in "ecstatic utterances" (*shathiyat*)—such as Mansur al-Hallaj's famous expression *ana al-haqq* (I am the truth [i.e., God])—and of Sufis who eat during Ramadan. Such stories seek to convey the notion that these Sufis, whose selves have been extinguished in God, operate with a *batin*-level of consciousness, which permits them to flout the customary sharia rules and regulations.

"Sober" and "Intoxicated" Sufism

The words "sober" and "intoxicated" have to do with the mystic's orientation toward the sharia. "Sober" mystics tend to stress the compatibility and points of contact between the law and mysticism, showing how mystical teachings take the individual into a deeper and more spiritual understanding of the law. On their reading, Sufism does not contradict or subvert the law but succeeds in facilitating the mystic's greater appreciation of it. The Sufi, then, is someone who understands the law and never seeks to transgress its principles.

Juxtaposed to the "sober" mystic is the "intoxicated" or "drunken" Sufi. If "sober" Sufism stresses the compatibility of mysticism and law, "intoxicated" Sufism tends to stress the spirit as opposed to the letter of the law. The goal of the latter type of Sufism is to pursue the intoxicating union with God at all costs. Among the most famous "intoxicated" Sufis are al-Hallaj (discussed more fully in the next section) and the Persian Abu Yazid al-Bistami (d. 875), who is reported to have uttered in the passion of an ecstatic union with God, "Glory to me! How great is My majesty!"[10] Although many "drunken" Sufis of the past were not opposed to the law, the potential for antinomianism in Sufism bothered people associated with the legal establishment, which perhaps explains the conservative criticism and persecution of Sufism down to the present day.

Some Key Figures

The list of key figures in the historical development of Sufism given here is by no means exhaustive, but it does seek to provide a sampling of the most important names.

RABIA AL-ADAWIYYA

Rabia al-Adawiyya (717?–801?) is often regarded as one of the most important female voices in early Islam and as a central figure in the development of the early mystical impulse. She left no writings, and what we do possess about her comes from much later male sources, in particular Farid al-Din Attar, whose goal, as we have already seen, was not so much historical accuracy, but the construction of Sufi hagiographies.

Rabia was born in Basra, Iraq, to an ascetic, once again showing how in the early Muslim mystical tradition ascetics had families, so that we should regard asceticism as a profession. She was the fourth daughter—hence, the name Rabia, which derives from the Arabic word for the number four. After the death of her family, Rabia was orphaned and subsequently sold into slavery, whereupon she encountered all sorts of hardships. Many men asked for her hand in marriage, but she always refused because she said that she was already married to God.

According to her hagiography, Rabia is the one whose life best symbolizes the virtue of ecstatic love (*mahabba*) of God. Rabia's love—expressed in terms of passion and intensity—was not based on fear of punishment or hope of reward; on the contrary, she describes with erotic undertones how only God could satisfy her. According to Attar, "It is related that Hasan said to Rabia, 'Would you like to take a husband?' She replied, 'The marriage knot ties only one who exists. Where is existence here? I am not my own—I am His and under His command. You must ask permission from Him.' 'O Rabia,' Hasan said, 'By what means did you attain this degree?' [She responded,] 'By losing in Him everything I had attained.' 'How do you know Him?' [She replied,] 'You know the how, I know the no-how.'"[11]

The truth of the matter is that we know next to nothing about Rabia. We know her story only as mediated by male Sufis for the consumption of other male Sufis. As such, she is constructed to do what few other women do: she refuses to increase her status (e.g., through marriage) and is thus content with her lot. Her story, as an object lesson for later Sufis, is one that ignores all attachments except to God. She symbolizes the Sufi virtues of *tawakkul*, *tawhid*, and negation of the *nafs*. Implicit in Attar's construction, it would seem, is that the ideal (male) mystic must become like a woman before God.

MANSUR AL-HALLAJ

Perhaps the best example of a "drunken" Sufi, Mansur al-Hallaj (ca. 858–922) was born in Persia, where he married. He subsequently made the pilgrimage to Mecca but decided to stay for one year, facing the mosque, as his biographers–hagiographers would say, and devoting himself to fasting and total silence. Implicit in this story is that whereas the average Muslim is content to go to Mecca for a few days as part of his or her religious duties, al-Hallaj was not content with such a *zahir*-based performance. His goal was to move toward the *batin*. After his stay in the city, he traveled extensively and wrote and taught along the way.

Many Sufi masters felt that it was inappropriate to share the mystical secrets of Islam with everyone, which is why the master–disciple relationship was so important to the development of Sufism: it cultivated the proper channels of transmission. However, al-Hallaj did share his message with all and sundry, so that he began to make enemies, both among other Sufis and the ruling authorities. This unwelcome approach was exacerbated by occasions when he would fall into trances and utter phrases such as "Ana l-haqq" (I am the Truth), which those unaccustomed to the mystical path took to mean that he was claiming to be God because *al-haqq* (the Truth) is one of the ninety-nine names of God. Al-Hallaj is also credited with uttering that "there is nothing wrapped in my turban but God." These utterances led to a long trial and his subsequent imprisonment for eleven years in a Baghdad prison. In the end, he was publicly crucified in 922. At his execution,

> When they cut off his hands, he burst out laughing, "What's there to laugh about?" They asked.
>
> "It's easy to cut off the hand of a person who's chained up. The true believer is one who cuts off the hand of attributes, swindling aspiration from the highest throne of heaven."
>
> When they chopped off his feet, he smiled and said, "With these feet I used to travel the earth. I have other feet that are traversing both worlds at this very moment. Cut off those feet, if you can." . . .
>
> Then they cut out his tongue. When they cut off his head, it was the hour of the evening prayer. As his head was being cut off, [Hallaj] smiled and died. The people roared. He shot the ball of his fate to the final goal of acceptance. From each one of his limbs came the cry "I am the Real." . . . None of the people of the path have had a victory like [al-Hallaj's].[12]

Like other "drunken" Sufis, al-Hallaj was so overcome by his ecstatic experiences that his bodily existence seems to have meant very little to him. Moreover, such mystics' utterances became more widely known than any actual teaching ascribed to them.

It should be noted, however, that much of what we know about al-Hallaj is based on later legendary accounts of his life, by which point he had become an important personality to whom any number of characteristics and sayings could be affixed. Indeed, some scholars think that al-Hallaj's execution had less to do with his mystical teachings than with various political intrigues at the Abbasid court in Baghdad.

ABU ʾL-QASIM AL-QUSHAYRI

The Persian Abu ʾl-Qasim al-Qushayri (986–1074) was the great theoretical systematizer of Sufi doctrine and teaching. His goal was to show the compatibility between mystical teaching and mainstream Sunni Islam. Although it is customary to say that this synthesis first occurred in the writings of al-Ghazali, it began, for all intents and purposes, with al-Qushayri. His major treatise, referred to as the "Qushayrian Treatise" or simply "the Treatise," is one of the most popular Sufi manuals and has served as a primary textbook for many generations of Sufi novices to the present.[13] In section three of the Treatise, al-Qushayri provides a taxonomy of key Sufi terms and concepts that theoretically and practically guide the mystic's journey.

Significantly, Qushayri also incorporated into his treatise the biographies of past masters, thereby providing a historical argument for Sufi legitimacy. His treatise was translated into Persian (under his supervision), which had the important repercussion of facilitating the dissemination of an increasingly systematized Sufism to the Persianate world.

ABU HAMID MUHAMMAD
IBN MUHAMMAD AL-GHAZALI

Abu Hamid Muhammad ibn Muhammad al-Ghazali (1058–1111) was not just an important Sufi thinker, but one of the most important thinkers in medieval Islam. He was a famous legal scholar and philosopher who taught at the prestigious Nizamiyya, an institution of higher education in Nishapur in northeastern Iran. His autobiography (*The Deliverance from Error*) describes his emotional breakdown from the weight of fame and prestige and his gradual rehabilitation through Sufism. He writes: "What is most distinctive of mysticism is something that cannot be apprehended by study, but only by immediate experience.... I apprehended clearly that the mystics were the men who had real experiences, not men of words, and that I had already progressed as far as possible by way of intellectual apprehension. What remained for me was not to be attained by oral instruction and study, but only be immediate experience and by walking in the mystic way."[14]

The term that al-Ghazali here uses for "experience," *dhawq*, literally means "taste" and is meant to show God's sensual and sensory nearness to the mystic. After his rehabilitation, al-Ghazali spent the next ten years of his life traveling, writing, and teaching; he eventually opened up a "retreat center" (*zawiya* or *ribat* in Arabic; *khanqah* in Persian), a place where mystics could go for spiritual retreats and support in the Islamic world. Ghazali was certainly not the first to open such a retreat; although their origins seem rather obscure, the first one documented appeared in the late eighth century and was associated with Abu Hashim al-Sufi (d. 768).

One of al-Ghazali's major works is *Ihya ulum al-din* (*The Revival of the Religious Sciences*), which, as the title suggest, is a compendium to virtually all fields of Islamic religious science (such as *fiqh* [jurisprudence] and *kalam* [theology]) filtered through the prism of Sufism. Owing to his earlier training in the Islamic legal sciences and building on the works of earlier Sufis such as al-Qushayri, al-Ghazali did more than anyone to bring Sufism into the heart of Sunni Islam. Rejecting the "intoxicated" variety practiced by al-Hallaj, he created a vision of Islam that used mystical teaching to inform traditional understanding of sharia.

IBN ARABI

If al-Ghazali was famous for his sobriety, Ibn Arabi (1165–1240) is well known for his theoretical sophistication. Born and raised in Muslim Spain (al-Andalus), he left the Iberian Peninsula at the age of thirty-five and set out for Mecca, where he began writing his *Al-Futuhat al-makkiyya* (*Meccan Illuminations*). He eventually left Mecca and died in Damascus, where his tomb is still an important pilgrimage site.

Ibn Arabi is most famous for his controversial theory of *wahdat al-wujud* (the oneness of being). According to him, all things in the universe are a manifestation of God in the sense that they derive their potency from

God's perception. Although critics would label this vision pantheistic (i.e., equating God with the world), Ibn Arabi's doctrine is much more nuanced and complex than such a moniker would suggest.

Central to Ibn Arabi's mystical theory is the concept of love—not only between the mystic and God, but as a principle that sustains the organic flow of the universe. Religions, individuals, indeed all phenomena differ little from one another in Ibn Arabi's singular vision:

> My heart has adopted every shape; it has become a pasture for a gazelles,
> and a convent for Christian monks.
> A temple for idols, and a pilgrim's Ka'ba, the tables of a Torah, and
> the pages of a Koran.
>   I follow the religion of Love; wherever Love's camels turn, there Love is
> my religion and faith.[15]

RUMI

Probably the most famous Sufi in the West is the great thirteenth-century poet Jalal al-Din Muhammad al-Rumi (1207–1273). He was born in what is now Tajikistan, and his name, Rumi, means "the Roman," because he lived in an area called Rum, which was once ruled by the Byzantine Empire.

Rumi composed thousands of rhymed couplets in Persian in a genre known as *mathnawi*. A collection of some 25,000 of them are known as the *Mathnawi*; it has been translated into many languages, and the English translation has made Rumi one of the most popular poets in the United States.

Following his death, his followers founded the Mawlawiyyah (or Mevlevi) Order, whose members are also known as the "whirling dervishes" because of their dance ceremony *sama*, a ritualized remembrance of God.

The following verse provides a sense of the evocative nature of Rumi's poetic voice:

> O you who've gone on pilgrimage
>   where are you, where, oh where?
> Here, here is the Beloved!
>   Oh come now, come, oh come!
> Your friend, he is your neighbor,

he is next to your wall
You, erring in the desert
   what air of love is this?
If you'd see the Beloved's
   form without any form
You are the house, the master,
   You are the Ka'ba, you! ...
Where is a bunch of roses,
   if you would be this garden?
Where, one soul's pearly essence
   when you're the Sea of God?
That's true—and yet your troubles
   may turn to treasures rich—
How sad that you yourself veil
   the treasure that is yours![16]

Institutional Sufism

Larger-than-life individuals tend to define the early or classical period of Sufism. Although individuals such as Hasan al-Basri (642–728) and Rabia al-Adawiyya were undoubtedly historical figures, their life stories—or, perhaps better, their hagiographies—were written and added to during the ensuing centuries. According to these sources, asceticism in the earliest centuries tended to be an elite preoccupation as opposed to a large-scale popular movement. The eleventh century, however, witnessed the rise of organized movements or associations, most likely brought on by the important synthesis between Sufi teaching and mainstream Islam achieved by mystics such as al-Ghazali. Indeed, as mentioned, al-Ghazali's name is often associated with those who established residential and self-governing brotherhoods of like-minded individuals (although these brotherhoods' origin seems to be even earlier). The brotherhoods would meet in retreats called either *khanqah* in Persian or *ribat* or *zawiya* in Arabic.

If in earlier centuries the *tariqa* referred primarily to the Sufi path to enlightenment, in the centuries after al-Ghazali it came to designate the various "orders" whereby initiates were instructed in the various stages of mystical experience. Although the relationship between the master (*shaykh* in Arabic; *pir* in Persian) and the disciple (*faqir* or *murid* in Arabic; *shagird* in

SUFISM, NEW AGE SPIRITUALITY, AND
THE INTERNET

In recent years, especially with the popularity of the Internet and the perceived lack of spirituality in the modern world, Sufism (much like Kabbalah, Jewish mysticism) has been co-opted into the New Age movement. Sufi poets such as Jalal al-Din al-Rumi (1207–1273) have now become almost household names in the West. Although many may well find benefit in this construction of Sufism, we should be aware that it largely strips Sufism of its historical, linguistic, and intellectual contexts in the service of some inchoate spirituality.

In this new configuration, Sufism often becomes "de-Islamicized" and part of a universal and perennial wisdom (*sophia perennis*), as in the following definition of Sufism: "[An] [a]ncient Persian mystical religious system which has been absorbed by Islam. Rather than focusing on the Five Pillars of Islam, Sufis seek ultimate religious experience through mystic trances or altered states of consciousness, often induced through twirling dances (the 'whirling dervish'). Although the Qur'an is considered scripture, many practitioners [of Sufism] have more in common with the New Age movement than with classic forms of Islam."*

Perhaps because Sufism is perceived as quietist and less political, it is often held up as the future of Islam or the "real" Islam. The Sufi convert Stephen Schwartz writes that Sufism holds itself out as the threshold to "global harmony": "I believe that the world needs Sufism. It is God's most deeply hidden treasure, *another Islam*, a miraculous sanctuary. One need not go all the way to Turkistan to find it, for it is present in the hearts of many who live throughout this world. Its gates are open; and in the world of Rumi it appeals to all believers: only come."† In his works, Schwartz seeks to create a distinction between the "religious" or "spiritual" forms of Islam (i.e., Sufism) and the "political" or "ideological" forms of tradition (e.g., alternatively referred to as "Wahhabism" or "Salafism" or "jihadism," all of which Schwartz often lumps together under the omnibus term "Islamofacism"). The result is a Manichean approach to Islam, wherein everything good apparently derives from Sufism, and everything bad emerges from Wahhabism.

*"Sufism," in *New Age Spirituality Dictionary on Sufism*, Global Oneness: Co-creating a Happy World, http://www.experiencefestival.com/a/Sufism/id/293028.

†Stephen Schwartz, *Other Islam: Sufism and the Road to Global Harmony* (New York: Doubleday, 2008), 239.

Persian) was common to all these orders, the orders tended to differ in the various techniques they used to achieve such enlightenment. The masters received their spiritual authority by tracing their mystical lineage (*silsila*) back to Muhammad. Consistency was maintained by the leader of the order passing on to the next generation the teachings that he had received from his shaykh. Disciples swore allegiance to their shaykh, thus further maintaining doctrinal consistency within each order. To this day in many Sufi communities, Sufism is disseminated and propagated through the teaching tradition, mediated between the intimate exchange between master and disciple, and experienced through ritual performance.[17]

The result of this method of dissemination was that by the thirteenth century, there existed numerous international *turuq*, such as the Mawlawi Order and Bektashiyya Order in Turkey, the Badawiyya Order in Egypt, the Suhrawardiyya Order in Pakistan and Bangladesh, the Tijaniyya in Africa, and the international Naqshbandiyya.

The Sufism associated with these various orders is frequently referred to as "popular Islam" because of its many heterogenous elements, which are often derived from syncretistic practices with local non-Muslim cultures and practices, and because of its wide appeal among so-called non-elites. The emphasis on pilgrimage to the tombs of saints or holy men, the celebration of their birthdays, and the practices often deemed "superstitious" by others make this form of Islam seem very real to its adherents, however. To call it "popular" is often a way of discrediting it, especially among ultraconservative forces (see the next section). Moreover, it is often very hard to teach about Sufism in the classroom because it often does not square either with assumptions of what Islam should be (e.g., radical monotheism) or with the "five pillars" to which we often reduce Islamic thought and belief.

Conservative Criticism of Sufism

As mentioned several times throughout this chapter, many conservative thinkers have labeled Sufism a *bida* (innovation). Its emphasis on the shaykh is accordingly seen as taking the Muslim away from an unmediated relationship with God. The visit to tombs and other such practices are likewise regarded as a form of *shirk* (polytheism). In the late nineteenth and early twentieth centuries, for example, Wahhabis—members of a conservative Islamic movement associated with the rise of modern Saudi Arabia—destroyed all shrines devoted to saints, including the tomb of Muhammad. The rationale was that such shrines contributed to idolatry. This is also the reason behind the destruction of the large Buddha statues in Bamiyan, Afghanistan, in 2001, which the Taliban regarded as intolerable monuments to polytheism.

In an attack against Sufism in the very conservative Muslim magazine *Nid'ul Islam*, Yusuf al-Hijazi summarizes many of the reasons why conservative authorities are mistrustful of Sufism and blame it for all the current ills in Islam:

Sufis distracted the Muslims from the teachings of the Quran and Sunnah towards the servitude of the Sheikh. Muslims thus became alienated from the teachings of Islam, and possessed no protection from the innovations and trappings of the deviant sects. . . . The Sufi's [sic] have left a lasting impression on the image of Islam, portraying it as one of peace and apolitical, and anyone who contravenes this is an impostor and considered an extremist. . . . The Sufi influence undoubtedly contributed greatly to the decline of the Ottoman Empire. The pacifist views they spread, the lack of Shariah knowledge, and their befriending of the disbelievers, made sure that no one would oppose the vast changes being made to the Ottoman Laws. . . . Whilst the masses were busy in the construction of extravagant mosques and spinning around in circles, the Ottoman Empire was overtaken by Masons and eventually torn to parts.[18]

Such criticisms have also entered the mainstream and occasionally appear in introductions to Islam meant for Western undergraduates and other readers. For example, in a relatively popular and otherwise very good introductory treatment of Islam, Fazlur Rahman—a Pakistani scholar and liberal Muslim reformer—writes of Sufism:

As it developed in the whole of the Muslim world, [it] is solely responsible for inculcating, spreading and perpetuating the most fantastic and grotesque beliefs in the miracles of saints. The network of superstitions such beliefs have engendered has simply enchained the minds and spirits of the credulous masses, and even the educated and the learned have fallen a prey to them in large numbers. . . . Tomb worship and the ills accruing from this have rendered the Muslim masses almost incapable of understanding the Islamic teaching.[19]

Lived Sufism Today

Such critical comments clearly reveal that many contemporary reformers regard Sufism as a pernicious influence in the modern world. This view, of course, says less about Sufism than about its critics, who seek to purge Islam of all Sufi influences. The role of Sufism in the spread of Islam to the far-flung reaches of the Muslim empire cannot be underestimated. Its use of mystically inspired poetry, the cult of saints, and practices geared to undertake mystical communion with God played a formative role in the spread of Islam.

Despite the vitriol that many reformers level against Sufism, it still plays an important role in the religious lives of Muslims around the world. Sufism today, as it has been throughout its lengthy history, remains a very diverse tradition that possesses much variation dependent on numerous regional and cultural contexts. Taking place within the channels of particular orders, teachings and knowledge are transmitted largely by the interpersonal teaching networks between masters and disciples. Within these orders, ritual performance, even more than teaching, remains the major vehicle of Sufi expression. Through activities such as dreams and dream interpretations, daily rituals of remembrance, and pilgrimage networks, Sufis struggle to attain spiritual enlightenment.

The quest for spiritual wisdom, in other words, is not found in books, but in the intimate face-to-face interaction with the master and in bodily practice. Within these contexts, stories about past masters are told and retold, initiates attend regular *dhikr* sessions and make pilgrimages to local shrines, and so on. The initiate's progress is charted by means of his or her practice of discipline, self-sacrifice, and ritual activity.

Although Sufism remains deeply rooted in everyday practice, it can also function as an important marker in regionalized networks of individual and group identity. In his analysis of the Chishti Sabiri Order in Pakistan, for example, Robert Rozehnal has shown that members of the order articulate and preserve an alternative identity independent of conservative Islam and the state through their piety and practices.[20]

NOTES

1. For example, Stephen Katz, "Language, Epistemology, and Mysticism," in Stephen Katz, ed., *Mysticism and Philosophical Analysis* (New York: Oxford University Press, 1978), 22–74.

2. See the comments in Ahmet T. Karamustafa, *Sufism: The Formative Period* (Berkeley: University of California Press, 2007), 1–3.

3. Peter Brown, *Authority and the Sacred: Aspects of the Christianisation of the Roman World* (Cambridge: Cambridge University Press, 1995).

4. For example, Richard W. Bulliet, *Conversion to Islam in the Medieval Period: An Essay in Quantitative History* (Cambridge, Mass.: Harvard University Press, 1979).

5. Karamustafa, *Sufism*, 56.

6. Quoted in Michael A. Sells, *Early Islamic Mysticism: Sufi, Quran, Miraj, Poetic, and Theological Writings* (New York: Paulist Press, 1996), 147–148.

7. See the discussion in Carl W. Ernst, *The Shambala Guide to Sufism* (Boston: Shambala, 1997), 102.

8. Farid ad-Din Attar, *Memorial of God's Friends: Lives and Sayings of Sufis*, trans. Paul Losensky (New York: Paulist Press, 2009), 98.

9. Farid ad-Din Attar, *The Conference of the Birds*, trans. Afkham Darbandi and Dick Davis (Harmondsworth: Penguin, 1984), 206.

10. Quoted in A. J. Arberry, *Sufism: An Account of the Mystics of Islam* (New York: Harper Torchbooks, 1970), 54.

11. Quoted, with slight modification, from Sells, *Early Islamic Mysticism*, 161–162.

12. Attar, *Memorial of God's Friends*, 406.

13. Abu ʾl-Qasim al-Qushayri, *Al-Qushayri's Epistle on Sufism: Al-Risala al-qushayriyya fi ʿilm al-tasawwuf*, trans. Alexander D. Knysh (Reading, Eng.: Garnet, 2007).

14. Quoted in W. Montgomery Watt, *The Faith and Practice of al-Ghazali* (London: Allen and Unwin, 1953), 56–57.

15. James T. Munroe, *Hispano-Arab Poetry: A Student Anthology* (Berkeley: University of California Press, 1974), 320.

16. Quoted in Annemarie Schimmel, *I Am Wind, You Are Fire: The Life and World of Rumi* (Boston: Shambala, 1992).

17. Robert Rozehnal, *Islamic Sufism Unbound: Politics and Piety in Twenty-first Century Pakistan* (New York: Palgrave Macmillan, 2007), 3–6.

18. Yusuf al-Hijazi, "Sufism: The Deviated Path," *Nidʾul Islam* 22 (1998), http://web.archive.org/web/20050803084708/http://www.islam.org.au/articles/22/sufism.htm.

19. Fazlur Rahman, *Islam*, 2nd ed. (Chicago: University of Chicago Press, 1979), 245–246.

20. Rozehnal, *Islamic Sufism Unbound*, 36–38.

SUGGESTIONS FOR FURTHER READING

Chittick, William C. *The Sufi Path of Knowledge: Ibn al-Arabi's Metaphysics of Imagination.* Albany: State University of New York Press, 1989.

Cornell, Vincent J. *Realm of the Saint: Power and Authority in Moroccan Sufism.* Austin: University of Texas Press, 1998.

Ernst, Carl W. *The Shambhala Guide to Sufism.* Boston: Shambhala, 1997.

Al-Ghazali. *Freedom and Fulfillment: An Annotated Translation of Al-Ghazali's "Al-Munqidh min al-dalal" and Other Relevant Works of al-Ghazali.* Translated by Richard Joseph McCarthy. Boston: Twayne, 1980.

Gruber, Christianne, and Frederick Colby, eds. *The Prophet's Ascension: Cross-Cultural Encounters with the Islamic Miraj Tales.* Bloomington: Indiana University Press, 2010.

Karamustafa, Ahmet T. *Sufism: The Formative Period.* Berkeley: University of California Press, 2007.

Knysh, Alexander. *Islamic Mysticism: A Short History.* Leiden: Brill, 2000.

Massignon, Louis. *The Passion of al-Hallaj: Mystical Martyr of Islam.* Translated by H. Mason. 4 vols. Princeton, N.J.: Princeton University Press, 1983.

Nicholson, Reynold A. *Studies in Islamic Mysticism.* Cambridge: Cambridge University Press, 1978.

Rozehnal, Robert. *Islamic Sufism Unbound: Politics and Piety in Twenty-first Century Pakistan.* New York: Palgrave Macmillan, 2007.

Schimmel, Annemarie. *Mystical Dimensions of Islam*. Chapel Hill: University of North Carolina Press, 1975.

Sells, Michael A. *Early Islamic Mysticism: Sufi, Quran, Miraj, Poetic, and Theological Writings*. New York: Paulist Press, 1996.

Watt, W. Montgomery. *The Faith and Practice of al-Ghazali*. London: Allen and Unwin, 1953.

Waugh, Earle H. *Memory, Music, and Religion: Morocco's Mystical Chanters*. Columbia: University of South Carolina Press, 2005.

PART III

BELIEFS AND PRACTICES

8

CONSTITUTING IDENTITIES

Beliefs and Schools

W HAT DO Muslims believe? It is as difficult to provide an answer to this question as it is to provide an answer to the question of what Jews, Christians, or Hindus believe. Even if we were to say, as many do, that Muslims are radical monotheists—believing in the complete transcendence and oneness of God—how do we fit the cult of saints discussed in chapter 7 into this framework? To claim that all Muslims from Tunisia to Bangladesh believe the same things and have the same encounter with their religion is, of course, ridiculous. For example, some Muslims believe that one should mark and celebrate the birthday of Muhammad, whereas other Muslims are steadfastly opposed to such a practice and argue that it is a form of polytheism that lifts Muhammad up to the level of a god. Is one of these beliefs better or more correct than the other? Is one authentically Muslim, and the other not? Such questions, more typically entertained by the theologian, cannot for obvious reasons concern us here.

Claims of what constitutes Muslim belief risk assuming that the millions of Muslims located in various geographic and cultural regions around the globe think about the religion in a unified manner. Moreover, such claims draw too sharp a distinction between Islam the religion that exists monolithically and the various cultures in which this Islam finds itself and that threaten to pollute it, distort it, or otherwise dismantle it (depending on one's point of view). Many anthropologists—from Clifford Geertz to Mark

Woodward to Laurence Rosen—have shown that great discrepancies exist between the theological and textbook presentations of Islamic doctrine, on the one hand, and the manifold ways that Muslims cobble together meaning from diverse local customs and beliefs, on the other. Many of these local customs are syncretistic, taking Muslim beliefs and practices and combining them with those that predate Islam in particular regions.[1]

To conceive of Islamic belief might also be to assume that Muslims actively think about their religion and conceive of it in ways that differ sharply and significantly from other aspects of their life. The fact of the matter is that, as other scholars have shown, the very term "religion" might not even be a useful one to apply to various cultures and eras.[2] Religion, at least as configured in the largely Protestant West, is often regarded as belonging to a particular sphere of the individual and his or her internal or spiritual piety, and it has been constructed largely as something that differs markedly from other spheres of life (e.g., the political and the economic) that have been signified as the so-called secular. Yet these dichotomies—religious/secular, internal/external, spiritual/mundane—often begin to break down and have limited utility when applied to other cultures.

Two major problems arise when discussing belief. First, there is often a tendency to construct *a*, *b*, and *c* as genuinely Islamic, but not *d*, *e*, and *f*. Why? What makes the former factors inherently Islamic, but not the latter? Is it because the former deal with what scholars in the West have decided to count as "religious" (e.g., prayer, death) and the latter with what they count as "secular" (e.g., legal rulings, economic transactions)? Although Westerners may be comfortable making such distinctions, many Muslims consider them spurious.

Second, we also tend to assume that all Muslims must necessarily believe what theologians have constructed as an authentically "Muslim" belief. But why must they? Or if they do, why must we assume that the belief means the same thing at different times or even in different geographic locations? All these issues pose numerous pitfalls for those wishing to understand Muslim belief except in the most basic of ways.

To try and negotiate these methodological difficulties, this chapter examines both the historical construction and the elucidation of certain concepts and ideals that have played a role in the formation of Islamic belief. The advantage of this two-pronged approach—as opposed to making the claim that all Muslims today believe the same things—is that it reveals something of the cultural, political, and ideological factors that have played a role in shaping Islamic identities both in the past and in the contemporary period.

The Rise of Muslim Theology (Kalam)

Central to every religion is the question of self-definition: How does religion, as a social and cultural form, enable its practitioners to imagine themselves as a community, and how is this community imagined to be different from rival communities? This question is, of course, as much political as it is religious. This is not to say that the earliest attempts to define terms such as "Islam" and "Muslim" were necessarily polemical; however, it is necessary to be aware that the need for self-definition corresponds to an awareness of difference and the attempt to make such difference into an ontological category.

At the time of Muhammad, when the Muslim community was just beginning to take shape as a historical and sociological entity, there had to be certain ways that believers could differentiate their belief from rival monotheisms within the Arabian Peninsula. Islam, like every religion, was engaged in a process of self-making, defining itself against various "others." Legal, social, religious, and political identities were formed in response to other such identities.

Once again, and this should come as no surprise, we have a paucity of historical sources to reconstruct the origins of Islamic theology—or, perhaps more accurately, the origins of what we might call early attempts by Muslims to carve out space for themselves in the crowded marketplace of both rival monotheisms and rival interpretations of Muhammad's message. This paucity is in part the result of the dearth of early sources, later sources pretending to be earlier ones, and the omnipresent problem of how to interpret the later material.

Although discussions concerning Islamic identity would emerge through the reading and interpretation of familiar literature such as the Quran and the materials comprising the Sunna, mature reflections on Islamic faith and belief took several centuries to develop. What we now consider to be hallmarks of Muslim faith (e.g., God's oneness, Day of Judgment) arose in response to a series of intercommunal debates (many of which we have encountered in previous chapters). These debates were responsible for the formation of what would emerge as "orthodoxy," further revealing that beliefs do not fall from heaven but develop in a utilitarian manner in response to the most mundane of needs.

However, a question that we must constantly ask ourselves whenever we encounter the term "orthodoxy" is, Whose orthodoxy? Part II pointed to the tendency to emphasize Sunni Islam as orthodox, but this emphasis is both problematic and incorrect. Even if we were to assume that it were true, we would then have to ask further: Which Sunnis? The mainstream Sunni viewpoint in the past, as now, was never a unified orthodoxy, but in a constant state of tension among various groups (e.g., rationalist, pietistic, traditionalist, universalist, and particularistic).

Indeed, this dialectic of contestation and synthesis is ultimately responsible for the formation of Muslim beliefs and identities. Again, however, there exists the caveat that beliefs (like identities) are rarely consistent, that they change over time, and that different sectarian movements possessed (and still possess) different—sometimes radically different—beliefs.

The Status of the Grave Sinner

One of the earliest of what we might in retrospect call theological debates within early Islam was whether the "grave sinner" (i.e., a murderer) could still be considered a believer and part of the community. This issue was not just legal, but practical, with many specific and practical connotations for the developing community, such as whether one could pray beside a "grave sinner" or marry one. The Kharijites—a group that split from the partisans of Ali when he agreed to arbitration with Muʿawiya (chapter 5)—held that the grave sinner threatened the true believers' purity and that such sinners, along with their families, should be executed. The Kharijites also tended to reject the emerging Sunna literature in favor of the Quran because of what they considered to be the Sunna's innovative nature. Although the Kharijites would be quickly marginalized, largely because they situated themselves in opposition to the ruling authorities, their influence would assert itself in various submovements throughout the Arabian Peninsula and North Africa, taking the more moderate position that only habitual sinners should be punished.

Another position on the issue of the "grave sinner" was taken by a group known as the Murjiʾa. Although critical of sin, this group held that

AL-QAEDA AND OTHER MODERN MILITANT ISLAMIC GROUPS AS "NEO-KHARIJITES"?

In the aftermath of the attacks on the World Trade Center and the Pentagon in the United States on September 11, 2001, numerous political commentators came up with the notion that those militant organizations responsible for these and other attacks resembled the Kharijite movement within Islam in its first hundred years. Hesham A. Hassaballa, writing for the American Muslim (an organization devoted to "peace, justice, and the reconcilia- tion of all humanity"—slippery signifiers like the Fox News "fair and balanced" motto), for example, argues,

> The murderous fanatics who kill in the name of Islam are trying to cast themselves as "Muslim heroes." They try to claim that they are "defending the ummah" with their acts of terrible destruction. Yet, we easily see through their facade of piety for the satanic murderers that they truly are. Just like the Kharijites, these fanatics consider all those Muslims who do not accept their twisted interpretation of Islam as "infidels," whose blood is lawful to be shed. Just like the Kharijites, these extrem- ists have committed a number of atrocities against their own co-religionists. Just like the Kharijites, these murderers threaten the safety and security of the Muslim ummah, and what is worse, today's "neo-Kharijites" even threaten the very exis- tence of the Muslim ummah.*

Although the use of terms from early Islamic history to refer to modern movements is certainly attractive to some, it is not without problems. First, many modern militant groups derive their understanding of Islam from modern thinkers (such as Muhammad ibn abd al-Wahhab and Sayyid Qutb [see chapter 10]) rather than from the ideology, whatever it might have been, of a seventh-century splinter group. The use of technol- ogy and *select* features of the modern world make groups such as al-Qaeda a decidedly modern religious phenomenon even though they certainly envisage their struggle to be an ancient one.

Individuals and groups are certainly free to use whatever terms they want to define themselves and others, considering that language evolves and changes through time. However, to avoid potential misunderstandings it is extremely important to be aware of the language that we and others use.

*Hesham A. Hassaballa, "Neo-Kharijites Not Islamic Fascists," American Muslim, October 2, 2006, http:// www.theamericanmuslim.org/tam.php/features/articles/neo_kharijites_not_islamic_fascists.

it was not within humans' power to decide the fate of the grave sinner. Only God can decide this question, and humans have no right to make decisions about what is right and wrong and thus about who is or is not within the community of believers. This position—and the more general position that only God knows the business of human affairs—would even- tually become the position taken by mainstream Sunni Islam and associ- ated with Abu Hanifa, especially the creedal statement attributed to him: al-fiqh al-akbar.[3]

Free Will and Predestination

Because the Kharijites argued that humans had the right to judge their fellows, it necessarily followed that they believed that humans had the freedom to choose whether to commit a particular action. This position of free will became most closely associated with another early group known as the Qadarites (the Arabic word *qadar* means "determination"). Once again, this theological debate was not simply theological, but intimately connected to contemporaneous political events emerging largely from the sectarian movement that became known as Shiʿism. Those who supported the Qadarite position were in favor of active rebellion against the ruling Umayyad forces, arguing that the community had the right to overthrow an unjust ruler, whereas those who supported the Umayyad political forces argued that their power to rule had been preordained by God. What would eventually become mainstream Muslim belief is actually a combination of these two principles: that God knows all, but that humans must act as if they have the freedom to act. If this freedom did not exist, there would be no need for the strictures of religion.

Mutazilites and the Doctrine of the Created Quran

As the early Islamic Empire moved into new areas, it was only a mater of time before earlier civilizations left their mark on Islamic thought. The Abbasids, as noted in chapter 4, came to power in the mid-eighth century, and they legitimated their rule in part on the establishment of cultural and scientific institutions. Part of this work included a massive translation movement of texts from Greek and Syriac into Arabic, which gave rise to a considerable body of Greek-inspired rationalism as texts by Plato, Aristotle, and others were translated into Arabic and subsequently interpreted and commented on by Muslim thinkers.

Another likely impetus behind the emergence of Muslim rationalism was the need to justify Islam and Muslim belief to non-Muslims. Early Muslim theological encounters with more sophisticated late antique Christianities seem to have encouraged some Muslim scholars to begin the study of non-Muslim rationalist texts and the reading of Muslim texts in their light. The fanciful anthropomorphisms in the Quran created the need among some Muslims to rationalize these anthropomorphisms, thereby bringing them under the control of human reason.

One of the earliest groups to engage in this sort of rationalist theological speculation was the **Mutazilites**. The origins of this group are obscure, with some sources claiming its members arose from among the group associated with Hasan al-Basri as an attempt to strike a middle way between earlier theological schools such as the Kharijites and the Murji'ites. Others argue that the Mutazilites were descendents of the Qadarites. Regardless of their origins, the Mutazilites referred to themselves as the *ahl al-adl wa'-tawhid* (People of [Divine] Justice and Unity), and they played a crucial role in introducing rationalism into Islam and then in developing Islamic sciences.

The result was the introduction of Greek rationalist speculation into Islam. It is important, however, not to regard the Mutazilites as philosophers, even though they used reason. They often knew their conclusions beforehand and so used rationalism to argue backward to formulate premises.

The Mutazilites used rationalist principles to articulate, as their name suggests, God's justice and unity. One sees, for example, the role of Greek rationality in the Mutazilite discussion of divine justice. According to them, God's justice necessarily equates with his goodness; as a result, God can do only that which we consider to be just and good acts. God, on this reading, can neither perform nor endorse (i.e., reward) unjust actions. Critics of this view not surprisingly argue that it is both impossible and ridiculous to limit God's actions by means of our own limited understanding of the words "justice" and "goodness."

The emphasis on justice led the Mutazilites to stress the importance of free will. If God rewards the righteous and punishes the wicked, it is important that humans have the ability to choose between good and evil. Evil actions must necessarily result from human decisions to act in a particular way, and because God is just, he can have nothing to do with that which is evil. God, according to the Mutazilites, is compelled to reward the righteous and to punish the sinner. To do otherwise would be unjust, something that God could never be, they argued.

Divine unity, the other major Mutazilite principle, emphasizes God's transcendence to the world. To describe God using too familiar language is to risk making God too much like humans. To say that God is "happy," for example, is to make God analogous to us, thereby compromising his unity. This issue led Mutazilite theologians to employ a form of negative theology

THE DEBATE BETWEEN AL-SIRAFI AND
MATTA B. YUNUS ON THE SCIENCE OF LOGIC

In an early dialogue supplied by Abu Hayyan al-Tawhidi (ca. 930–1023), we get a good sense of the debate over the role that Greek science has played in Islam. Al-Tawhidi provides us with the "transcript" of a debate between Abu Bishr Matta b. Yunus (d. 940) and Abu Saʿid al-Sirafi (d. 979). Yunus, the teacher of the famous Abu Nasr al-Farabi (870–950), argues that logic is a universal science that is central to clear thinking. Al-Sirafi, in contrast, holds that logic is not universal, but a Greek linguistic habit that is both unnecessary and unhelpful to Arabic speakers, who have all they need in the rules of Arabic grammar.

> AL-SIRAFI: If logic be the invention of a Greek made in the Greek language and according to Greek conventions, and according to the descriptions and symbols that Greeks understand, whence does it follow that the Turks, Indians, Persians, and Arabs should attend to it?
> MATTA B. YUNUS: This follows because Logic is the discussion of accidents apprehended by reason, and ideas comprehended thereby, and the investigation of thoughts that occur, and notions that enter the mind. Now in matters apprehended by the intellect all men are alike, as for example, four and four are eight among all the nations.*

*The entire debate can be found in D. S. Margoliouth, "The Merits of Logic and Grammar," *Journal of the Royal Asiatic Society* (1905): 79–129.

in which the only things that can legitimately be said of God ought to be said in negatives (e.g., "God is not sad") because only negatives do not impinge on God's absolute unity.

This understanding of language and the view of God led to the reinterpretation of the Quran, especially those verses that stress God's anthropomorphic qualities. Those verses, for example, that describe God's body parts (e.g., his face in 6:52) or God sitting on a throne (e.g., 2:255) cannot literally be true and therefore have to be understood as metaphors. "God's face," according to their reading, actually means God's essence; "God's hand" refers to his "power," and so on.

In order to protect God's absolute unity, the Mutazilites further stressed the created nature of the Quran. According to them, an eternal Quran would not only jeopardize God's unity (i.e., it would make something coeternal with him) but also limit humans' free will because it would mean that God would have known of the fate or choices of characters within the Quran before these figures themselves did (e.g. the condemnation of Abu Lahab in sura 111). The Quran was therefore created in time. This position, especially given the way that Islam was developing, would come under widespread attack by what was gradually emerging as Sunni orthodoxy.

The Mutazilites, however, had the political support of the Abbasid caliph, al-Mamun (r. 813–833). According to traditional accounts, al-Mamun, in order to systematize belief, gave the Mutazilites permission to create an "inquisition" (*mihna*), wherein Muslim jurists were posed the question whether they believed in the created nature of the Quran. Those who held that it was created were allowed to remain in their positions; those who argued that it was eternal were stripped of their position, and some—for example, Ahmad ibn Hanbal (discussed in chapter 6 and later in this chapter)—were thrown in jail. However, there is some ambiguity regarding who the actual players were in the inquisition. It was most likely carried out by the caliph, not the Mutazilites, perhaps as a way to create something like a centralized "church" that would enforce belief, establish orthodoxy, and so on.

The early Abbasid era (starting in 750) was really the heyday of the Mutazilites. The relatively small number of Mutazilites and their increasing lack of touch with what was emerging as Sunni consensus about God and the role of reason largely meant that they would eventually fall out of favor. Those influenced by their teachings would periodically emerge in the coming centuries, and their biggest influence would be on Shi'i legal theory.

Ahmad ibn Hanbal

We have already encountered the conservative Ahmad ibn Hanbal (d. 855)—the founder of one of the four Sunni schools of law—as one of the instrumental figures in the development of Sunni legal theory (see chapter 6). During the Mutazilite-fueled and caliphal-sanctioned inquisition, ibn Hanbal was one of the few scholars who refused to back down to the caliph and deny the Quran's createdness. He was steadfastly opposed to the employment of rationalist theology to elucidate Islamic principles. He was imprisoned, and while in jail, his partisans tell us, he was tortured in order to make him renounce his position. He refused and quickly became a symbol of defiance for all those who held his position. In 847, ibn Hanbal was set free by the caliph al-Mutawakkil (r. 847–861), whereupon his stature as a legal scholar and critic of rationalism further increased.

The importance of ibn Hanbal's position cannot be underestimated. Up until his time, the institution of the caliphate seemed to be the primary arbiter of law and theology within Islam. His successful challenge to this status quo effectively increased the power of the *ulama* at the expense of the caliph. This shift would have tremendous repercussions on the role and influence of the *ulama* down to the present.

The Asharites

The chief intellectual rivals to the Mutazilites were the Asharites, a group founded by Abu al-Hasan al-Ashari (ca. 873–935). Al-Ashari was not op-posed to the Mutazilites in the same manner that ibn Hanbal was, and in many ways he created a position in between the two: one that also sought to use rationalist principles, but to articulate a position more in harmony with what he perceived to be "orthodox" Islam. It is important, however, not to regard the Asharites as "irrational" or "antirational." On the con-trary, they represent a rationalist theology that was on par with the Mu-tazilites' theology, but that argued for different principles. Whereas the Mutazilites argued for God's absolute justice, the Asharites emphasized God's absolute omnipotence. Many of the post-Ghazali writings of the Asharites—for example, those by Saʿad al-Din al-Taftazani (d. 1390)—dis-play an extremely sophisticated rationalism.[4]

The Asharites came down on the opposite side regarding many of the Mutazilites' key principles. Whereas the Mutazilites stressed free will, the Asharites emphasized determinism in order to protect God's omnipotence and omniscience. According to classical Asharite theory (in many ways influenced by Greek atomism), God creates the potentiality for people to act, and even though he ultimately knows what decisions they will make, humans must take responsibility for all that they do. Al-Ashari writes: "No human act can occur without [God's] willing it because that would imply that [the act] occurred out of carelessness and neglect or out of weakness and inadequacy on [God's] part to effect what He wills."[5]

According to al-Ashari's formulation, God continually creates the world anew and that what we think of as cause and effect (e.g., where there is smoke, there is fire) is an illusion. Given God's absolute omnipo-tence, there may well be situations that human categories cannot sup-port. Although it may seem that fire produces smoke, there may be a time in the future when this is not the case at all. This position enabled Asharites to protect divine miracles. What we see as cause and effect is simply a product of God's mercy. Both the fire and the smoke are the effects from God, and for our benefit he causes both (most of the time) to follow each other.

The view of God as the only creator posed a problem for the concept of free will. If humans possess free will, then they, too, are creators in the sense that they create their actions. In order to mediate between these positions, al-Ashari developed the position of "acquisition" (iktisab), in which humans acquire the will to perform a particular action because God creates the will in the first place. For example, when I walk to the store, God creates both the will and power in me to walk.

Related to God's absolute omnipotence is the Quran's use of terminology to describe him. Because the Asharites rejected the Quran's creation in time, they held that its language had to mean what it said and could not be interpreted away by employing allegorical exegesis. If the Quran speaks of God's hand or God's face, then, by this view, these expressions must signify God in some way. Because applying human characteristics (e.g., face, hand) to God might pose certain categorical problems, however, Asharites contended that when the Quran speaks of, for example, God's hand, the term "hand" has to be understood "without knowing how or what" (bila kayf) it actually means. This view became known as the principle of **balkafa**. Later Asharites, however, developed other, primarily philological means of dealing with anthropomorphic terms in the Quran and hadiths, such as looking for second-order meanings. Many of these Asharite positions would in fact become orthodoxy in Sunni Islam. The concepts of determinism, the eternality of the Quran, and, to a certain extent, the principle of balkafa still largely hold for many Muslims. One of the most important of the later Asharites was Abu Hamid Muhammad ibn Muhammad al-Ghazali (d. 1111), whom we encountered in reference to Sufism in chapter 7.

The Maturidis

Abu Mansur al-Maturdi (d. 944), born in Samarqand (modern-day Uzbekistan) in Central Asia, was another important tenth-century theologian who, especially after his death, played an important role in the emergence of Sunni Islam. Like al-Ashari, he followed a middle path that stressed both traditionalism and rationalism, and in his *Kitab al-tawhid* (*Book of Unity*) he argued that reason is God given and must be employed to judge other sources of knowledge. Although he believed in free will, like al-Ashari he argued that individuals "acquire" their actions because only God, whose existence alone is necessary and eternal, can create.

Many of al-Maturdi's theological positions became associated with the Hanafi legal school, which had spread to Central Asia at this time. The school's spread and eventual success seem to have been a result of the conversion of many Turks to a Hanafi/Maturdi version of Islam. The Maturdi school of theology would subsequently become the main theological school of the Ottoman Empire. Turkish expansion through the Ottoman Empire in turn enabled the Hanafi and Maturdi schools to spread throughout western Persia, Iraq, Anatolia, and Syria.

Al-Maturdi's theological position is witnessed in the creed (*aqida*) penned by Najm al-Din al-Nasafi (d. 1142). This creed presents an outline of Muslim belief, beginning with sources of knowledge before moving on to discuss God, his nature and attributes, belief, communication of God to his messengers, and life in this world. The creed subsequently gave way to many commentaries, one of the more important being by the fourteenth-century Ashari theologian al-Taftazani.[6]

Medieval Islamic Philosophy

Beginning in the tenth century, a group of individuals sought to show the fusion between Islam and the thought of Plato, Aristotle, and other philosophers of late antiquity. Although perhaps drawing on the Mutazilites' earlier arguments, these new thinkers were not nearly as interested in apologetical claims, and many were unwilling to accept conclusions that revealed scripture told them had to be true. This reluctance led to the redefinition of many traditional Muslim concepts, such as creation, prophecy, and redemption.

Many of these philosophers were also scientists, and they engaged, commented on, and made advances in the scientific theories handed to them from late antiquity in such fields as optics, medicine, mathematics, and astronomy. Because many of the Islamic philosophers were heavily invested in the Greek philosophical sciences at this time, they worked with

THE VIRTUOUS CITY

Abu Nasr al-Farabi (870–950) on the characteristics of the perfect ruler–lawgiver:

The supreme ruler without qualification is he who does not need anyone to rule over him in anything whatever, but has actually acquired the sciences and every kind of knowledge, and has no need of a man to guide him in anything. He is able to comprehend well each kind of the particular things that he ought to do. He is able to guide well all others to everything in which he instructs them, to employ all those who do any of the acts for which they are equipped, and to determine, define, and direct thee acts toward happiness. This is found only in the one who possesses great and superior natural dispositions, when his soul is in union with the Active Intellect. . . . For man attain revelation only when he attains this rank, that is, when there is n longer an intermediary between him and the Active Intellect. . . . The men who are governed by the rule of this ruler are the virtuous, good, and happy men. If they form a nation, then that is the virtuous nation.*

Al-Farabi on the superiority of philosophy over religion:

According to the ancients, religion is an imitation of philosophy. Both comprise the same subjects and both give an account of the ultimate principles of the beings. Both supply knowledge about the first principle and the cause of the beings, and both give an account of the ultimate end for the sake of which man is made—that is, supreme happiness—and the ultimate end of every one of the other beings. In everything of which philosophy gives an account based on intellectual perception or conception, religion gives an account based on imagination. In everything demonstrated by philosophy, religion employs persuasion. Philosophy gives an account of the ultimate principles as they are perceived by the intellect. Religion sets forth their images by means of similitudes of them taken from corporeal principles and imitates them by their likenesses among political offices. . . . Also, in everything of which philosophy gives an account that is demonstrable and certain, religion gives an account based on persuasive arguments. Finally, philosophy is prior to religion in time.†

*Abu Nasr al-Farabi, "The Political Regime," trans. Fauzi M. Najjar, in Ralph Lerner and Muhsin Mahdi, eds., *Medieval Political Philosophy* (Ithaca, N.Y.: Cornell University Press, 1963), 36–37.

†Abu Nasr al-Farabi, "The Attainment of Happiness," trans. Muhsin Mahdi, in ibid., 77–78.

the notion that the world was not created but eternal (à la Aristotle) and tended to naturalize traditional Muslim concepts such as prophecy and the afterlife. Their theories not surprisingly met with severe criticism by more orthodox authorities.

One of the earliest Islamic philosophers was Abu Nasr al-Farabi (ca. 870–950). Although al-Farabi made many contributions to the fields of logic and mathematics, his most famous work is his *Al-Madina al-fadila* (*The Virtuous City*), wherein he tries to imagine the ideal state. In this work, he argues that religion is a symbolic rendering of philosophical truths meant for the masses. Like Plato, he argues that the philosopher's duty is to provide guidance to the state, which is ideally ruled by the prophet-philosopher-king.

According to al-Farabi, following Aristotle and the Aristotelian tradition, God is an Intellect and by definition cannot know particulars. This means that the God of the philosophers cannot know individual actions and thus takes no active role in human affairs. Although nonphilosophers work on the assumption (or "noble lie") that God rewards the good and punishes the evil, the philosopher realizes the importance of ethics as the sole arbiter of human conduct.

Al-Farabi—like many of the philosophers who would follow in his wake—also controversially argued that the afterlife was not based on the resurrection of the body, but on the eternal existence of the soul (often called the intellect), which loses its distinguishing features when the body dies because, again following the ancient Greek philosophical tradition, it is the essence of the individual, with the body simply being its temporary material casing.

Another important medieval Islamic philosopher is the Persian Ibn Sina (Abu Ali al-Husayn ibn Abd Allah) (ca. 980–1037), known in the West as Avicenna. His fourteen-volume *Al-Qanun fi-al-tibb* (*The Canon of Medicine*) was a standard medical text in Europe and the Islamic world up until the eighteenth century. In addition, his *Kitab al-shifa* (*The Book of Healing*) is a scientific and philosophical encyclopedia that covers all the main sciences of the day, from logic to physics to metaphysics.

Al-Ghazali was extremely critical of al-Farabi and Avicenna. He wrote a work titled *Tahafut al-falasifa* (*Incoherence of the Philosophers*), wherein he accuses them of *kufr* (unbelief) on many accounts, the most serious being (1) their denial of the world's creation, (2) their denial that God can know particulars, and (3) their denial of bodily resurrection. Some have argued that al-Ghazali's critique all but ended philosophical speculation in much of the Islamic world.

Perhaps the most famous medieval Islamic philosopher is Abu'l-Walid Muhammad ibn Ahmad Ibn Rushd (1126–1198), best known in the West by the name Averroes. Born in Córdoba (Muslim Spain), he was appointed a judge (*qadi*) in 1160. His legal stature led him to compose a work titled *The Decisive Treatise*, which provided a legal ruling (fatwa) that good Muslims must engage in the study of philosophy because the Quran and the hadith command such activity. His use and praise of philosophy, however, would

AVERROES AND THE LEGAL OBLIGATION TO
STUDY PHILOSOPHY

Thus spoke the lawyer, imam, judge, and unique scholar Abu al-Walid Muhammad ibn Ahmad Ibn Rushd:

We say: if the activity of philosophy is nothing more than the study of existing beings and reflection on them as indications of the Artisan, that is, inasmuch as they are products of art, and if the Law has recommended and urged reflection on beings, then it is clear that what this name signifies is either obligatory or recommended by the Law.

That the Law summons to the reflection on beings, and the pursuit of knowledge about them, by the intellect is clear from several verses of the Book of God, Blessed and Exalted, such as the saying of the Exalted, "Reflect, you have vision" [Quran 59:2]: this is textual authority for the obligation to use intellectual reasoning, or a combination of intellectual and legal reasoning. Another example is His saying, "Have they not studied the kingdom of the heavens and the earth, and whatever things God has created" [7:185]: this is a text urging the study of the totality of beings. Again, God, the Exalted, has taught that one whom He singularly honored by this knowledge was Abraham, peace on him, for the Exalted said, "So we made Abraham see the kingdom of the heavens and the earth, that he might be [and so on to the end of] the verse [6:75]. The Exalted also said, "Do they not observe the camels, how they have been created, and the sky, how it has been raised up? [88:17–18]; and He said "and they give thought to the creation of the heavens and the earth [3:191], and so on in countless other verses.

Since it has now been established that the Law has rendered obligatory the study of beings by the intellect, and reflection on them, and since reflection is nothing more than inference and drawing out of the unknown from the known, and since this is reasoning or at any rate done by reasoning, therefore we are under an obligation to carry on our study of beings by intellectual reasoning.*

*Averroes, "The Decisive Treatise, Determining What the Connection Is Between Religion and Philosophy," trans. George F. Hourani, in Ralph Lerner and Muhsin Mahdi, eds., *Medieval Political Philosophy* (Ithaca, N.Y.: Cornell University Press, 1963), 164–165.

soon go up against the more conservative and "fundamentalist" beliefs of the Almohad dynasty, which conquered Muslim Spain in 1170. As a result, Averroes was banished to Morocco, and his library was confiscated. Near the end of his life, he was reinstated as a *qadi*, and he devoted the rest of his life to his philosophical writings.

Because Averroes found so many contradictory ideas circulating in the name of Aristotle, he decided to clarify exactly what the Greek philosopher's ideas were. As a result, he wrote not just one but three commentaries to each of Aristotle's philosophical works. These commentaries are referred to as the short, middle, and long commentaries, and they were responsible for introducing the Latin West to Aristotelianism when they were translated from Arabic to Latin, often by Jewish translators familiar with both intellectual cultures. In fact, Averroes's interpretation of Aristotle became known as "Averroism" and was one of the major schools of philosophy among Jews and Christians up until the Renaissance in the sixteenth century. Averroes also wrote a treatise defending philosophy against the attacks by al-Ghazali, which he entitled *Tahafut al-tahafut* (*The Incoherence of the Incoherence*).

What happened to the study of philosophy in Islam after the death of Averroes is a matter of some debate with fairly important repercussions about how we think about Islam. Some argue that Averroes's death marked the end of Islamic rationalism, the rise of religious obscurantism, and the subsequent decline of Islam.[7] Others, however, argue that philosophy's center of gravity switched from the West to the East, especially to Iran, where it took on a set of different emphases under the name "Illuminationism," expounded by important philosophers such as Shihab al-Din al-Suhrawardi (1155–1191), who is mistakenly called a Sufi in some literature, and Sadr al-Din Muhammad Shirazi, also known as Mulla Sadra (1571–1641).[8]

Although the philosophers' ideas may not have been representative of "average" Muslims, they are nevertheless important when examining the breadth of Islamic belief and its intersection with other cultures. Such ideas, in other words, reveal that Islamic beliefs did not develop in a vacuum, but in conversation with ancient Greeks, Jews, and Christians. Moreover, it also reveals how the Islamic philosophical tradition is an intimate part of the Western philosophical heritage.

The Five Doctrines of Islamic Faith

As stated at the beginning of this chapter, any attempt to claim that all Muslims believe the same thing proves difficult to maintain. As a result, most of the chapter has covered many different beliefs in Islam, including the opposition that they engendered. In this last section, I survey five doctrines that in the classical formulations came to define the faith (*iman*) of the believing Muslim (referred to as a *mumin*). The gateway to these five doctrines is called the *shahada* (testimony): "There is no god but God, and Muhammad is the messenger of God" (la ilaha illa Allah wa-Muhammad rasul Allah). This phrase is ideally uttered to the newborn and to the dying Muslim, and the convert repeats it when he or she accepts Islam because it theoretically makes the rest of the beliefs in Islam possible.

The two statements of the *shahada*—that there is no god but God and that Muhammad is his messenger—are nowhere found as a single statement in the Quran. We first encounter the statement on early coins from the Umayyad dynasty and in hadith literature, where there are certain variations on it. The *shahada*, as we now know it, seems to date from roughly two hundred years after Muhammad's death.

FAITH

The first doctrine followed by the believing Muslim is the faith that he should have in God and his absolute unity (*tawhid*). Anything that comes in the way of believing in this unity is referred to as *shirk,* or "associating" someone or something with God. But, again, this unity needs to be nuanced in such a manner that it includes potentially paradoxical beliefs. For example, some argue that the belief in saints that some Muslims have does not compromise God's unity, but others argue that such a belief does. Both concepts—and many others relating to faith—often sit awkwardly and seemingly paradoxically under the canopy of faith.

ANGELS

The belief that angels function as messengers and helpers of God is the second doctrine of belief. These angels include those familiar to a Judeo-Christian audience (e.g., Jibril/Gabriel and Mikal/Michael). The Quran mentions that whereas humans are made of clay, angels are made of light. In between humans and angels exists another genus: the *jinn* (sing., *jinni*), who are made of fire. These creatures can be either good or evil and are often used to explain various aspects of life (e.g., the uncanny, the strange). Iblis or Shaytan—who, along with his retinue, tempts humans—is also made of fire, according to the Quran.

PROPHETS AND SCRIPTURES

According to the Islamic tradition, Muhammad was but the last prophet to bring a scripture to his people. In this regard, there is an awareness that there existed other messengers and prophets before his time. Some of these prophets are familiar to Jews and Christians (Moses, Jesus); other are less familiar (Hud, Salih); and others are familiar in name but not in terms of prophetic stature (David, Aaron). In Islam, all these prophets are considered to be Muslim and to have brought more or less the same message.

Although one might think that this belief in other prophets would lead to a form of ecumenicism, classical Muslim orthodoxy maintains, as we have seen, that other scriptures have been "tampered" with. This doctrine, *tahrif*, means that many Muslims believe that the Hebrew and Christian Bible have been falsified and that references to Muhammad therein have been removed. On this reading, then, there exists only one "untampered" scripture: the Quran.

THE FINAL JUDGMENT

The fourth doctrine refers to the End of Days, when the righteous will be rewarded and the wicked punished. According to the Quran, each individual stands before God without intermediary (although there are some interpretations that Muhammad can intercede for believers) to receive his or her judgment. The wicked will be cast to hell (*jahannam*), where they will be punished by angels without respite. Paradise is referred to as "the Garden" (*al-janna*) inhabited by beautiful young women (*huris*) and wine that does not make one drunk. Whether such imagery is interpreted literally or symbolically depends on the individual Muslim and the type of Islam he or she follows.

PREDESTINATION

We have already seen in this chapter how the thorny question of free will and determinism played a key role in some of the earliest theological debates within Islam. The fifth and final doctrine of faith is referred to as *al-qada wa'l-qadar* (the divine decree and predestination). As this doctrine came to be understood, it argues that God knows and determines everything in the universe and that every human action is recorded. According to a hadith, "Abdallah b. Amr reported God's messenger as saying 'God recorded the fates of all creatures 50,000 years before creating the heavens and the earth, and His throne was upon the water.' "[9]

According to this passage and many others like it, God has preordained all our actions. This proposition, of course, seems to nullify human freedom to act. Regardless, however, Muslim doctrine holds that God is far beyond human comprehension and that humans must behave and act in their lives as if they do have the possibility to choose.

This chapter has attempted to show the breadth and depth of Muslim belief across the centuries. It is next to impossible to capture the complexity and diversity of this belief in a few pages, so suffice it to say that Muslims' belief structures are not static, that they have developed over time, and that they have played a key role in the shaping of diverse Muslim identities.

NOTES

1. See, for example, Clifford Geertz, *Islam Observed: Religious Development in Morocco and Indonesia* (Chicago: University of Chicago Press, 1968); Mark Woodward, *Islam in Java: Normative Piety and Mysticism in the Sultanate of Yogyakarta* (Tucson: University of Arizona Press, 1989); and Laurence Rosen, *The Culture of Islam: Changing Aspects of Contemporary Muslim Life* (Chicago: University of Chicago Press, 2002).

2. See, for example, Talal Asad, *Genealogies of Religion: Disciplines and Reasons of Power in Christianity and Islam* (Baltimore: Johns Hopkins University Press, 1993); Russell T. McCutcheon, *Manufacturing Religion: The Discourse on Sui Generis Religion and the Politics of Nostalgia* (New York: Oxford University Press, 2003); and Timothy Fitzgerald, *The Ideology of Religious Studies* (New York: Oxford University Press, 2003).

3. A. J. Wensinck, *The Muslim Creed: Its Genesis and Historical Development* (Cambridge: Cambridge University Press, 1932), chap. 6.

4. Richard M. Frank, *Texts and Studies on the History of Kalam*, vol. 3, *Classical Islamic Theology: The Asharites* (London: Ashgate, 2007).

5. Abu al-Hasan al-Ashari, *Abu'l-Hasan Ali ibn Ismail al-Ashari's "Al-Ibanah an usul ad-diyanah"* (*The Elucidation of Islam's Foundation*), trans. Walter C. Klein (New Haven, Conn.: American Oriental Society, 1940), 47.

6. "A Commentary on the Creed of Islam: Saʿd al-Dīn al-Taftāzāni on the Creed of Najm al-Dīn al-Nasafī," trans. Earl Edgar Elder, http://marifah.net/articles/A_Commentary_on_the_Creed_of_Islam.pdf.

7. This opinion is given, for example, in Bernard Lewis, *What Went Wrong? Western Impact and Middle Eastern Response* (New York: Oxford University Press, 2001).

8. John T. Walbridge, *The Leaven of the Ancients: Suhrawardi and the Heritage of the Greeks* (Albany: State University of New York Press, 2000).

9. Al-Baghawi, *Mishkatat al-Masabih*, trans. James Robson, 29 vols. (Lahore, Pakistan: Sh. Muhammad Ashraf, 1965–1966), 1:23, quoted in Frederick Mathewson Denny, *An Introduction to Islam*, 3rd ed. (New York: Macmillan, 2005), 102.

SUGGESTIONS FOR FURTHER READING

Fakhry, Majid. *A History of Islamic Philosophy*. 3rd ed. New York: Columbia University Press, 2004.

Frank, Richard M. *Texts and Studies on the History of Kalam*. 3 vols. London: Ashgate, 2007.

Goldziher, Ignaz. *Introduction to Islamic Theology and Law*. Translated by Andras Hamori and Ruth Hamori, with an introduction and additional notes by Bernard Lewis. Princeton, N.J.: Princeton University Press, 1981.

Macdonald, Duncan B. *Development of Muslim Theology, Jurisprudence, and Constitutional Theory*. London: Routledge, 1903.

Madelung, Wilferd. *Religious Schools and Sects in Medieval Islam*. London: Variorum, 1985.

Martin, Richard C., and Mark R. Woodward, with Dwi S. Atmaja. *Defenders of Reason in Islam: Mutazilism from Medieval School to Modern Symbol*. Oxford: Oneworld, 1997.

Pines, Shlomo. *Studies in Islamic Atomism*. Translated by Michael Schwartz. Jerusalem: Magnes Press, 1997.

Rahman, Fazlur. *Prophecy in Islam: Philosophy and Orthodoxy*. Chicago: University of Chicago Press, 1979.

Rosenthal, E. I. J. *Political Thought in Medieval Islam: An Introductory Outline*. Cambridge: Cambridge University Press, 1958.

Van Ess, Joseph. *The Flowering of Muslim Theology*. Translated by Jane Marie Todd. Cambridge, Mass.: Harvard University Press, 2006.

Watt, W. Montgomery. *The Formative Period of Islamic Thought*. Edinburgh: Edinburgh University Press, 1973.

Wensinck, A. J. *The Muslim Creed: Its Genesis and Historical Development*. Cambridge: Cambridge University Press, 1932.

Wolfson, Harry A. *The Philosophy of the Kalam*. Cambridge, Mass.: Harvard University Press, 1976.

9

THE PERFORMANCE OF
MUSLIM IDENTITIES

A S IN the previous chapter, here we again run up against the thorny problem of what constitutes a particular practice or action as distinctly "Muslim." Are the various actions that a Muslim performs during the course of his or her day considered religious actions? We may consider some Muslim activities religious simply because they are activities that the modern West has deemed "religious" (e.g., prayer, going to a mosque), but what do we do with all those other activities that we conceive of as secular or nonreligious (e.g., cooking or crossing the street)? More controversially, where do we place the actions of those who do bad things (e.g., kill) in the name of Islam? Are these actions also to be considered Muslim religious practices?

To get at these and related difficulties, let us further complicate the examples given here so far. According to Muslim thought, only those ritual actions performed with the correct intention (*niyya*) are considered valid. So what do we do with the actions of a Muslim who prays but lacks the proper *niyya*? Or what if the individual recites the *basmala* ("in the name of God, the Compassionate, the Merciful . . .") before cooking or uses his right foot to enter a room (an action that hadith reports tell us Muhammad would perform when entering a room or beginning a journey)? Do these seeming nonreligious acts now become religious? Finally, although many might well say that those who commit murder in the name of Islam are not really Muslims or that they misunderstand their religion, what do we do when such individuals find legal precedent for their action and thereby define themselves and their actions not only as Muslim, but as the most authentically Muslim?

Some have argued that one of the major problems of religious studies is that over the course of its history it has taken all those actions that Protestant Christianity has deemed "religious" and then exported this model in its attempt to understand the various religions of the globe.[1] Many non-Protestant religions do not classify the world according to such an inner/outer, religious/secular dichotomy. However, without such conceptual modeling, we are left with the assumption that everything that is done in a particular religion is sui generis or unique. The goal of our analysis, then, must be to use preexistent categories that the study of religion has bequeathed to us, yet at the same time to realize that such categories need to be applied in such a manner that they can be nuanced and expanded in the process.

This chapter seeks to provide a series of insights into Muslims' religious practices with the qualification that the adjective "religious" itself is potentially problematic. The default position for such an exploration is to discuss the so-called five pillars of Islam—the religious actions that Muslims are obligated to perform on a daily and annual basis throughout the course of their lives (even though we should not assume that they all do). The danger of such a presentation is that it risks assuming that all Muslims enact or perform their identities monolithically. It also risks assuming that Muslim identity—as opposed to *identities*—is recuperated or simply subscribed to by performing such acts as opposed to constructed, imagined, and contested through their performance. It is quite simply impossible to ascertain what Muslims think about when they perform actions that either the tradition or we as Western interpreters have constructed as "Muslim." Moreover, we should also realize that *some* Muslims do not perform any of the actions associated with pillars yet still regard themselves quite contentedly as "Muslims."

Given the problems associated with the rather vague adjective "religious," it is important to be aware of the political, ideological, and cultural aspects of ritual. Many actions that we deem "religious" actually have several overlapping meanings. A perfect example is the *hijab*, the covering or veil that some Muslim women wear (discussed more fully in chapter 11). In the modern period, for example, some women in the West freely choose to wear a *hijab* to assert their Muslim identity—the veil, on this level, is how some women "perform" their identity, how they identify as belonging to a distinct religion that others can recognize they are a part of. However, in other areas (e.g., Saudi Arabia, Afghanistan), men force Muslim women to cover themselves—in which case the veil becomes a sign of oppression or, at the very least, the way that men "perform" their identities by trying to control women's bodies. Religious actions and rituals are multivalent, and we, as interpreters of Islam, must be cautious of not conflating the two instances. Problems of understanding arise when individuals, for whatever reason, seek to lock a particular symbol or action into one meaning.

The same can be said for all Muslim actions. It is necessary to keep an open mind about all practices Muslims follow, realizing that they are ways that Muslims establish, maintain, create, and renew identities. The meanings that these practices take on and the ways in which they are understood are dependent not only on temporal and geographic context, but also on the individual who performs them.

The Mosque

Despite the fact that a mosque (*masjid*) is not absolutely necessary for one to carry out one's ritual obligations (especially prayer), it has become a central focus of life for many Muslims around the world (figure 7). Mosques have become an important symbol for Muslim life; this may be especially true for Muslims who live in largely non-Muslim environments (figure 8). In such places, mosques serve as a place where Muslims can come together for prayer, socialization, information, education, and dispute settlement. Some American mosques, for example, host voter registration and other civic-participation drives that seek to involve Muslims, many of whom are often first- or second-generation immigrants, in the political process.

Three architectural structures define the mosque. The first is the **mihrab**, or niche in the wall that indicates the *qibla*, the direction of the Ka'ba in Mecca, toward which Muslims face during prayer. The second is the **minbar**, a pulpit from which the imam delivers his sermon (*khutba*). And, finally, the **minaret** is a tall spire that is often free standing and that is taller than

FIGURE 7 Grand Mosque, Mecca, Saudi Arabia. (Photograph by Basil D. Soufi; courtesy of Wikimedia Commons)

the mosque itself. In addition to its distinctive architectural features, the minaret provides a vantage point from which the **muezzin** issues the call to prayer, or *adhan* (five times each day: dawn, noon, midafternoon, sunset, and night). In most modern mosques, however, this call is made via a microphone inside the mosque that is connected to a speaker on the minaret.

The appointment of a prayer leader is considered desirable, but not always obligatory. This leader is referred to as an imam (not to be confused with the Shiʿi Imams encountered in chapter 5). This prayer leader is authoritative in religious matters and should be a fair arbiter of disputes. In mosques constructed and maintained by the government, the ruler frequently appoints the imam, whereas in private mosques members vote on the issue. According to the Hanafi school of law, the person who built the mosque has a strong claim to the title of imam, but the other schools do not share this view.

In the modern period, especially in those countries and places where Muslims are a minority, the imam is usually recruited from outside the

FIGURE 8   Mother Mosque of America, Cedar Rapids, Iowa. (Photograph by Rifeldeas; courtesy of Wikimedia Commons)

country. This practice not infrequently creates a series of tensions because this de facto leader, the imam, is often unfamiliar with the various local customs and habits that the community has developed as a way to negotiate often conflicting demands with non-Muslims and non-Muslim society. Moreover, in the new setting the imam must often take on roles that are more than just religious (e.g., he must be a marriage counselor, visit hospitals, engage in interfaith dialogue groups, and so on).

According to a saying attributed to Muhammad, "The best mosques for women are the inner parts of their houses." Although Muhammad did not forbid women from entering mosques, Islamic law eventually required gender segregation in the prayer hall. In some mosques, women must occupy the rows behind the men; most mosques, however, put women behind a barrier or partition or in another room altogether. Some mosques do not admit women at all due to the lack of space and the fact that some prayers, such as the Friday afternoon prayer, are mandatory for men but optional for women.

Ritual Action

Perhaps owing to the need to draw a sharp line between the time Muhammad shared his message and the period immediately before it on the Arabian Peninsula, there is a distinct antimythological strain in Islam. There seems to be little connection, for example, to earlier planting and harvest festivals, as there is in, say, Judaism or Christianity. And although many of the rituals discussed here are commemorative in the sense that they remember past actions by Muhammad or Abraham or other important figures, there is very little desire for the person to inhabit the past. Rituals are not perceived as sacraments wherein God is said to be active or present, but as occasions to express one's belief and piety in a highly formalized and stylized setting.

In the modern period, many of the actions and symbols associated with Muslim ritual behavior are increasingly ways in which individuals—especially in Western countries—seek to define themselves against the mainstream. This view has contributed to the "politicization" of these activities.[2] Even though the five pillars are the bedrock of Muslim practice, the interpretation of them has remained neither theoretically nor practically constant. Like so much in Islam, they have become tropes or symbols that various actors—seeking legitimization for their particular understanding of Islam—have sought to mold to fit their concerns.

All the modern variations of Islam discussed in chapter 10 have something to say about the place of Muslim ritual in the life of both the individual and society. The politicization of belief and practice in a world perceived to be increasingly secular (and, accordingly, hostile) and the growing migration of Muslims and their new status as minorities have made the performance of Islam one of the primary sites for creating and contesting identity, both personal and collective. It is thus important to be aware of the five pillars' ideological power in the quest for identity formation.

The Five Pillars

As noted, Muslims are in theory required to perform a set of basic, minimal acts of devotion. These acts are referred to as *ibadat* (sing., *ibada* [acts of worship]) but are customarily called the "five pillars" in English or *arkan* in Arabic. The Islamic legal codes are quick to mention that one must perform these ritual actions with both the right intention (*niyya*) and in a state of ritual purity (*tahara*). To ensure that the believer carries a "proper" mental and religious attitude into the action to be performed, he or she must make a specific utterance before performing that action. Being in a state of both physical and mental purity denotes the ability to perform these actions. There exist varying degrees of impurity that bar Muslims, again in theory, from performing these actions. Physical impurities—such as bodily discharges, menstruation—can be removed through ritualized ablutions (*wudu*) and baths (*ghusl*).

It is difficult to ascertain at what historical point the community imagined these five pillars as *the* ritual component of Islam. Although some of the pillars are mentioned in the Quran, none receives full elaboration

WHEN DID THE FIVE PILLARS OF FAITH BECOME THE FIVE PILLARS?

The Quran does not fully articulate the requirements for any of the five pillars of faith. Moreover, they all seem to have their own histories that predate the arrival of Islam. As a result, it is very difficult to establish when exactly the five pillars of faith were imagined together and at what date their performance was imposed on Muslims as a religious obligation. One thing that does seem clear is that it is highly unlikely that these five acts would have been imposed on believers from the beginning as the way to be a "good Muslim."

Although the term *arkan* (pillars) did not emerge until the tenth century, by the eighth century—that is, about 150 years after Muhammad's death—numerous individuals began to mention that Islam is based on five practices. Some of the earliest formulations of these practices occur in the hadith collections of Muhammad ibn Isma'il al-Bukhari (d. 870) and Muslim ibn al-Hajjaj (d. 875). Even earlier than these collections is the description found in the *Risala* of Muhammad ibn Idris al-Shafi'i (d. 822):

> The sum-total of what God has declared to His creatures in His book, by which he invited them to worship him in accordance with His prior decision, includes various categories. One of these is what He declared to His creatures by texts [in the Quran], such as the aggregate of duties owing to Him: That they shall perform the prayer, pay the *zakat* [alms tax], perform the pilgrimage, and observe the fast. And that He has forbidden disgraceful acts—both visible and hidden—and in the [textual prohibition] of adultery, [the drinking of] wine, eating [the flesh of dead things and of blood and pork; and he has made clear to them how to perform the duty of [the major] ablution as well as other matters stated precisely in the text [of the Quran].[*]

Although al-Shafi'i mentions these elements as important practices, he nowhere articulates the position that they are the defining element of Islam.

[*]Muhammad ibn Idris al-Shafi'i, *Islamic Jurisprudence: Shafi'i's "Risala,"* trans. Majid Khadduri (Baltimore: Johns Hopkins University Press, 1961), 67–68.

therein. Certainly the hajj resignifies an earlier Arabian ritual, but its precise reformulation or resignification is difficult to reconstruct from the Quran or other sources. Although some of the earliest hadith collections—both those collected by Muhammad ibn Isma'il al-Bukhari and those collected by Muslim ibn al-Hajjaj—mention that Muhammad said that Islam is based on these five pillars, the earliest theological explication of them does not occur until the tenth century. To frame this conundrum somewhat differently, even though these five pillars seemed to have played a role in the development of Muslim identity from a fairly early period, it is hard to know at what point they became the primary ritual markers of this identity.

THE WITNESS TO FAITH

We have already encountered the importance of the witness to faith (*shahada*) in chapter 8, whose words—"There is no god but God, and Muhammad is the messenger of God"—serve as the segue not only into the other pillars, but into the very heart of Islam. The theologian Abd al-Qahir al-Baghdadi (d. 1037) stated that the individual must utter this phrase "out of understanding and with heartfelt sincerity."[3] The convert to Islam utters it when he or she enters the community, but every Muslim must also say it on a daily basis as part of the prayer cycle. Shi'is add to it the phrase "and Ali is the friend of God."

Even though both clauses that comprise the *shahada* are found in the Quran, they are nowhere found together or attached. Moreover, various coins and inscriptions dating to the early empire have different variations of the phrase, attesting to the fact that the actual phrasing of the *shahada* may not have appeared until perhaps as late as the tenth century, when it is first encountered in the work of writers such as al-Baghdadi.

PRAYER

Although the Quran speaks frequently of prayer (**salat**), nowhere does it stipulate that Muslims are to perform this ritual five times a day. Muslim theologians subsequently elaborated on the Quranic injunction and developed the form of prayer that we today recognize as Muslim. Even in the early Umayyad Empire, there seems to have been some discrepancy among the various legal schools as to what constituted the actual performance of the *salat*.

Muslims are supposed to pray five times during the course of every day: early morning (*salat al-fajr*), noon (*salat al-zuhr*), midafternoon (*salat al-asr*), sunset (*salat al-maghrib*), and evening (*salat al-isha*). No matter where Muslims are in the world, they pray in the direction of Mecca (in mosques, as noted, the proper direction is indicated by the mihrab). Following the ritual ablution, Muslims make a series of recitations and engage in ritually proscribed movements, plus perhaps supplemental acts derived from the various legal schools to which each person happens to belong.

Although the daily prayers can be said anywhere and by oneself (although saying them in the company of others is preferred), the Friday noon prayer is held in the mosque. An imam, or prayer leader, leads this prayer, and a sermon is delivered by the **khatib**, who is frequently the same person as the imam. In the modern period, this sermon, depending on the place and time, may well be a highly politicized one that critiques the moral turpitude of the secular government that is perceived to be hostile to Islam or a critical assessment of U.S. foreign policy, the evils of the State of Israel, or the like.

Prayer in Islam is not restricted to the five daily prayers. Another type of prayer, the **du'a'**, is a nonritualized prayer wherein the individual may make private addresses to God. In addition, the *wird* is a ritualized private prayer.

CHARITY

The Quran speaks frequently of the importance of giving alms to the poor—"You will not attain piety until you expend of what you love; and whatever thing you expend, God knows of it" (3:86)—but supplies very few details. It also says much about helping those less fortunate than oneself and gives some definition to this group:

> The freewill offerings are for the poor and needy
> Those who work to collect them, those whose hearts are
> Brought together [converts?], the ransoming of slaves, debtors
> In God's way, and the traveler; so God ordains; God is
> All-knowing, All-wise. (9:60)

This verse attests to the vagueness of the Quranic message. Even much of the hadith literature is unclear when it comes to setting guidelines for giving to the groups mentioned in the verse. As a result, like so much of Islamic thought and theology, it was left to later jurists to work out the moral and legal implications of such statements.

The legal schools had to develop the details of what constitutes charity (*zakat*), including the percentage of one's wealth. Although some of the details differ in terms of the particular school, and there exist many complicated formulas about what does and does not count as taxable income, for the most part *zakat* involves 10 percent of one's crops and roughly 2.5 percent of one's cash, gold, and silver merchandise.

In classical times, the government collected the *zakat* and distributed to the less fortunate. Today, however, where and whether the *zakat* is given is primarily a matter of the individual's conscience, each Muslim giving money to a particular cause that he or she deems worthy of receipt.

FASTING

Muslims are required to fast (*sawm*) during the ninth month of the Muslim calendar. Both the month and the fast are referred to as Ramadan. For the thirty days of the month, from sunrise until sunset, Muslims are forbidden to eat, drink, or engage in sexual relations. Although this thirty-day period offers a month of introspection for Muslims, it is not regarded as a somber time: evenings are spent breaking the fast in the joyous company of family and friends. It should also be recalled that Muhammad instituted this fast as an act of self-definition for his nascent community. Before he did so, his followers had fasted on the holiest day of the Jewish calendar, Yom Kippur, the Day of Atonement.

Ramadan is a time when Muslims are encouraged to slow down from worldly affairs in order to focus on spiritual cleansing and enlightenment. Each individual is ideally to try and establish a link between himself or herself and God through prayer, supplication, charity, good deeds, and helping others. Because Ramadan is also a festival of giving and sharing, Muslims prepare special foods and buy gifts for their family and friends and for the poor and needy. The evening meal that breaks the fast every night during the month is called *iftar*.

According to Muslim belief, the Quran was first revealed during this month (2:182) on an evening that is marked as *laylat al-qadr* (the evening of power).[4] As a result, it is regarded as especially meritorious for Muslims to read the entire book during this month. The Quran is accordingly divided into thirty sections, one of which should read each day during Ramadan.

Id al-Fitr (Festival of Breaking the Fast) marks the end of the fasting period of Ramadan and the first day of the following month. Food is donated to the poor (a practice referred to as *zakat al-fitr*), and everyone is encouraged to put on their best clothes that day. Communal prayers are held in the early morning, followed by feasting and visits to relatives and friends.

Fasting is not limited to Ramadan. Quran 5:90 mentions a three-day fast required for breaking an oath; in 5:95, a fast is enjoined on those who mistakenly kill an animal during the pilgrimage to Mecca. Other times are also set aside for fasting during the Muslim year—for example, any six days during the month of Shawwal or the ninth, tenth, and eleventh days of Muharram.

PILGRIMAGE TO MECCA

The pilgrimage to Mecca (hajj), the fifth pillar, is probably the best known of the Muslim holidays. It is held annually during the first weeks of the last month of the Muslim calendar, Dhu al-Hijja. It is required once during a Muslim's life, provided he or she does not have to go into debt to perform it. With Quranic references in 2:193–200 and 5:95–100, the hajj has become a powerful symbol for the worldwide Muslim community as individuals from everywhere converge on Mecca and stand side by side with one another, all wearing only a white cloth (*ihram*) wrapped around them.

Before the hajj begins in earnest, pilgrims circumambulate the Kaʿba seven times and run seven times between al-Safa and al-Marwa, two small hills beside the Kaʿba (today joined to the central mosque by a covered arcade), a distance that Hagar is said to have run searching for water when Ibrahim cast her and her son Ismail out of his house. It is then that God, according to tradition, miraculously caused the Zamzam Well to appear. On the seventh day of the month, the hajj begins. It involves the following rituals: walking to the Plain of Arafat and the Mount of Mercy (about ten miles [fifteen kilometers] east of Mecca), where pilgrims pray and contemplate from sunrise to sunset; making a journey to Mina via Muzdalifa, where each pilgrim throws seven stones at a pillar said to represent Satan;

MALCOLM X'S LETTER ON THE HAJJ

Never have I witnessed such sincere hospitality and overwhelming spirit of true brotherhood as is practiced by people of all colors and races here in this ancient Holy Land, the home of Abraham, Muhammad and all the other Prophets of the Holy Scriptures. For the past week, I have been utterly speechless and spellbound by the graciousness I see displayed all around me by people of all colors.

I have been blessed to visit the Holy City of Mecca, I have made my seven circuits around the Ka'ba, led by a young Mutawaf named Muhammad, I drank water from the well of the Zam Zam. I ran seven times back and forth between the hills of Mt. Al-Safa and Al Marwah. I have prayed in the ancient city of Mina, and I have prayed on Mt. Arafat.

There were tens of thousands of pilgrims, from all over the world. They were of all colors, from blue-eyed blondes to black-skinned Africans. But we were all participating in the same ritual, displaying a spirit of unity and brotherhood that my experiences in America had led me to believe never could exist between the white and non-white.

America needs to understand Islam, because this is the one religion that erases from its society the race problem. Throughout my travels in the Muslim world, I have met, talked to, and even eaten with people who in America would have been considered white—but the white attitude was removed from their minds by the religion of Islam. I have never before seen sincere and true brotherhood practiced by all colors together, irrespective of their color.

You may be shocked by these words coming from me. But on this pilgrimage, what I have seen, and experienced, has forced me to rearrange much of my thought-patterns previously held, and to toss aside some of my previous conclusions. This was not too difficult for me. Despite my firm convictions, I have always been a man who tries to face facts, and to accept the reality of life as new experience and new knowledge unfolds it. I have always kept an open mind, which is necessary to the flexibility that must go hand in hand with every form of intelligent search for truth.

During the past eleven days here in the Muslim world, I have eaten from the same plate, drunk from the same glass, and slept on the same rug—while praying to the same God—with fellow Muslims, whose eyes were the bluest of blue, whose hair was the blondest of blond, and whose skin was the whitest of white. And in the words and in the deeds of the white Muslims, I felt the same sincerity that I felt among the black African Muslims of Nigeria, Sudan and Ghana.

We were truly all the same (brothers)—because their belief in one God had removed the white from their minds, the white from their behavior, and the white from their attitude.

I could see from this, that perhaps if white Americans could accept the Oneness of God, then perhaps, too, they could accept in reality the Oneness of Man—and cease to measure, and hinder, and harm others in terms of their "differences" in color.

With racism plaguing America like an incurable cancer, the so-called "Christian" white American heart should be more receptive to a proven solution to such a destructive problem. Perhaps it could be in time to save America from imminent disaster—the same destruction brought upon Germany by racism that eventually destroyed the Germans themselves.

Each hour here in the Holy Land enables me to have greater spiritual insights into what is happening in America between black and white. The American Negro never can be blamed for his racial animosities—he is only reacting to four hundred years of the conscious racism of the American whites. But as racism leads America up the suicide path, I do believe, from the experiences that I have had with them, that the whites of the younger generation, in the colleges and universities, will see the handwriting on the walls and many of them will turn to the spiritual path of truth—the only way left to America to ward off the disaster that racism inevitably must lead to.

> Never have I been so highly honored. Never have I been made to feel more humble and unworthy. Who would believe the blessings that have been heaped upon an American Negro? A few nights ago, a man who would be called in America a white man, a United Nations diplomat, an ambassador, a companion of kings, gave me his hotel suite, his bed. Never would I have even thought of dreaming that I would ever be a recipient of such honors—honors that in America would be bestowed upon a King—not a Negro.
> All praise is due to Allah, the Lord of all the Worlds.
> Sincerely,
> Al-Hajj Malik El-Shabazz (Malcolm X)
>
> *Malcolm X, with Alex Haley, *The Autobiography of Malcolm X* (New York: Grove Press, 1966), excerpted at Ummah Forum, http://www.ummah.com/forum/showthread.php?30889-Malcolm-X-s-Letter-from-Hajj.

returning to Mecca and, if not done prior to the hajj, circumambulating the Ka'ba and running between al-Safa and al-Marwa; celebrating for three days, which includes praying and again walking around the Ka'ba; and, finally, returning to one's home country or, for most, to Medina.

During this time, the second major festival in Islam is carried out. Id al-Adha (Festival of the Sacrifice)—in theory, performed by all Muslims, not just those on the pilgrimage—sees the mass slaughter of sheep, goats, and camels. This festival is meant to commemorate the event that witnessed Ibrahim slaughter an animal as opposed to his son. In recent years, because of the very large number of people who go on the hajj each year (roughly 1 million), the individual slaughtering of animals is impossible, so this practice has given way to the practice of buying vouchers to ensure that an animal is killed ritually in an abattoir and then frozen to be distributed later to Muslim refugee populations throughout the world.

A Sixth Pillar: The Case of Jihad

Some Sunni scholars add a sixth pillar to the standard five: **jihad** (literally, "striving"). The Quran states: "Therefore, obey not the unbelievers, but strive against them with a great striving" (25:54), and "Permission is given to fight because they are oppressed—God is able to grant them victory—expelled from their homes without right, except that they say: 'Our Lord is God'" (22:39–40). It is accordingly all Muslims' duty to strive against unbelievers and those who take offensive action against Muslims. Although the

JIHAD AND JUST-WAR THEORY

Just-war theory is based on a system of ethics that maintains that a military conflict can meet the criteria of religious and political justice when it follows certain conditions. This system includes the conditions for going to war in the first place (e.g., all other means of putting an end to the conflict must have been shown to be impractical or ineffective) and the conditions for battle (e.g., the use of arms must not produce evils and disorders graver than the evil to be eliminated).

Many Islamic jurists both in the past and in the present have attempted to articulate the conception of jihad to clarify the nature of the Islamic community, the proper leadership of that community, and the community's relations with the non-Islamic world. Central to this conception is a legal division of the world into two realms: the *dar al-Islam* (house of Islam), or those areas where Muslims can practice their religion freely, and the *dar al-harb* (house of war), or those areas of the world where Islamic law is not in place.

Islamic law stipulates certain conditions that must be met when Muslim armies go to war. These stipulations differ depending on whether the conflict is offensive or defensive and whether it occurs in the *dar al-Islam* or the *dar al-harb*. A declaration of jihad within the *dar al-Islam*, for example, is theoretically based on a set of rules that govern everything from the caliph's authority to a clear declaration of hostilities and eventual peace to the disposition of spoils by the ruling authority.

A question that often arises is: If classical just-war theory in Islam is based on a set of ethical obligations, what about those who do not follow this theory yet who feel quite comfortable declaring jihad against the West (e.g., Osama bin Laden)? One tendency in the secondary literature is to argue that individuals such as Osama bin Laden do not engage in *real jurisprudential* thinking and thus have no right to declare jihad on anyone, be it the West or other Muslims.[*] Although this may be true, it certainly does not make the declarations by people such Osama bin Laden illegitimate in either their own eyes or their followers' eyes. A more realistic account would say that terms such as "jihad" are contested by various Muslim actors and that attempts to control or manipulate these terms play an important role in shaping manifold Muslim identities in the present.

[*]See, for example, John Kelsay, *Arguing the Just War in Islam* (Cambridge, Mass.: Harvard University Press, 2007).

---

term "jihad" is often translated as "holy war," some sources and modern commentators point out that this translation indicates only one aspect of the phenomenon.

In classical Islamic jurisprudence, the word "jihad" refers to warfare with the aim of expansion and defense of Islamic territory. In the classical manuals of Islamic jurisprudence, the rules associated with armed warfare are covered at great length. Such rules include not killing women, children, or noncombatants and not damaging cultivated or residential areas. Today, Muslim authors recognize as legitimate only those wars with the aim of defense of territory or the defense of religious freedom.[5]

As mentioned, some people tend to emphasize the nonmilitant aspects of jihad. Within this context, it can simply mean striving to live a moral and virtuous life, spreading and defending Islam, as well as fighting injustice and oppression, among other things. This peaceful form of inner jihad is called the "greater jihad" (al-jihad al-akhbar), whereas the physical and militaristic version is referred to as the "lesser jihad" (al-jihad al-asghar). The relative importance of these two forms of jihad is a matter of controversy. David Cook, for instance, argues that

> in reading Muslim literature—both contemporary and classical—one can see that the evidence for the primacy of spiritual jihad is negligible. Today it is certain that no Muslim, writing in a non-Western language (such as Arabic, Persian, Urdu), would ever make claims that jihad is primarily nonviolent or has been superseded by the spiritual jihad. Such claims are made solely by Western scholars, primarily those who study Sufism and/or work in interfaith dialogue, and by Muslim apologists who are trying to present Islam in the most innocuous manner possible.[6]

Ritual Practice in Shi'ism

In addition to the pillars, Twelver Shi'is have other ritual practices, referring to them collectively as the "Ten Practices of Religion."[7] The first four are the shahada, prayer, fasting, and alms, and then the fifth is the khums, or 20 percent tax on income, half of which is considered to be the Imam's share. The sixth is jihad. The seventh is "commanding what is just," which calls for every Muslim to live a virtuous life and to encourage others to do the same. The eighth is "forbidding what is evil," which enjoins Muslims to refrain from vice and evil actions and to encourage others to do the same. The ninth is to love the ahl al-bayt, the family of Muhammad, from which the Imams come. The tenth and final act is to dissociate from the enemies of the ahl al-bayt.

In addition to these practices, Twelver Shi'is also make pilgrimages to the shrines of the tombs of the Imams—for instance, the shrine of Ali at Najaf and the shrine of Husayn at Karbala, both located in modern-day Iraq. Elaborate rituals were drawn up for undertaking these pilgrimages that parallel in detail the hajj to Mecca.

Extremely important to Shi'i religious practice are the rituals surrounding the assassination of Husayn on the plains of Karbala. These rituals are performed during the month of Muharram, which is the first month of the Muslim calendar and culminates on the tenth day, known as Ashura. How the event is commemorated depends on the particular branch of Shiʿism followed and the practitioner's ethnicity. Many tend to embark on a pilgrimage to the Imam Husayn Shrine in Karbala, one of the holiest places for Shiʿis outside Mecca and Medina. Others gather in "Hussainias," congregation halls built explicitly for mourning. Others participate in Muharram processions, some of which involve self-flagellation. Another form of mourning is the theatrical reenactment of the Battle of Karbala, often called the *taziya*.

Muhammad's Birthday

Muhammad's birthday (*mawlid al-nabi*) is fixed as the twelfth day of the Islamic month Rabi I, although Shiʿis tend to observe the event on the seventeenth day of that month, coinciding with the birth date of Jaʿfar al-Sadiq, the sixth Imam. It is usually marked by large street processions and the decoration of homes and mosques in the color green (said to be Muhammad's favorite color and thus, by extension, the "official" color of Islam). Charity and food are distributed, and stories about Muhammad's life are narrated. In many Islamic countries, with the notable exception of ultraconservative Saudi Arabia, it is an official holiday.

In the modern world, many conservative theologians regard the celebration of *mawlid al-nabi* as an innovation (*bida*). Although all Muslims certainly agree that the birth of Muhammad was the most significant event in Islamic history, they point out that Muhammad's Companions did not celebrate his birthday, nor did Muhammad advise his followers to observe his birthday.

"Popular" Islam

Many commentators tend to signify by the problematic term "popular Islam" the majority of beliefs and practices that Muslims engage in throughout the world. These beliefs and practices—including the cult of saints, mediation between the believer and God, pilgrimages to shrines, even the celebration of Muhammad's birthday—often seem to contradict the theological tenets as elaborated in the various legal codes. The fact is that the five pillars tend to overlook these diverse practices. In many places—from Nigeria to Morocco, Malaysia to Pakistan—numerous syncretistic elements combine Islamic doctrine and local customs. Conservative critics are often quick to point out that popular Islam is not really Islam or not the real Islam, but an Islam that has been corrupted by local cultures. But religion does not exist apart from culture, so it is impossible to say what is "real" Islam and what is "fake" or "popular." It is important to be aware, however, that these theological debates struggle over what Islam should be.

In addition to the "popular" rituals such as the cult of saints and so on, another practice that problematizes the difficulty of neatly separating the religious from the cultural is female circumcision. Is it a Muslim ritual? Many are quick to say that it is not and that Islam does not condone its practice,[8] yet it is popular in many Muslim countries (Saudi Arabia, Jordan, and some countries in Africa), and *for some* it is in fact a marker of Muslim identity.[9] A definitive answer cannot be given here, but it can safely be said that female circumcision shows both the ambiguity of the religious/cultural binary and its contestation in that some regard it as a religious practice, whereas others do not.

Sufism

In chapter 7, we looked at Sufi *dhikr* (remembrance) and the ways in which it is achieved. Many ritual practices are meant to focus the Sufi's inner eye by denigrating the *nafs* in the soul's quest for conjunction with God. Such *dhikr* practices include but are certainly not limited to ritual dance, recitation, music, and yoga. The type of *dhikr*, it should be recalled, is dependent on the particular Sufi *tariqa*, or order.

This chapter has presented an overview of the various rituals that have contributed to Muslims' self-identity through the centuries. We should be cautious of assuming that they have meant the same things to people in the past and people in the modern period. Not all Muslims perform the actions described, and if they do, they may not have the same intentions or desires.

We have seen how aspects of Muslim practice, such as the hajj, have transformed pre-Islamic Arabian ritual activity, although the sources themselves are unclear as to how this activity occurred in the early period; regarding the hajj, they merely say that Muhammad cleared the idols from the Kaʿba and rededicated it to God. In like manner, the fast that Muhammad instituted during the month of Ramadan was clearly an attempt to define the nascent Islamic polity in the light of perceived rival monotheisms in the Arabian Peninsula.

This idea of ritual activity as a marker of religious identity certainly carries into the modern period. As the secular forces of modernity are perceived to encroach on religious life, ritual activity has increasingly become one of the few constants for Muslims in a sea of uncertainty. The performance of ritual is one of the primary sites where Muslims perform their identity, marking themselves off or setting themselves in counterpoint to forces that they increasingly see as hostile. The slogan that Islam is that which encompasses all of life (see chapter 10) is in many ways a political slogan that responds to the secularism of the modern world.

It would certainly be a mistake to assume that in the premodern world the rituals or religious actions described in this chapter were stable. Over the centuries, they have been flexible as many Muslims have tried to perform them in different circumstances with changing demands on them. Many of these rituals have also been manipulated for political and ideological purposes in times of upheaval (e.g., the Iranian Revolution of 1979, the events of September 11, 2001). Finally, it should be pointed out that in the modern world the performance of Muslim ritual is a convenient way for Muslims to recuperate a perceived lost identity, the place where they can identify with other Muslims and can signal their difference from the "West" and all the evils associated with it.

NOTES

1. See, for example, Daniel Dubuisson, *The Western Construction of Religion: Myths, Knowledge, and Ideology*, trans. William Sayers (Baltimore: Johns Hopkins University Press, 2003).

2. Charles J. Adams, "Islamic Resurgence: Religion and Politics in the Muslim World," in Nigel Biggar, Jamie S. Scott, and William Schweiker, eds., *Cities of Gods: Faith, Politics, and Pluralism in Judaism, Christianity, and Islam* (New York: Greenwood Press, 1986), 167–191.

3. "Al-Baghdadi on the Pillars of Islam," in Andrew Rippin and Jan Knappert, eds., *Textual Sources for the Study of Islam* (Chicago: University of Chicago Press, 1990), 90.

4. For a full treatment of the Quran, see K. Wagtendonk, *Fasting in the Qur'an* (Leiden: Brill, 1968).

5. Rudolph Peters, *Jihad in Classical and Modern Islam* (Princeton, N.J.: Wiener, 2005), 125.

6. David Cook, *Understanding Jihad* (Berkeley: University of California Press, 2005),165–166.

7. Moojen Momen, *An Introduction to Shi'i Islam: The History and Doctrines of Twelver Shi'ism* (Oxford: Ronald, 1985), 179–180

8. See, for example, "Gender Equity in Islam," *Jannah*, http://www.jannah.org/genderequity/equityappendix.html. But note that even this Web site states that the former "rector of Al-Azhar University, Sheikh Gad Al-Haque, argued that since the Prophet did not ban female circumcision, it falls within the category of the permissible."

9. See, for example, Sami A. Aldeeb Abu Sahlieh, "To Mutilate in the Name of Jehovah or Allah: Legitimization of Male and Female Circumcision," *Medicine and Law* 13, nos. 7–8 (1994): 575–622.

SUGGESTIONS FOR FURTHER READING

Bowen, John R. *Muslims Through Discourse: Religion and Ritual in Gayo Society*. Princeton, N.J.: Princeton University Press, 1993.

Cook, David. *Understanding Jihad*. Berkeley: University of California Press, 2005.

Geertz, Clifford. *Islam Observed: Religious Development in Morocco and Indonesia*. Chicago: University of Chicago Press, 1968.

Halevi, Leor. *Muhammad's Grave: Death Rites and the Making of Islamic Society*. New York: Columbia University Press, 2007.

Long, David. *The Hajj Today: A Survey of the Contemporary Makkan Pilgrimage*. Albany: State University of New York Press, 1979.

Metcalf, Barbara D., ed. *Making Muslim Space in North America and Europe*. Berkeley: University of California Press, 1996.

Peters, Rudolph. *Jihad in Classical and Modern Islam*. Princeton, N.J.: Wiener, 2005.

Rosen, Lawrence. *The Culture of Islam: Changing Aspects of Contemporary Muslim Life*. Chicago: University of Chicago Press, 2002.

Schubel, Vernon. *Religious Performance in Contemporary Islam: Shi'i Devotional Rituals in South Asia*. Columbia: University of South Carolina Press, 1993.

Waugh, Earle H. *Memory, Music, and Religion: Morocco's Mystical Chanters*. Columbia: University of South Carolina Press, 2005.

Wheeler, Brannon. *Mecca and Eden: Ritual, Relics, and Territory in Islam*. Chicago: University of Chicago Press, 2006.

Woodward, Mark R. *Islam in Java: Normative Piety and Mysticism in the Sultanate of Yogyakarta*. Tucson: University of Arizona Press, 1989.

PART IV

MODERN VARIATIONS

10

ENCOUNTERS WITH MODERNITY

IN AUGUST 1797, the French emperor Napoleon Bonaparte initiated a military expedition to take control of Egypt, then a province of the Ottoman Empire, in order to protect French trade interests and undermine Britain's access to India. The subsequent campaign, although ultimately unsuccessful, would have a powerful impact on the Ottoman Empire in general and the Arab world in particular. Among other things, the invasion demonstrated the military, technological, and organizational superiority of the western European powers over the Middle East. The encounter between Europe and Islam, long a complex one, would in the ensuing centuries create a set of profound social, intellectual, and religious changes in the region. Not only did Napoleon's invasion open the region up to Western technology, but it also introduced numerous ideas, such as liberalism and nationalism. Some scholars argue that Napoleon's arrival in Egypt marks the beginning of the modern Middle East.[1]

Islam's encounter with the West is highly charged and complex and so demands nuance in its description. A complex dialectic is at work here: modernity becomes a force or set of forces against which Muslim identities are formed and manipulated. Once formed, however, these manifold Muslims identities become invested in shaping the modern world to their own perceptions of what Islam should be. Within these many formulations, Islam serves an interpretive strategy to explain or account for the rise of modernity and to counter an increasingly unfriendly and powerful European bloc. So even the most extreme rejection of the modern world paradoxically needs selected elements of modernity to define its rejection and, in the process, its vision of Islam.

The categorical mistake in this complicated dialectic is to assume that there was or has been a monolithic Islamic response to modernity. A host of books on "modern Islam" that seek to portray a "clash of civilizations" or of a religion that is incapable of adapting to the modern world has made this mistake.[2] There are almost as many different Muslim responses to modernity as there are Muslims. There is, however, a tendency among many scholars and theologians (both Muslim and non-Muslim) to try and sort through these myriad constructions and choose, depending on the perspective to be argued, a particular version of Islam that appears to be most "authentic." This choice is often made for various political reasons, usually either to discredit Islam by implying that all Muslims are angry and violent or to show that Islam is compatible with modernity because certain groups are. Such interpretative frameworks make various parts stand for the whole in the service of some larger ideological agenda.

Many take events such as the attacks on September 11, 2001, as a filter to examine the entire history of Islam. Some commentators or pundits say that events in the historical record such as the violence of the sectarian Kharijites or Muhammad's purported assassination of a Jewish tribe in Medina demonstrate that Islam was violent or anti-Semitic from the beginning. Yet others take various hadith reports to construct a proto-democratic, proto-feminist, or proto-humanist Muhammad. Once again, however, we are left with the rhetoric of authenticity,[3] the attempt to impose a normative Muslim identity on a complex web of historical and mythological projections. The "real" Islam as defined by each group is singled out from all the sources and interpretations and made to fit effortlessly with the needs, political or otherwise, with those doing the interpreting.

But if the chapters in this book have shown anything, it is that there is no such thing as a monolithic Islam or a singular Muslim identity. On the contrary, terms such as "real Islam" and "real Muslims" are highly charged and, as such, highly contested. Various actors and various groups have constantly been caught up in the struggle to make their version of Islam normative or authentic, and so, by extension, they define the Islams of their competitors as innovations, misinterpretations, or bastardizations.

It is imperative that we be self-reflective regarding the language and categories we employ as we wade through these various contestations and try to be mindful of the ideological skirmishes that occur around the fault lines of identity. This chapter shows just how many of the issues raised in the previous chapters—questions about sources, ideology, and legitimacy—remain. The previous chapters, in other words, present not just the stuff of history, but the prime ingredients in the ongoing construction of Muslim identities and the debates to which such constructions inevitably give rise.

Definitions of Modernity

Modernity is a difficult concept to define owing largely to its ability to cover under its broad canopy any number of social, economic, political, and intellectual forces. As a movement, modernity tends to coincide with the rise of capitalism, secularization, and the emergence of postindustrial life—as well as with all the consequences to which these changes gave rise. The sociologist Anthony Giddens, for example, writes,

> At its simplest, modernity is a shorthand term for modern society, or industrial civilization. Portrayed in more detail, it is associated with (1) a certain set of attitudes towards the world, the idea of the world as open to transformation, by human intervention; (2) a complex of economic institutions, especially industrial production and a market economy; (3) a certain range of political institutions, including the nation-state and mass democracy. Largely as a result of these characteristics, modernity is vastly more dynamic than any previous type of social order. It is a society—more technically, a complex of institutions—which, unlike any preceding culture, lives in the future, rather than the past.[4]

Modernity has forced Islam—indeed, as it has forced all religions—to intersect, both willingly and unwillingly, the traditional with the modern, the religious with the scientific, and the particular with the universal. The modern era has witnessed the rise of various types of social, political, and authority structures that religious practitioners frequently perceive as pernicious to "true" religious belief. The quest for authenticity—how to create the idyll of Muhammad's Medina, for example—accordingly becomes a major force at work in the modern period. How, so the question goes, can we return to the way the religion was perceived to be practiced in the past? The answers to this question—from adapting to the modern period to completely rejecting it—are as manifold as those seeking the answer. The only mistake that can be made here is to assume either that there is only one response to this question or that one response is more valid or authentic than others.

Colonialism and Orientalism

Colonialism and Orientalism have been instrumental in modern constructions of Islam. Colonialism, driven largely by economic considerations, can be defined as the process of building and maintaining colonies and plantations in one territory by elites living elsewhere, referred to as the "metropole" (e.g., London, Paris). Once the new territory was defeated militarily, the metropole often sought to impose new governments and, not infrequently, new social structures and economies on the colonies with the aim of "civilizing" them and helping them enter the modern world and its mercantile economy.

Much of European colonialism occurred in areas whose main inhabitants happened to be Muslim (e.g., Middle East, South Asia). Islam accordingly became the religion that European colonialists associated with backwardness and rigidity when it came to adapting to modernity. Behind this assessment, of course, lingered medieval polemics between Europe and Islam, perhaps the only major civilization that constantly threatened European interests in the premodern world.

A case study of colonialism can be seen in the partitioning of the Ottoman Empire at the end of World War I (1914–1918).[5] The huge conglomeration of territories and peoples that the sultan of the Ottoman Empire had ruled continuously from the thirteenth century to the beginning of the twentieth was now divided into several new nation-states by the victorious European powers. The League of Nations dismantled the Ottoman Empire and under the Sykes-Picot Agreement (1916) gave England and France the power to govern different parts of it. France was to have a mandate over the newly formed nation-states of Syria and Lebanon, and England was to possess mandates over Jordan and Palestine. These new countries, although staples of twentieth-century conflict, had never existed in the premodern world, and they for all intents and purposes became European colonies under the political, social, cultural, and linguistic control of the superpowers of the day.

Orientalism is often seen as the handmaiden of colonialism, the intellectual and artistic activity that manufactured "the Orient" for Western consumption. The term was given prominence by Edward Said (1935–2003) in his highly influential work *Orientalism*, published in 1978. For him, intellectual production (e.g., literature, operas) and imperial control reinforce each other because the former provides the latter's legitimization and dehumanization. For Said, Orientalism exists before there is colonialism. He defines Orientalism in the following terms: "Orientalism can be discussed and analyzed as the corporate institution of dealing with the Orient—dealing with it by making statements about it, authorizing views of it, describing it, by teaching it, settling it, ruling over it: in short, Orientalism as a Western style for dominating, restructuring, and having authority over the Orient."[6]

For Said, the entire Western apparatus used to understand the East—from the discipline of Arabic and Islamic studies in academia to literature to opera—was and still is complicit in attempts to control the Orient and thus heavily invested in the colonial enterprise. Although some scholars have tried to temper the overgeneralizations of Said's critique,[7] the fact remains that scholarship about Islam is often tied to broader geopolitical forces, whether vitriolic or apologetical.

Maximalism and Minimalism

Before we can create and analyze a typology of Muslim responses to modernity, we might find it useful to distinguish between what Bruce Lincoln calls "maximalist" and "minimalist" understandings of religion.[8] These two understandings concern the role that religion plays or is perceived to play in society. It is a distinction that by no means is confined to Islam; rather, it can easily be applied to all religions in the modern world. Lincoln locates this distinction in the Enlightenment, a period that witnessed, among other things, the desire to curtail the influence of religion in the public sphere—a process or set of processes that led to the foundation of the modern nation-state.[9] Out of this worldview there emerged the idea that religion should play a "minimalist" role in society, confined largely—as the philosopher Immanuel Kant (1724–1804) would have it—to the realms of aesthetics and ethics.

The curtailment of the function and place of religion in society necessarily led to the rise of individuals, groups, and movements highly critical of the perceived immortality, sexual depravity, and moral laxity that emerges when religion is marginalized. Such groups sought a "maximalist" role for religion in society, seeking to reintroduce it whenever and wherever they could and—depending on the group—by any means at their disposal.

A reproduction of Lincoln's chart emphasizing the differences between these two worldviews is helpful:

Maximalist	Minimalist
Religion = the central domain of culture, deeply involved in ethical and aesthetic practices constitutive of the community.	Economy = the central domain of culture; religion restricted to private sphere and metaphysical concerns.
Cultural preferences constituted largely as morality and stabilized by religion.	Cultural preferences constituted largely as fashion and opened to market fluctuations.
Religious authority secures coherent, ongoing order.	Capitalist dynamism effects rapid expansion of wealth and power.
Minimalist system experienced as powerful and intrusive, a serious temptation for would-be elites and a dangerous threat to all.	Maximalist system experienced in two ways: a quaint, seductive diversion for some, and a resentful atavism, capable of reactionary counterattacks.[10]

This distinction is useful on several levels. First, it shows that the dichotomy can be usefully applied to all religions (including those in contemporary America), not just Islam, which can thus no longer be singled out as the "problem" religion. Second, it should force us to be cautious of applying simplistic phrases such as "clash of civilizations" because it reveals that the real clashes go on not between religions, but between various incarnations (whether in the Muslim world, in Israel, in America) of maximalists and minimalists. Third, the conflicts—perhaps we might even define them as "cultural wars"—are a distinct hallmark of modernity, where maximalists perceive the space for religion as ever shrinking owing to the pernicious forces of secularization.

The Versatility of Islam in the Modern World: An Overview

"Islam in the modern world" is truly a vague rubric. Rather than envisage an Islamic take on the modern world, it might make more sense to imagine

Islam as an interpretive strategy that can be used in the service of numerous local and global agendas. In many ways, Islamic ideologies represent Islamic interpretations of global ideologies (e.g., a nationalist movement, a social movement, and increasingly an ethnic movement). This section seeks to show some of the manifold ways that Islam was imagined over the course of the twentieth century and presents numerous case studies of these various interpretations in detail.

The degradation of Islamic societies into objects of European colonialism after the end of the nineteenth century led to various responses, most of which sought to redefine Islam in light of European charges of "backwardness." By the beginning of the twentieth century, for example, roughly 80 percent of Muslims were ruled by at least eleven different colonial powers (from Great Britain and France to China). In response, many of these colonial subjects increasingly began to conceive of Islam in the service of nationalism. From the Syrian Muhammad Rashid Rida (1865–1935) to the Turk Mehmet Ziya Gokalp (1876–1924), Muslim intellectuals constructed Islam as forming the basis of various nationalist causes. It is worth noting that these individuals were not interested in creating an "Islamic republic" as conceived of today, but in using Islam as the realization of a system of government based on state institutions and political ethics. In places and movements as diverse as the Muslim Brotherhood in Syria and Nasserism in Egypt, Muhammad could easily be celebrated as the founder of a socialist movement, someone whose goals in the seventh century C.E. were not unlike the goals pursued by twentieth-century nationalist reformers.

These various modern movements increasingly used an early Islamic context—even when such a context went against their own ideals—to attract and unify diverse groups in newly created states. Various national movements—in Algeria, in Egypt, increasingly in Palestine and elsewhere—tended to be portrayed mythically as Islamic expressions or to present Islam as the so-called ideology of Third World liberation, the voice of the dispossessed in colonies seeking their independence from Europe.

Within such contexts, some began to conceive of Islam as a transnational force, something to give the "Islamic public" or umma—nationally and regionally fragmented—a unified entity. Such efforts were no doubt aided by humanist causes (e.g., the plight of the Palestinians at the hands of the Israelis) and oil wealth in places such as Saudi Arabia. The latter, for example, created the Muslim World League of Mecca in 1972 with an eye toward Islamic unity.

The 1970s also witnessed the rise of Islam as the perfection of all ideological thought.[11] This new interpretation conceived of Islam as superior to all Western ideologies, the best of which, it was claimed, were already preexistent within Islam. Islam, in other words, now held the solution to the West's secular malaise and, because of this, was actually superior to the West. This view led to the formation of a distinct Islamic political language that could be employed to justify and legitimate "Islamic states" and "Islamic revolutions." Not coincidentally, the Iranian Revolution occurred in the year 1979 (see the section "Ruhollah Musavi Khomeini").

Islam now was perceived as the ideology to liberate the deprived in places as diverse as Iran, North Africa, and Indonesia and to guarantee a new transnational Islamic identity or consciousness. Islam also became the ideology to critique and offer alternatives to various governments perceived to be either "un-Islamic" or not Islamic enough. The use of this ideology could be witnessed in various attempts to topple governments (e.g., in Saudi Arabia in 1979) and to go to war with other Islamic countries (e.g., Iran–Iraq War).

The years 1979 to 1989 increasingly witnessed the fragmentation of Islamic voices and the rise of new interpretations of Islam. As Reinhard Schulze points out, Islam "was no longer considered as an objective, social state of affairs, but as a hermeneutic process of interpretations."[12] This fragmentation led in some quarters, especially among French-inflected intellectuals in North Africa, to a liberal Islam that sought to reject polygamy and jihad in favor of what they perceived to be more modern—and thus more "Islamic"—norms. In other quarters, it meant that Islam became a symbol worth fighting for. Hamas and other Islamic groups that sought wide appeal among Muslims whether at home or abroad gave the Israeli–Palestinian conflict an Islamic veneer, so much so that even the secular, Marxist Palestine Liberation Organization had to adopt Islamic themes and symbols for its voice to be heard.

The past few decades—with the Gulf War, the U.S.–Iraq War, the various wars in Afghanistan, and so on—have increasingly made various subgroups more militant against what they perceive to be the West's excesses and its neocolonialism. These diverse groups, collectively forming what is referred to as the "Islamic jihad movement," is perhaps best—or, at least, famously—symbolized by Osama bin Laden and his al-Qaeda network (see chapter 12). In many of these groups, local causes or worldviews have often intersected with the global vision of a jihad movement.

Typology of Responses to Modernity

Lincoln's division between minimalist and maximalist approaches to the place of religion in society suggests a convenient way to establish a taxonomy of Muslim encounters with modernity. Such a taxonomy, although by no means accurately mirroring the complexity of Islamic voices on the ground, should provide a convenient context to begin the process of sorting through at least some of these competing voices heard from Islam. Most important, it should also avoid the common assumption that all Muslims, whether synchronically or diachronically, speak with one voice or that they all react in the same manner to external or internal stimuli.

For sake of convenience, I divide these voices into the following types: *fundamentalism*, *modernism*, and *nationalism*.[13] They are certainly meant as ideal types or various theoretical markers, between which reside more complex, variegated, and realistic formations. Individuals, let alone groups, can rarely be placed neatly into watertight categories. Such categories likewise admit of neither nuance nor change. What constitutes a modernist version of Islam today may not be the same as what constituted such a movement fifty or even ten years ago. Moreover, these categories masquerade a stability that often does not exist in reality, especially as groups change, modify, and reconfigure with others dependent on larger political and social contexts.

Common to most of these types, however, is the notion that some monolithic or essentialist Islam is in need of reform. Where they differ, not surprisingly, is in the kind of reform required or in the means and end of the reform process. In this regard, all these types look to the past, albeit a past that is constructed and romanticized based on all that is perceived to be wrong with the present. From the present, there is the desire to create a Muslim identity that coincides with this ideal past variously configured. These Muslim identities are not simply inherited or ascribed but actively cobbled together from the shards of memory and desire. In this respect, modern Muslim identity formations are no different from premodern ones: both are predicated on various constructions of who Muhammad was or should be, what the Quran is or should be, and the ideals imagined to be embodied in the nascent Muslim polity.

This section offers a description of each type of Muslim encounter with modernity and provides examples of individual voices that are constitutive of yet also show the diversity within each type.

FUNDAMENTALISM

"Islamic fundamentalism" is an omnibus term used to describe any number of religious ideologies that advocate a return to the so-called fundamentals of Islam (e.g., the Quran and the Sunna). It is also a potentially misleading term because it often includes under its large canopy individuals and groups with radically different agendas: some are intolerant of outsiders, whereas others are more pluralistic; some are democratic, others authoritarian; some are pacifist, others violent. To label all these groups as "fundamentalist" is accordingly problematic. A cognate term used to describe Muslim fundamentalism is "**Islamism**" ("Islamist" in the adjective form). The latter term possesses a greater political valence than does "fundamentalism" and accordingly implies a greater activity in the political arena in order to bring about an Islamic state.

Muslim fundamentalists hold that the perceived current political and military weakness of Muslims stems from the fact that many have strayed away from the fundamentals of Islam and have instead become influenced by secularism, often defined synonymously with the "West" or the United States. The only way to overcome this current malaise, according to this view, is to "return" to Islam—that is, to the fundamentalists' particular reading of Islam—by implementing the sharia to govern all aspects of life.

Several scholars have questioned the utility of employing the word "fundamentalist"—a term originally used by certain American Protestants in the early twentieth century to describe their struggle against modernism and their desire to return to the "fundamentals" of their tradition.[14] Protestant fundamentalists stressed biblical inerrancy, individual salvation, and the redemptive qualities of Jesus—all of which are far removed from Islam. Moreover, whereas these Protestant fundamentalists used the term "fundamentalist" to refer to themselves, Westerners tend to use it strictly to describe Muslims, who do not call themselves by this name.

The crucial difference between early Protestant fundamentalists and Muslim fundamentalists is that whereas the former tended to shy away from the political stage (although this is certainly not the case today), the latter have a political agenda—to implement Islam into all areas of life. And whereas Protestant fundamentalism had its origins in the reaction against modernity, the origins of Islamic fundamentalism did not.

In this regard, the origins of Islamic fundamentalism are usually attributed to Taqi al-Din Ahmad Ibn Taymiyya (1263–1328), whose life dates should caution against the simple importation of the twentieth-century category "fundamentalism" into Islam. Ibn Taymiyya was highly critical of Sufism and Sufi practice, which he believed had infiltrated all spheres of Islamic life—for example, celebrating Muhammad's birthday, using music, making pilgrimages to shrines, practicing excessive asceticism, and claiming miracles. (Ibn Taymiyya paradoxically articulated these criticisms even though he was a member of the Qadiri Sufi order.) Working out of the conservative Hanbali legal school, he sought to purge such beliefs and practices from Islam. Anything that could not be justified by appeals to the Quran and Sunna had to be rejected. Ibn Taymiyya also believed that Shi'ism was a heretical movement, and he consequently sought to refute it and sanctioned violence against Shi'is.

Islamic militant groups (chapter 12) usually derive their rhetoric from this ideal type and, in this regard, should be classified as a species under the broader genus "fundamentalist."

Wahhabis

Inspired by the teachings of Ibn Taymiyya, Muhammad Ibn abd al-Wahhab (1703–1792) sought to return to the "fundamentals" of the tradition—the Quran, the Sunna, and the Hanbali school's legal positions. Everything else, in his and his followers' opinion, was *bida* (innovation). Based in the Arabian Peninsula, the Wahhabis, as his followers were called, accordingly destroyed many mosques, shrines, and tombs on the peninsula that they believed to be dedicated to the memory of Sufi saints. In 1802, they also attacked and destroyed the Shi'i Holy City of Karbala. It is also important to note that although others use the name "Wahhabi" to refer to this group, members of the group tend to refer to themselves as "Salafis," the "pious ancestors" who were the first followers and Companions of Muhammad.

Wahhabism might well have been only a fairly minor movement in a desert backwater were it not for the establishment of a pact between the emerging House of Saud and Ibn abd al-Wahhab, the former pledging to implement the latter's teachings and enforce them on neighboring towns in return for his political support. The House of Saud sought to seize control of Arabia and its environs and finally did so in 1932 with the establishment of the modern Kingdom of Saudi Arabia. Because the kingdom never severed its alliance with the Wahhabi religious ideology, this ultraconservative movement became the de facto state religion.

The Wahhabis became a quasi-religious police that continues to enforce morality throughout the kingdom and beyond. Forced attendance at prayer, dress codes, strict separation of the sexes, and restrictions on women driving have been part of this group's vision of what Islam should be.

As the Saudi family's prestige increased throughout the Muslim world—largely because of its vast oil wealth (discovered in the 1930s) and control of Mecca and Medina, the two holiest places in Islam—the Wahhabis' puritanical vision has exerted a tremendous influence on other Muslim groups. Because of Saudi Arabia's wealth, it often funds the construction of mosques in other countries, the publication and dissemination of religious literature, and the training of religious leaders throughout the Islamic world. All these acts have meant that Wahhabism has moved far beyond the borders of Saudi Arabia and has influenced other highly conservative reform movements across the modern Muslim world, including the Taliban in Afghanistan.

Muslim Brotherhood and Sayyid Qutb

The Muslim Brotherhood (al-Ikhwan al-Muslimun) was a religiopolitical movement based in Egypt. Founded in 1928 by Hasan al-Banna (1906–1949), the movement sought to purify Islam of what it perceived to be the West's corrupting influences. Al-Banna desired to ban all Western ideas from the Egyptian educational curriculum, arguing that primary schools should be part of the mosque infrastructure. He also wanted a ban on political parties and democratic institutions other than the *shura* (electoral council of elders), which had been used, for example, to elect Uthman after the death of Muhammad. Al-Banna also rejected as unsound the hadith calling the internal jihad of greater importance than the external one: "Supreme martyrdom is only conferred on those who slay or are slain in the way of God," he argued. "As death is inevitable and can happen only once, partaking in jihad is profitable in this world and the next."[15]

The Muslim Brotherhood sought to replace Egypt's secularism with its vision of an all-embracing Islam that would govern all aspects of modern Egyptian life. The movement received renewed impetus in 1948 with the establishment of the State of Israel, perceived to be a hostile Other imposed by imperialist forces on Egypt's eastern border.

After the attempted assassination of Gamal abd al-Nasser in 1954, the authorities accused the brotherhood of the plot. Nasser then abolished the brotherhood and imprisoned and punished thousands of its members. Although outlawed in theory, the Muslim Brotherhood continues to operate in Egypt through a network of social services in local neighborhoods and villages, and it still runs candidates in elections, albeit as "independents." Muslim Brotherhoods also now exist in many countries in Africa, the Middle East, and beyond. Recent political upheavals in Egypt associated with the so-called Arab Spring have meant that the Muslim Brotherhood there has entered the political mainstream.

Sayyid Qutb (1906–1966) is arguably the most important and influential of the fundamentalist thinkers. Like his contemporary Hasan al-Banna, Qutb played an important role in the Muslim Brotherhood, providing an intellectual impetus both to the brotherhood and to those Islamist movements that would come after it in Egypt and elsewhere. Said to have memorized the Quran at the age of ten, Qutb originally seems to have been fond of certain aspects of Western civilization, but he grew increasingly dismayed by it in the aftermath of 1948, the year in which the State of Israel was founded.[16]

In 1948, he published *Al-Adala al-ijtimaʿiyya fiʾl-Islam* (*Social Justice in Islam*), in which he argued that Muslims needed to return to Islam, which, he claimed, provides a complete and total way of life based on equilibrium in the social, economic, political, and legal spheres of life. Any insertion of foreign (i.e., Western) elements into this total way of life was a form of corruption and would ultimately weaken Islam, something that he saw happening in his own day. After publishing the work, Qutb traveled to the United States and described what he saw there:

> I saw them there as nervous tension devoured their lives despite all the evidence of wealth, plenty, and gadgets that they have. Their enjoyment is nervous excitement, animal merriment. One gets the image that they are constantly running from ghosts that are pursuing them. They are machines that move with madness, spend, and convulsion that does not cease. Many times I thought as though the people were in a grinding machine that does not stop day or night, morning or evening. It grinds them and they are devoured without a moment's rest. They have no faith in themselves or in life around them.[17]

Upon his return to Egypt, Qutb joined the Muslim Brotherhood. He also published his important and massive thirty-volume commentary on the Quran, *Fi zilal al-Quran* (*In the Shade of the Quran*), in which he articulated further his vision of Islam and Muslim identity as the perfect system representing all aspects of life.

After the Egyptian Revolution of 1952 and the ensuing Nasser years, the Muslim Brotherhood was made an outlawed political organization, as it was until 2011. Qutb's critiques of the government ensured that he spent time in prison. In 1964, he wrote his most important and influential work, *Ma'alim fi-l-tariq* (*Milestones*).

One of Qutb's most important aims in *Milestones* was the resignification of the term *jahiliyya*, which, as noted in chapter 1, refers to a mythical "age of ignorance" on the Arabian Peninsula prior to the advent or reestablishment of Islam.[18] Qutb transformed this term so that it would refer to all those systems of thought—including what we even tend to think of as "Muslim"—that elevate humans to the status of God. He juxtaposed these systems with his own purified vision of Islam: "Today we are in a similar or darker *jahiliyyah* than that contemporaneous to early Islam. All that surrounds us is *jahiliyyah*, people visions, beliefs, their habits and customs, their source of knowledge, art, literature, rules and laws, even what we consider as Islamic education, Islamic sources, Islamic philosophy and Islamic thought—all of it is the product to *jahiliyyah*."[19]

After its publication, *Milestones* became a manual of Islamic revival. In 1965, Qutb was arrested for plotting to overthrow the state and then executed a year later. He was buried in an unmarked gave, but he continues to be considered an important martyr and a symbol of Islamic revival throughout the Islamic world to this day. Sayyid Qutb's writings have inspired many other fundamentalist reformers, including the Muslim Brotherhoods outside Egypt and Hamas in the Palestinian Territories, and his writings played an important role in the intellectual development of Ayman al-Zawahiri and Osama bin Laden, the founders of al-Qaeda.

Mawlana Abu'l-Ala Mawdudi

Mawlana Abu'l-Ala Mawdudi (1903–1979) was the founder of the Islamic Association (Jamaat-i-Islami) in Lahore, Pakistan, in 1941 during the closing days of the British Raj. Highly critical of British imperialism, Mawdudi wanted to secure the existence of a Muslim community overwhelmed by the Hindu population on the Indian subcontinent.

As a newspaper journalist and editor, Mawdudi used as his main platform the journal *Tarjuman al-Quran*, which was highly critical of the Indian Nationalist Congress's nationalist aspirations. According to Mawdudi, Islam was steadfastly opposed to nationalism, which often coincided with a secular state, and Muslims were bound together based solely on their religious commitment to God, which took precedence over language, race, or culture. However, he wrote, "the reforms which Islam wants to bring about cannot be carried out merely by sermons. Political power is essential for their achievement. . . . [T]he struggle for obtaining control over the organs of the state when motivated by the urge to establish the *din* [religion] and the Islamic *shariah* and to enforce the Islamic injunction is not only permissible but is positively desirable and is such obligatory."[20]

Although originally critical of the nationalist aspirations to create a Muslim homeland, Pakistan, after partition occurred in 1947, Mawdudi was forced to flee there, and from there he began to argue that the new state's constitution should be based solely on Islamic principles. Creating such a constitution would lead to the renaissance of Islam in the modern world by creating a social order that he—like al-Banna and Qutb—imagined to be at work in Muhammad's time and in the period immediately thereafter. It was only in the ensuing years, so the argument went, that Islam gradually became corrupted as it encountered and absorbed foreign ideas and practices.

The Islamic Association is still a political party in Pakistan, and its goal remains the establishment of a pure Islamic state governed by the sharia as well as opposition to Westernization and its concomitant ideologies capitalism, socialism, and secularism. In recent years, Indian and American politicians have argued that the Islamic Association forms the political wing of more radical militant groups (such as Party of Jihadists [Hizbul Mujahidin]) in Pakistan.

Ruhollah Musavi Khomeini

Ruhollah Musavi Khomeini (1902–1989)—often referred to as "Ayatollah Khomeini"—was the spiritual head of the Iranian Revolution in 1979. When the shah attempted to nationalize the Shi'i *ulama*, a group of clerics led by Khomeini opposed the monarchy's autocracy and its desire to monitor and control the religious institutions associated with southern Iran. After a series of large-scale demonstrations, Khomeini was arrested and deported to Iraq.

Although Khomeini would eventually become the poster boy in the West for militant and intolerant Islam, he was someone who was interested in Western philosophy, was himself a poet, and—unlike some of the other individuals discussed so far—was firmly entrenched in the classical sources of the tradition. In exile, Khomeini also encountered the works of Islamist thinkers such as Hasan al-Banna and Sayyid Qutb, who although Sunnis, spoke openly of the conflict between the West and Islam, the forces of secularism, and Muslim fundamentals.

In exile, Khomeini published an innovative tract on the traditional Shiʿi concept of *wilayat al-faqih* (the legal scholar's mandate), in which he argued that in the absence of the Imam, qualified religious scholars can assume the right to rule. It was this theory that brought Khomeini to power in 1979 when the shah left Iran.[21] He wrote, for example, that "the acquisition of knowledge and expertise in various sciences—is necessary for making plans for a country and for exercising executive and administrative functions; we too will make use of people with those qualifications. But as for the supervisions and supreme administration of the country, the dispensing of justice and the establishment of equitable relations among the people—these are precisely the subjects that the *faqih* [religious scholar] has studied."[22]

Khomeini's supporters used the imagery of the martyrdom of Husayn in the seventh century to symbolize their struggle. The shah became associated with the forces of Yazid, and Khomeini and his followers were associated with the moral and spiritual superiority of the *ahl al-bayt*, Muhammad's family. Khomeini was able to take the historically quietist position of Shiʿism, which emerged out of particular historical contexts (see chapter 5), and turn it into political activism.

Under Khomeini's rule, sharia was introduced in Iran, and the Islamic Revolutionary Guard enforced an Islamic dress code and morality for both men and women. For instance, women were required to cover their hair, and men were not allowed to wear shorts. Alcohol, most Western movies, and the practice of men and women swimming or sunbathing together were banned. The educational curriculum was Islamized at all levels, and any music other than that composed for martial or religious purposes was banned. Khomeini was also responsible for issuing the fatwa calling for the assassination of the British novelist Salman Rushdie for his publication of what many Muslims considered to be the defamatory *Satanic Verses* (see chapter 3).

Although the majority of Iranians welcomed Khomeini with open arms in 1979, the effects of the revolution are anything but clear today. Many Iranians have grown disaffected with the revolution and have called for an end to the theocracy of the Shi'i *ulama*. Elections, widely regarded as rigged, have secured the status quo, and there is great unease between the populace and many religious leaders, who control the government and its policies (there are reformist religious scholars, but they tend to be harassed and marginalized).

MODERNISM

If fundamentalists seek a return to the ideals that they perceive to have been at work in the sacred past when Muhammad lived, modernists try to adapt the past and its teachings to the contemporary world. This distinction does not make the claim that modernists are secular or that they reject Islam—this would effectively take them beyond the pale of the religion, although there are certainly many secular Muslims. Where modernists differ from such secularists is in their desire to ground change in the Quran and Sunna, albeit in a much more liberal fashion than the fundamentalists advocate. "Modernist" is the umbrella term that refers to all those Muslims who believe that Islam and modernity are compatible with each other, at least when both are properly configured.

Whereas fundamentalists drew and continue to chart their identity formations against the perceived bedrock of an immutable past to which the present must be made to conform, modernists acknowledge the instability of social formation and try to recast Islamic principles accordingly. Whereas fundamentalists are quick to posit the self-sufficiency of Islam, modernists are not afraid to admit that certain Western ideals are compatible with Islam (this view sometimes leads to the apologetic claim that Western political ideals such as democracy and minority rights are actually Islamic as opposed to European in origin).

Islamic modernism has its roots in the nineteenth century and was most likely connected to the age of colonialism and imperialism. It is, in certain ways, based on the European critique of Islam as backward. The development of the modernist position is tied to the notions that Islam is currently flawed and that its regeneration requires that *certain* aspects of it need to be changed. In many ways, this position is based on the modern European distinction between the religious and the secular: modernists tend to see Islam as the basis for religious life that informs more secular political ideals such as democracy, liberalism, and tolerance.

Although modernists do attempt to limit the binding authority of the past, they are quick not to deny its authority. Their goal is not to re-create Muhammad's polis in the modern period, but to distill the essence of Islam, which can in turn be infused into the present period.

Muhammad Abduh

Muhammad Abduh (1849–1905) was born to a poor peasant family in Upper Egypt before going on to study at al-Azhar in Cairo, where he would eventually become its first modernizing rector. He was a student of Jamal al-Din al-Afghani (1839–1907), a philosopher and religious reformer who advocated Pan-Islamism to resist European colonialism.[23] Like all reformers—fundamentalist, modernist, and nationalist—Abduh perceived the Islam of his contemporaries to be in a state of decay and in need of resurrection.

Seeing the religious sphere in a state of demise and the Western-inspired secular sphere threatening to overturn Islam, Abduh sought to harness them to each other. His rational and rationalist construction of Islam would enable Muslims to thrive in the modern world, he believed, helping a new learned class to select what was necessary from modernity and then show how it can be made to be compatible with Islam.

The way that Abduh sought to make Islam compatible with nineteenth-century rationalism was by opening up the gates of *ijtihad* (independent reasoning), a move that struck many conservatives and traditionalists as highly controversial. In taking this approach, he was highly critical of what he considered to be the old-fashioned notions of *fiqh* (jurisprudence) and *taqlid* (imitation), which offered only an overreliance on previous legal reasoning and curtailed present concerns. Muslims, according to him, could not simply rely on medieval interpretations of texts but needed to use reason to keep up with changing times.

Keeping up with the times, of course, did not mean abandoning traditions. Although Abduh preached the compatibility between religion and science, he encouraged believers to look beyond the laws of nature to their source in a creator. He composed a modernist commentary on the Quran—which he regarded, along with the Sunna, as the key to Islamic renaissance in the modern period.

Muhammad Iqbal

Sir Muhammad Iqbal (1877–1938) was born in Sialkot in the Punjab, where he was educated at the Scotch Mission before going on to study philosophy in Lahore. He subsequently studied in Cambridge, Heidelberg, and Munich, where he completed a doctorate in 1908 with the dissertation "The Development of Metaphysics in Persia." He returned to Lahore and established a law practice but concentrated primarily on writing poetry and various scholarly works on politics, philosophy, and religion.

Drawing on his studies in Europe and his own perception of the current weakened state of contemporary Indian Muslim society, Iqbal sought to reinvigorate Islam by detaching it from Sufi pantheism and Hindu intellectualism. He argued that one of the main ways to accomplish this task was to establish an Islamic state founded on the principle of absolute equality. He argued apologetically that this democratic principle had existed at the beginnings of Islam but was gradually curtailed during the decades of Islamic expansions. Now, he wrote, "democracy [which] has been the great mission of England in modern times . . . is one aspect of our own political ideal that is being worked out in it. It is . . . the spirit of the British Empire that makes it the greatest Muhammadan Empire in the world."[24]

Muslim democracy, however, was far from realizable until Muslims developed their potential as Muslims and, as such, became active participants in the betterment of society. Once this happened, Muslim countries around the globe could form their own "League of Nations": "It seems to me that God is slowly bringing home to us the truth that Islam is neither Nationalism nor Imperialism but a League of Nations which recognize[s] artificial boundaries and racial distinctions of reference only and not for restricting the social horizons of its members."[25]

Iqbal, as the president of the India Muslim League, was one of the first in India to argue for the creation of a separate Muslim state. However, he also argued that "a false reverence for past history and its artificial resurrection constitute no remedy for a people's decay."[26] Like the fundamentalists, Iqbal thought that the main problem plaguing the modern Muslim world was its departure from Islamic principles, so he desired to find in an imagined past a model for present (and future) regeneration. However, he differed from the fundamentalists in the assertion that the past must be shaped and molded to address contemporary concerns rather than the reverse.

Fazlur Rahman

Fazlur Rahman (1911–1988) was born in the Hazara area of British India (now Pakistan), received a doctorate in Islamic philosophy from the University of Oxford, and went on to teach at, among other places, McGill University in Canada and the University of Chicago. He briefly interrupted his academic career from 1962 to 1968 to become the director of the Islamic Research Institute in Pakistan, which the Pakistani government set up to implement Islam into the nation's daily dealings. However, owing to conservative criticism, he was forced to leave both the institute and the country.[27]

Rahman was highly critical of the classical Islamic legal tradition. He argued that much of this tradition had ignored the spirit or moral of the sources in a literal reading of them. He also adopted an historicist position, arguing that it is imperative to examine both historically and critically how the Quran and other sources have been understood and by whom. For Rahman, this process enables us to see what is essential to Islam and what is historically conditioned.

His search, then, like those of the others examined in this chapter, was for a pristine Islam that exists outside the historical, the cultural, or the political. However, the articulations of this nebulous Islam, as should be clear, reveal more about the interpreters' hermeneutical stance that they do about Islam.

Abdolkarim Soroush

Abdolkarim Soroush (b. 1945) was educated in Iran and England before returning to Tehran after the revolution in 1979. He was thereupon appointed director of the Islamic Culture Group at the Tehran Teacher's Training College and was a member of Khomeini's Advisory Council of the Cultural Revolution. The latter organization was responsible for closing Iran's universities and restricting free speech.[28] Despite his initial support for the revolution, Soroush became increasingly critical of what he considered to be the Shi'i clerics' authoritarian and fundamentalist nature.

During the 1990s, Soroush became highly critical of the political role played by the Iranian clergy. He wrote, for example, that, "rather than guiding and criticizing the ruler, [the seminaries] offer opinions and issue *fatwas* that meet [the rulers'] tastes, or they will close the door to debate concerning various theoretical issues. If in the seminaries, for example, the right to discuss the issue of *vilayat-i faqihi* [guardianship of the religious scholars] is not exercised, and opposing and supporting opinions are not freely exchanged, this is an indicator of a problem that must be removed."[29]

Soroush also cofounded the magazine *Kiyan*, in which he published articles in support of religious pluralism, tolerance, and human rights. The religiopolitical authorities clamped down on *Kiyan* and other magazines in 1998, however, and Soroush became subject to harassment and state censorship, in addition to losing his job. From the year 2000 on, he has resided outside Iran, teaching at various Western universities, such as Harvard and Princeton.

NATIONALISM

A third way to deal with the "Islamic question" in the modern world has been nationalism, which emerged in the twentieth century largely as a reaction to European domination yet paradoxically under the influence of European ideas about nation-states. The central idea in nationalism focuses on how a particular group (e.g., Arabs, Turks, Persians) unified by language and a shared sense of history has been long divided and dominated by outside powers. The various nationalist movements of the twentieth century were often secular—although they certainly incorporated select aspects of the Islamic past—and sought to create a strong nation to check colonialist powers.

Arab nationalism offers a telling example. By the 1950s and 1960s, largely owing to the articulation by the Egyptian leader Gamal abd al-Nasser and by various political parties such as the secular Ba'ath (Resurrection or Renaissance) Party found throughout the Arab world, nationalism was very popular in most of the more than twenty independent states of the Arab world. The nationalists believed that the Arab nation had existed as a historical entity for centuries and constellated around the twin notions of Arabic as the language of communication and Islam as the religion and culture in the region.

Even though largely secular, these movements, like every other movement in Islamic history, made appeals to select aspects of the Islamic past—scientific developments, political hegemony, and so on—as the antidote to modern ills. Many of these nationalist movements would often make appeals to Islam when it politically suited them. For instance, Saddam Hussein added the words "Allahu Akhbar" (God is Great) to the Iraqi flag in 1991, presumably as a way to turn the war with the Americans into a religious war and thereby to garner support among other Muslim nations. Not surprisingly, the establishment of the State of Israel in 1948 provided a catalyst to various Arab nationalist movements. Israel was regarded largely as a colonialist imposition on Arab soil and, as such, an imposition that threatened the greatness of both specific Arab nation-states and the pan-Arabic nation.

Although nationalism still remains a potent political force today, the Arab defeat by Israel in the Six-Day War in June 1967—which Nasser had dubbed the "Battle of Destiny"—and Nasser's death in 1970 weakened faith in this ideal early on. Moreover, the increasing brutality by which some nationalist leaders have kept in check various opposition movements, rising unemployment and nepotism, and, increasingly, charges that the nationalists are in power because of their willingness to protect American interests in the region have further eroded belief in the ideal. Islamic fundamentalist movements—for example, in Egypt, Iran, Palestine, and Iraq—have attempted to fill the political vacuum left behind by these movements.

Mustafa Kemal Atatürk

Mustafa Kemal Atatürk (1881–1935) was born in Salonika (now Thessaloniki) in what was then the Ottoman Empire. In 1919, he began a nationalist revolution in Anatolia, organizing resistance to the peace settlement imposed on the Ottoman Empire by the victorious Allies. His successful military campaigns led to the liberation of the country and to the establishment of the modern nation-state of Turkey. During his presidency, Atatürk embarked on a program of political, economic, and cultural reforms. An admirer of the European Enlightenment, he transformed the former Ottoman Empire into a modern and secular nation.

His reforms included the emancipation of women; the abolition of all Islamic institutions; the introduction of Western legal codes, dress, and calendar; and the replacement of the Arabic script with a Latin one. Although he did much to dismantle the state's Islamic infrastructure, he also sponsored Turkish translations of the Quran, which were read publically, as well as a Turkish-language modernist *tafsir* (interpretation) of the Quran. Many Turks could not read Arabic, so Atatürk was worried that religious affairs would be the domain of the few as opposed to open to all.

Gamal abd al-Nasser

Gamal abd al-Nasser (1918–1970) is generally considered to be one of the most important figures in the twentieth-century Arab world. He led a bloodless coup that toppled the monarchy in Egypt in 1952, thereby heralding a new period of modernization and socialist reform. He introduced numerous modernizing measures in Egypt, which included nationalizing companies; bringing al-Azhar, one of the most distinguished institutions of Sunni legal thought, under state control; and providing housing and health care to all Egyptians.

Nasser's domestic and foreign policies increasingly clashed with the colonial interests of European powers in the region—Britain and France. In addition, Nasser's neutrality, his recognition of the Communist People's Republic of China, and his arms deals with the Soviet bloc also alienated American support for his regime. In 1956, when Nasser announced the nationalization of the Suez Canal Company, a company in which the French and British had major shareholdings, these two countries, along with Israel, invaded Egypt and took over the Suez Canal. However, the Eisenhower administration in the United States publically condemned the raid and demanded the withdrawal of the three states from Egyptian territory. This show of support did much to raise Nasser's political capital both in Egypt and throughout the Arab world.

Nasser is probably best known for his vision of pan-Arabism, a movement that calls for the unification of the peoples and countries of the Arab world from the Atlantic Ocean to the Arabian Sea. It is a concept that is often used interchangeably with Arab nationalism, the idea that Arabs constitute a single nation. The pan-Arabism movement reached its height during the 1960s under the guidance of Nasser, and it was a largely secular and socialist political ideology that opposed Western political involvement in the Middle East. In 1958, Nasser helped form the United Arab Republic, a union between Egypt and Syria, which lasted little more than three years, with Syria seceding from the union in 1961. In April 1963, Egypt, Syria, and Iraq agreed to form a new United Arab Republic, which was to be entirely federal in structure, leaving each member state its identity and institutions. This union was finally abolished in 1971 owing to irreconcilable differences between Syria and Egypt.[30]

Pan-Arabism was strongly hurt following Israel's defeat of the Arabs in the Six-Day War. Moreover, many countries' inability to get along and to generate economic growth contributed to its demise. The Ba'ath Party in Syria and Iraq (until the U.S. invasion of Iraq in 2003) is still in principle committed to the notion of pan-Arabism. In many parts of the Islamic world today, however, the religious notion of Islam as opposed to the secular notion of nationalism seems to be ascendant.

Saddam Hussein

A very competent officer in the Iraqi Ba'ath Party, Saddam Hussein (1937–2006) was regarded by U.S. intelligence officials as an important individual in the fight against Communism in the Arab world during the 1960s and 1970s. After the Ba'athists took power in 1968, the party focused on achieving stability in a nation riddled with profound social, ethnic, religious, and economic tensions.

As Iraq's de facto ruler, Saddam Hussein actively fostered the modernization of the Iraqi economy and the creation of a strong security apparatus to prevent coups within the power structure and insurrections apart from it. Ever concerned with broadening his base of support among the diverse elements of Iraqi society and mobilizing mass support, he closely followed the administration of state welfare and development programs.

He was greatly aided in achieving his agenda owing to the oil crises of 1973, his nationalization of foreign oil companies in the country, and the dramatic increase in oil prices that followed.

Angering many conservatives, Hussein's party greatly increased Iraqi women's freedoms and social mobility, including their entrance into high-level government and industry jobs. He also created a Western-style legal system, making Iraq the only country in the Persian Gulf not ruled according to sharia.

After a long-drawn-out war (1980–1988) with Iran—a war that saw the use of chemical weapons, the death of up to 500,000 soldiers and civilians, but no change in borders—Hussein sought to get the Kuwaitis to forgive his war debt (up to $30 billion), but they refused. He then asked the Organization of Petroleum Exporting Countries to raise the price of oil by cutting production, but it refused, largely owing to Kuwait's opposition. So on August 2, 1990, Hussein invaded and annexed Kuwait, sparking an international crisis. Although the United States had provided assistance to Saddam Hussein in the war with Iran, it now led a coalition that relatively quickly drove Iraq's troops from Kuwait in February 1991. The Gulf War ended on February 28, 1991.

The United States continued to view Hussein as a tyrant who threatened the region's stability. The sanctions imposed on Iraq during the Gulf War were never lifted afterward, and it was hoped that his political enemies within the country would overthrow him. This position changed, however, following the attacks of September 11, 2001. President George W. Bush spoke of Iraq as a key player in the "axis of evil" (which also included Iran and North Korea). He also announced that he would possibly take action to topple the Iraqi government because of the alleged threat of its "weapons of mass destruction."

On March 20, 2003, the United States (as part of what it called a "coalition of the willing") invaded Iraq, and Hussein's government toppled within a matter of weeks. Hussein was found hiding underground at a farmhouse in his native province of Tikrit, was put on trial in 2006, and, after being found guilty of crimes against humanity, was quickly executed. Since the American-led invasion, the Ba'ath Party has been banned in Iraq.

This chapter has tried to clarify the complex relationship that has emerged from Islam's encounter with modernity. Although this response has been presented as taking three different approaches—fundamentalist, modernist, and nationalist—it is important to be aware that these rubrics are theoretical. What defined fundamentalism at the beginning of the twentieth century and the ways perceived to implement Islamic principles in society, for example, were often much different from what they are in the present. In like manner, it is not out of the question that a nationalist group might align itself with a fundamentalist ideology (e.g., as Hamas has done in Palestine). It is good to be aware of the potential fluidity between these rubrics.

Although the imagined role that Islam is to play in the modern world is common to all these responses to modernity, it is always necessary to remember that Islam has never been a stable factor in all these conversations. It is, on the contrary, a contested and highly politicized factor that is defined differently by the various actors involved—which is why some can say that Islam is compatible with democracy, but others can deny such commensurability. Islam in the modern period is as invested in the formation and maintenance of various Muslim identities as it was in the late antique and medieval periods.

Islam's encounter with modernity has been tantamount to its encounter with the West. The colonial powers (e.g., Britain, France, America)—their ideas of progress, the nation-state, and so on—have been instrumental in defining the terms of reference that have driven the conversations within Islam. Imperialistic desires, political ideologies, and market forces have contributed to the manifold Muslim identities that have emerged from modernity. Even the idea that Islam is a total and holistic way of life can be read as a direct response to the notion of a separation between church and state that has played such a large role in thinking about religion and its place in society in the contemporary West.

Edward Said argued that the West has always imagined "the Orient" as the opposite of itself and as a way to define itself better. The case, of course, can also be made that Muslim thinkers have also imagined "the West" selectively and for their own purposes of self-definition. Rather than talk about the "clash of civilizations," as so many want to at the present moment, it might be more productive to pay attention to the polyphonous voices (not voice!) that have emerged from Islam's encounter with the modern West and vice versa.

NOTES

1. See, for example, Roger Owen, *State, Power, and Politics in the Making of the Modern Middle East*, 3rd ed. (London: Routledge, 2004), 5–38.

2. For example, Samuel P. Huntington, *The Clash of Civilizations and the Remaking of the World Order* (New York: Simon and Schuster, 1998). Huntington's thesis has been picked up, most notably for Islamic studies, by Bernard Lewis in *What Went Wrong? Western Impact and Middle Eastern Response* (New York: Oxford University Press, 2001).

3. For an in-depth study of the uses of the term "authenticity" in the study of religion more generally, see Russell T. McCutcheon, *Manufacturing Religion: The Discourse on Sui Generis Religion and the Politics of Nostalgia* (New York: Oxford University Press, 1997).

4. Anthony Giddens, *Conversations with Anthony Giddens: Making Sense of Modernity* (Stanford, Calif.: Stanford University Press, 1998), 94.

5. See, for example, Mustafa Aksakal, *The Ottoman Road to War in 1914: The Ottoman Empire and the First World War* (Cambridge: Cambridge University Press, 2008); and Karen Barkey, *Empire of Difference: The Ottomans in Comparative Perspective* (Cambridge: Cambridge University Press, 2008), 264–295.

6. Edward W. Said, *Orientalism* (New York: Vintage, 1978), 3.

7. See, for example, Aaron W. Hughes, *Situating Islam: The Past and Future of an Academic Discipline* (London: Equinox, 2007), 9–32.

8. Bruce Lincoln, *Holy Terrors: Thinking About Religion After September 11* (Chicago: University of Chicago Press, 2003), 56.

9. Ibid., 57–58.

10. Ibid., 59.

11. Reinhard Schulze, *A Modern History of the Islamic World*, trans. Azizeh Azodi (London: Tauris, 2002), 221–222.

12. Ibid., 244.

13. This division of voices in Islam is loosely based on the classification in William E. Shepard, "Islam and Ideology: Towards a Typology," *International Journal of Middle Eastern Studies* 19 (1987): 307–336.

14. On the problems and utility of using "fundamentalist" as a comparative term, see Martin E. Marty and R. Scott Appleby, "Conclusion: An Interim Report on a Hypothetical Family," in Martin E. Marty and R. Scott Appleby, eds., *Fundamentalisms Observed* (Chicago: University of Chicago Press, 1994), 814–842.

15. Hasan al-Banna, *Five Tracts of Hasan al-Bannā (1906–1949): A Selection from the "Majmuʿat Rasaʾil al-Imam al-Shahid*," trans. Charles Wendell (Berkeley: University of California Press, 1978), 155–156.

16. A good discussion of these and related issues can be found in Yvonne Y. Haddad, "Sayyid Qutb, Ideologue of the Islamic Revival," in John Esposito, ed., *Voices of Resurgent Islam* (New York: Oxford University Press, 1983), 67–98.

17. Quoted in Yvonne Y. Haddad, *Contemporary Islam and the Challenge of History* (Albany: State University of New York Press, 1982), 90.

18. William E. Shepard, "Sayyid Qutb's Doctrine of *Jahiliyya*," *International Journal of Middle Eastern Studies* 35 (2003): 521–545.

19. Sayyid Qutb, *Milestones* (Indianapolis: American Trust, 1990), quoted in Haddad, "Sayyid Qutb," 85.

20. Mawlana Abuʾl-Ala Mawdudi, *Islamic Law and Constitution*, ed. and trans. Khurshi Ahmad, 10th ed. (Lahore: Islamic Publications, 1990), 177.

21. Hamid Enyat, "Iran: Khumayni's Concept of the 'Guardianship of the Jurisconsult,'" in James Piscatori, ed., *Islam in the Political Process* (Cambridge: Cambridge University Press, 1983), 160–180.

22. Quoted in Michael M. J. Fischer, "Imam Khomeini: Four Levels of Understanding," in Esposito, ed., *Voices of Resurgent Islam*, 158.

23. A full biography and analysis of Muhammad Abduh can be found in Mark Sedgwick, *Muhammad Abduh* (Oxford: Oneworld, 2009).

24. Muhammad Iqbal, "Islam as a Moral and Political Ideal," in *Thoughts and Reflections of Iqbal*, ed. S. A. Vahid (Lahore, Pakistan: Sh. Muhammad Ashraf, 1964), 52.

25. Muhammad Iqbal, "The Principle of Movement in the Structure of Islam," in *The Reconstruction of Religious Thought in Islam* (Lahore, Pakistan: Sh. Muhammad Ashraf, 1968), 159, quoted in John L. Esposito, "Muhammad Iqbal and the Islamic State," in Esposito, ed., *Voices of Resurgent Islam*, 183.

26. Iqbal, "Principle of Movement," quoted in Esposito, "Muhammad Iqbal," 151.

27. For more on Fazlur Rahman, see Earle H. Waugh and Frederick M. Denny, eds., *The Shaping of an American Islamic Discourse: A Memorial to Fazlur Rahman* (Atlanta: Scholars Press, 1998).

28. See the comments in Valla Vakili, "Abdolkarim Soroush and Critical Discourse in Iran," in John L. Esposito and John O. Voll, eds., *Makers of Contemporary Islam* (New York: Oxford University Press, 2001), 150–176.

29. Quoted in ibid., 167.

30. Libya's Muammar Gaddafi also attempted to form pan-Arab movements—the Federation of Arab Republics and the Arab Islam Republic—but neither of them ever got off the ground. The seven Arab emirates that today form the United Arab Emirates is perhaps the only example of a successful unification between Arab neighbors.

SUGGESTIONS FOR FURTHER READING

Antoun, Richard T. *Muslim Preacher in the Modern World: A Jordanian Case Study in Comparative Perspective*. Princeton, N.J.: Princeton University Press, 1989.

Eickelman, Dale F., and James Piscatori. *Muslim Politics*. 2nd ed. Princeton, N.J.: Princeton University Press, 2004.

Esposito, John L., ed. *Voices of Resurgent Islam*. New York: Oxford University Press, 1983.

Esposito, John L., and John O. Voll, eds. *Makers of Contemporary Islam*. New York: Oxford University Press, 2001.

Gibb, Hamilton A. R. *Modern Trends in Islam*. Chicago: University of Chicago Press, 1947.

Hourani, Albert. *Arabic Thought in the Liberal Age, 1798–1939*. 2nd ed. Oxford: Oxford University Press, 1983.

Kurzman, Charles, ed. *Liberal Islam: A Sourcebook*. New York: Oxford University Press, 1998.

Lawrence, Bruce B. *Defenders of God: The Fundamentalist Revolt Against the Modern Age*. San Francisco: Harper & Row, 1989.

Lincoln, Bruce. *Holy Terrors: Thinking About Religion After September 11*. Chicago: University of Chicago Press, 2003.

Qutb, Sayyid. *Ma'alim fi-l-tariq*. Cairo: Kanzi, 1964.

——. *Milestones*. Indianapolis: American Trust, 1990.

Rahman, Fazlur. *Islam in Modernity: The Transformation of the Intellectual Tradition*. Chicago: University of Chicago Press, 1982.

Said, Edward. *Orientalism*. New York: Vintage, 1978.

Schulze, Reinhard. *A Modern History of the Islamic World*. Translated by Azizeh Azodi. London: Tauris, 2002.

Sivan, Emmanuel. *Radical Islam: Medieval Theology and Modern Politics*. Enlarged ed. New Haven, Conn.: Yale University Press, 1985.

Soroush, Abdolkarim. *Reason, Freedom, and Democracy in Islam: Essential Writings of Abdolkarim Soroush*. Translated and edited by Mahmoud Sadri and Ahmad Sadri. New York: Oxford University Press, 2000.

Voll, John O. *Islam: Continuity and Change in the Modern World*. 2nd ed. Syracuse, N.Y.: Syracuse University Press, 1994.

11

CONSTRUCTING MUSLIM WOMEN

O NE OF the most visible markers of Muslim identity in the modern world is the veil. In Europe, many see the veil as a sign that Islam is not compatible with liberal European values, and in specific countries, most noticeably France, some regard the veil as an infringement on secular society and consider it a risk to the traditional separation of church and state. In 2004, for instance, the French government banned head coverings and other overt symbols of religious faith from schools. On the other side of the debate, some Muslims argue that legislation against veiling is a form of religious discrimination and an attempt to discredit Islam and impose secular values on Muslims.

In Muslim countries, especially ones that have been more secular either traditionally or politically (e.g., Turkey, Palestine, Lebanon), the veil has increasingly become more widespread, and some see this change as a gauge of the influence and popularity of Islamism. It would seem, then, that the various types of head coverings are not simply about women and Islam's perceived treatment of them but have become a symbol of particular Muslim identities. As we should come to expect, there is no simple "Muslim perspective" on the veil and veiling; there are as many different perspectives on it as there are types of modern Islam (as indicated in the typology outlined in chapter 10).

Regardless of country—whether in Europe, America, the Middle East, or Africa—women's bodies are increasingly the site where Muslim identities, both male and female, are played out and contested. This situation is probably not surprising given the fact that from the earliest centuries those doing the most to think about women, women's bodies, and the place of women in society have been men, especially male scholars. Discussions of women in Islam often say as much about men as they do about women. Any discussion of gender in Islam, therefore, must be aware of the fact that until the modern period men have been the ones responsible for defining the "correct" place for women within the family and society. But recent years have witnessed the rise of Muslim or Islamic feminists who seek to address the changing role of women in Muslim society.

Modern Attempts to Re-create Women's Lives During the Time of Muhammad

Any attempt to write about anything that occurred during Muhammad's lifetime returns us to the conundrum that arose in the first three chapters of this book: we know virtually nothing about the earliest centuries of Islam because all the materials that claim knowledge of this period are from much later periods. This problem, however, has not stopped various interested parties from attempting to portray the lives of women during the time of Muhammad. They usually do so for apologetic purposes, to show that the earliest period was marked by a type of gender equality preached by Muhammad, which later eroded when male elites began to corrupt his message by increasingly circumscribing women's role and place in Muslim society.[1]

As for so many other issues, the time of Muhammad served as a canvas on which later sources painted their own visions and agendas regarding women and Islam. The case is not much different today. For some, the advent of Islam empowered women, giving them a set of rights unheard of until relatively recently in the West.[2] Such interpreters contrast the message of Islam, as we saw in chapter 1, with the *jahiliyya* (period of ignorance), when it is said the Arabs practiced female infanticide and gave women no rights. Others, however, find sources that demonstrate the opposite: women enjoyed power and prestige in the pre-Islamic period, and the Quran initially reflected this status but was subsequently misinterpreted to deprive women of their rights.

MUHAMMAD AS FEMINIST

As we saw in chapter 2, many modern treatments of Muhammad seek to portray or define him in the light of contemporary and anachronistic categories. The modern Muslim commentator Tariq Ramadan, for instance, seeks to show "the spiritual and contemporary teachings in the life of the last prophet." In his desire to accomplish this task, he provides an imaginative account of Muhammad's treatment of women and, by extension, Islam's high regard for women. He writes, for instance:

> Inside the mosque, the women would line up behind the men's ranks, as the postures of prayer, in its various stages, require an arrangement that preserves modesty, decency, and respect. Women prayed, studied, and expressed themselves in that space. Moreover, they found in the Prophet's attitude the epitome of courtesy and regard: he demanded that men remain seated in order to let women leave first and without inconvenience, there was always gentleness and dignity in his behavior toward women, whom he listened to, and whose right to express themselves and set forth their opinions and arguments he acknowledged, protected, and promoted.*

Such a reading is virtually impossible to verify let alone support given the paucity of sources available to us. As such, it is important to regard Ramadan's account here as a theological and necessarily apologetic treatment of Muhammad.

*Tariq Ramadan, *In the Footsteps of Muhammad: Lessons from the Life of Muhammad* (Oxford: Oxford University Press, 2007), 148.

On this reading, Islam—at least according to its subsequent theological elaboration—is a large part of the problem of subjugating women. Both of these interpretations still possess much currency in the modern period.

The fact of the matter, however, is that these interpretations, at least from the historian's perspective, are absolutely impossible to verify. Attempts to show women in power in the pre-Islamic world are not made to raise the status of women, for example, but to lend credence to an ethos that gives women power over men—an ethos that Islam was perceived to correct. Those who wish to point to the positive treatment of women in early Islam, on the contrary, are usually drawn to a number of key females associated with Muhammad: Khadija (his first wife), Aisha (his last wife), and Fatima (his daughter). The goal of the analysis here is to show how these individuals function in the construction of modern Muslim, in particular female Muslim, identity.

KHADIJA

According to the biography of Muhammad (*sira*), Khadija bint (daughter of) Khuwaylid (ca. 555–619), a wealthy trader, was Muhammad's first wife.

Some sources depict her as a widow; yet others, owing to the problems that this status might pose (i.e., that Muhammad's first wife had been with another man), deny this characterization. Again according to the later biography, Khadija proposed marriage to Muhammad; she was the first convert to Islam; she provided great moral and emotional support to Muhammad; and while she was alive, Muhammad took no other wives. In his fourteenth-century commentary on the Quran, Isma'il Ibn Kathir (1301–1373) writes: "Once Aisha asked him if Khadija had been the only woman worthy of his love. The Prophet (peace and blessings of Allah be upon him) replied: 'She believed in me when no one else did; she accepted Islam when people rejected me; and she helped and comforted me when there was no one else to lend me a helping hand.'"[3]

Muhammad and Khadija had two sons, Qasim and Abd-Allah (both of whom died very young), and four daughters: Zaynab, Ruqayya, Umm Kulthum, and Fatima. However, most Shi'is debate the paternity of the first three, arguing that they were the products of previous marriages and claiming—as a way to protect the sanctity of the *ahl al-bayt* and the lineage of the Imams—that only Fatima is the true daughter of the union between Muhammad and Khadija.

AISHA

Aisha bint Abu Bakr (d. ca. 678) was one of Muhammad's first wives after the death of Khadija and was, as her name suggests, the daughter of the first successor to Muhammad, Abu Bakr (see chapter 4). She is quoted as a source for many hadiths, especially those concerning aspects of Muhammad's personal life. Many later Muslims regard Aisha, given her role in the transmission of hadith, as a learned woman who tirelessly recounted stories from the life of Muhammad and who explained the earliest history and traditions to a new generation of the followers of Muhammad's message. As the most prominent of Muhammad's wives, she is revered as a role model by millions of Muslim women.

Although certain details of Aisha's situation do not bother some Muslims, they do raise issues, perhaps of more contemporary concern, that nevertheless must be addressed. According to sources, Aisha was betrothed to Muhammad when she was six or seven years old, and the marriage was consummated when she was nine. Although child marriages were and still are relatively common in Bedouin societies, many modern critics of Islam use Muhammad's marriage to Aisha as evidence to discredit him as a pedophile, especially those who for a variety of reasons are critical of Islam to begin with (e.g., Ayaan Hirsi Ali, the Somali Dutch former Muslim politician who now lives in the United States). Denise Spellberg offers perhaps the most interesting and plausible defense of Muhammad, arguing that Aisha's young age might have been a later construction or interpolation to assure everyone that Muhammad's "favorite wife" was a virgin at marriage.[4]

Another problem is that some of Muhammad's enemies accused Aisha of committing adultery. When she was traveling with Muhammad and some of his followers on one occasion, she left camp in the morning to search for a lost necklace and, upon returning, found that the men had dismantled the camp and left without her. A man named Safwan eventually rescued her, which led to speculation that she and Safwan had committed adultery. Shortly after this incident, Muhammad announced that he had received a revelation from God confirming Aisha's innocence and directing that charges of adultery thereafter be supported by four eyewitness (Quran 24:4).[5]

Because of her young age at the time of marriage, Aisha lived for a significantly long period after Muhammad died. As chapter 4 notes, she was involved in an early and unsuccessful uprising against Ali in the Battle of the Camel. Some Muslim feminists have thus argued that Aisha provided a role model for women's political participation in Islamic communities and that women became marginalized in Islamic polity following her defeat at this battle.[6]

FATIMA

Fatima (ca. 605–632) was one of Muhammad's daughters—for Shi'is, the only daughter—from his first wife, Khadija. She remained at her father's side through the years of persecution that he suffered at the hands of the Quraysh in Mecca. After the *hijra* to Medina, she married Ali ibn Abi Talib, who became the fourth caliph and the first Imam. Regarded as "the mother of the Imams," Fatima plays a special role in Shi'i piety. She has a unique status as Muhammad's only surviving child; the wife of Ali, the first Imam; and the mother of Hasan and Husayn. She is believed to have been immaculate and sinless—a role model for Muslim women. Although said to have led a life of poverty, she shared whatever she had with others, according to Shiʿis.

Because of her marriage to Ali, Fatima is often imagined in later Shiʿi sources as a critic of the Abu Bakr and Umar caliphates. After the death of Muhammad, for instance, she opposed the election of Abu Bakr and supported Ali's claims. It is said that in the ensuing years she had many grievances with both Abu Bakr and Umar concerning a host of issues from the political and the genealogical to the financial. Later Shiʿi historians tell of how Umar called for Ali and his men to come out and swear allegiance to Abu Bakr. When they did not, Umar broke into their house, with the result that Fatima's ribs were broken when she was pressed between the door and the wall; this injury caused her to miscarry and led to her eventual death. She also laid claim to her father's property rights and challenged Abu Bakr's refusal to cede them. Such stories about Fatima, including the ones recounted earlier concerning her refusal to submit to the first caliph's will and the violence directed toward her, undoubtedly contributed to the pathos of later Shiʿism. In this regard, Fatima became an important symbol in the evolution of Shiʿi identity, functioning as a feminine image to sanctify the Prophet's family, on the one hand, and to reinforce the domestic role of Shiʿi women within a patriarchal system, on the other.[7]

Gender and the Construction of Female Mystics

Many modern commentators who are interested in reconciling Islam and women's rights frequently point to Sufism, wherein it is said that "women enjoy full equal rights."[8] Such comments, however, are difficult to sustain given the fact that, as witnessed in chapter 7, male scholars have largely been responsible for creating the various stories about female Sufi saints bequeathed to us. These male scholars, writing centuries after the fact, have constructed female mystical identities as a way to show that although these figures are women, they are unlike most women who desire marriage, children, and various accoutrements. In fact, the sources render these female mystics, if they in fact existed, as the ideal from male Sufis' perspective: lowly individuals, acutely aware of their inferiority, who were marginalized from the rest of society, thereby enabling them to contemplate God in relative isolation. In reference to the female mystic Rabia al-

Adawiyya, Sufi hagiographer Farid al-Din Attar states, "When a woman becomes a man in the path of God, she is a man and one cannot any more call her a woman."[9] Although such anecdotes might initially strike us as gender bending, they in fact reinforce the male as the ideal.

The Veil: A Contested Symbol

As noted at the beginning of this chapter, one of the most visible and contested symbols in Islam is the veil. In order to get a better sense of its manifold meanings, it is important to put this symbol in historical context so that we may see how it has been deployed, used, and understood over the centuries.

The term *hijab*—which can refer specifically to a veil (head scarf) or more generally to the concept of modesty—initially appears in the Quran. It is used in particular in the context of instructing male believers to talk to Muhammad's wives behind a *"hijab"* (33:53). Some have accordingly argued that the *hijab* referred to here was not the personal veil of later centuries, but a large curtain used to ensure the sanctity of Muhammad's wives. Other Quranic verses that are used to support veiling include the following:

And say to the believing women, that they cast down their eyes and guard their private parts; and reveal not their adornment save such is outward; and let them cast their veils over their bosoms, and reveal not their adornment save to their husbands, or their fathers, or their husbands fathers, or their sons, or their husband's sons, or their brothers, or their brothers' sons, or their sisters' sons, or their women, or what their right hands own, or such men as attend them, not having sexual desire, or children who have not yet attained knowledge of women's private parts; nor let them stamp their feet, so that their hidden ornament may be known. And turn all together to God, O you believers; happily so you will prosper. (24:31)

Children of Adam! We have sent down on you a garment to cover your shameful parts, and feathers; and the garments of the godfearing—that is better; that is one of God's signs; haply they will remember. (7:26)

O Prophet, say to your wives and daughters and the believing women, that they draw their veils close to them (when they go abroad). That will be better, so it is likelier that they will be known, and not hurt. God is All-forgiving, All-compassionate. (33:59)

All these verses, however, are extremely vague; none specifically refers to practice of women veiling, and they all can seemingly be interpreted in any number of ways. Regardless of the actual contents of such verses, however, they were subsequently generalized in the later legal tradition to establish the often rigid segregation of Muslim men and women. With these aforementioned vague verses in the background, all four major Sunni legal schools (Hanafi, Shafiʻi, Maliki, and Hanbali) today hold that a woman's entire body, frequently but not always with the exception of her face and hands, is considered part of her *awrah*, that part of the body that must be covered in public settings.

Some commentators in the modern period argue that there is nothing specifically Islamic about such covering because the practice already existed in pre-Islamic Arabia. Leila Ahmed, for example, contends that because of this preexistence, veiling is not or should not be mandatory in Islam.[10]

John Esposito, a scholar of Islam, argues that Muhammad's wives were the only ones to wear veils as a symbol of their status and that only later did Muslim women more generally take up the practice. At this later period, he asserts, Muslims were influenced by upper- and middle-class Persian and Byzantine women, who wore the veil as a sign of their rank to separate themselves not from men, but from the lower classes.[11]

There is obviously some debate as to the origins of the veil in Islam. This debate typically revolves around whether the veil is a cultural or a religious symbol. However, the line separating the religious from the cultural in seventh-century Arabia (or even in today's world) is anything but clear.

In recent years, the debate about veiling has shifted from a question about its origins to a question regarding the status of women in Islam. Owing to its visibility, veiling has become one of the few practices involving Muslim women that Westerners are aware of. Many point to it as a sign of the seclusion and oppression of women in Muslim societies and, when coupled with news that women are forbidden to drive in Saudi Arabia, as further proof of their complete marginalization. It is important to be aware of the various sides of the debate here. There are not simply two sides: Muslims who support the veil and non-Muslims who regard it as a symbol of misogyny. The fact of the matter is that many Muslims are opposed to the veil and contend that issues of modesty should be contingent on the society in which particular Muslims happen to find themselves.

Those who see the veil in a more favorable light argue that rather than regard it as a sign of female oppression, we need to see it as a sign of their freedom. An anonymous author on a fundamentalist Web site, for example, argues that, "contrary to popular belief, the covering of the Muslim woman is not oppression but a liberation from the shackles of male scrutiny and the standards of attractiveness. In Islam, a woman is free to be who she is inside, and immune from being portrayed as sex symbol and lusted after. Islam exalts the status of a woman by commanding that she enjoys equal rights to those of man in everything, she stands on an equal footing with man, and both [men and women] share mutual rights and obligations in all aspects of life."[12] Although this example may well offer an extreme view, it does show what is at stake for those who support the veiling of women. For them, the veil is not a cultural symbol, but a religious one that is required—morally, legally, and socially—for all Muslim women.

Rather than enter into the debate as to whether veiling is good or bad, religious or cultural, it is perhaps better to regard the veil in all its many manifestations as a contested symbol around which all sorts of actors skirmish in their desire to define what is authentically "Muslim." How, for example, can the veil be a symbol of a woman's freedom when in *certain* Muslim countries (most notably Saudi Arabia and Iran) women are not only forced to wear them, but forced to do so *by men*? Yet surely we need not regard every woman who wears the veil as a victim of male oppression. In many countries, such as the United States, some Muslim women freely and willingly wear the *hijab* as a sign of their Muslim identity and an expression of their choice of Islam over Western secularism. Just as we should not assume that every women in Iran wears the veil against her will, however, we should not assume that there are no cases in places such as America in which women are forced to veil, whether by husbands, brothers, or fathers.

It is also important to be aware that at stake in much of the public discourses concerning the veil is the perceived role and place of Islam in the West today. It is perhaps unfortunate that political discourse in Europe over banning the veil presents a stark binary—Muslims can choose to be "modern and European" or "backward and Oriental"—and, as such, a "with us or against us" mentality. All these debates, of course, transcend the veil and instead revolve around the perceived integration (or not) of Islam into America and Europe.

Traditional Patterns

Islam, like most religions, is patriarchal. As such, women have been excluded from many areas of public life and ritual activity. Menstruation, for example, puts women in a state of ritual impurity that prevents them from becoming full participants in Muslim ritual, especially prayer. This practice is sometimes presented apologetically, as it is also in Orthodox Judaism, with the argument that women might prove a distraction for men at prayer, thereby preventing both genders from achieving their proper intentions and goals during this important activity. It is also contended that women occupy a different sphere than men and, as such, have different sets of responsibilities that take place largely within the context of the home (e.g., looking after children).

In many places in the Islamic world, women have naturally gravitated to more "popular" forms of religious devotion, such as saint worship and the practices associated with the tombs of such saints. This type of devotion, as some scholars have shown, has provided women with a different form of ritual life and in certain instances given them a sense of solidarity and independence from men.[13] Conservative Muslim groups—whose members, as a subset of religious fundamentalists, have been signified as male given the terms and concepts they use—have labeled such practices, perhaps not surprisingly, as "un-Islamic."[14]

These traditional patterns are predicated on the notion of **purdah**, a Persian concept that denotes the sharp separation between men and women. In Arabic, the word *hijab* denotes this concept in that it can refer both to the actual veil, the physical segregation of the sexes, and to the requirement that women cover their bodies and conceal their form. Women in total seclusion, even though they are granted little or no restrictions within the house, must be escorted in public by a close male relative, be covered so that men may not see them, and must not mix with men who are not related to them unless they need to.

It is important to nuance the concept of purdah with several caveats. First, not all Muslim women exist in such a state of seclusion. Its practice often depends on geographic location in the Muslim world (for example, it is practiced in ultraconservative Saudi Arabia but not in more liberal countries such as Indonesia), on social status, and on other such factors. And as Islam finds a place for itself in the modern world, especially in the multicultural and multiethnic West, Muslim families are often caught between cultures and generations, with traditional parents trying to enforce their religious and cultural values on children brought up in an environment with a different ethos. These intrafamilial and intercultural tensions can usually be negotiated, but they occasionally cannot, and in such case we sometimes hear of violence committed against women in which a male relative (usually a father or brother) harms a woman who refuses to obey him and in this way is perceived to threaten the family's good name. This violence is usually directed against women for being immodest according to conservative tenets—desiring to break off an arranged marriage, seeking a divorce, committing adultery, or even being sexually assaulted. Although such crimes against women—in their most extreme form they are called "honor killings"—tend to be more common in the Islamic world, they do happen in places not in the Islamic world, such as America, as well. The United Nations Population Fund estimates the annual worldwide total of honor-killing victims at five thousand (although it is probably much higher).[15]

Another aspect of the debate regarding seclusion is whether it is Islamic or cultural in origin. One commentator aptly concludes,

> As is frequently the case, this is as much a matter of definitions of words as anything else. The total veiling of women—taken as a way of implementing a "moveable seclusion"—is not stated as a requirement in the Quran and, on that basis, is often suggested to be simply a cultural trait and not part of Islam. Such is true only, however, if attention is paid to the outer form clothing alone. Veiling is, in fact, the logical (although, strictly speaking, perhaps not necessary) outgrowth of various Quranic statements taken to their limits.[16]

Finally, it must be remembered that women's status is currently in flux. As economic, demographic, and sociological conditions change, it is often no longer viable to have only males working outside the home and women, indeed sometimes very well-educated women, confined to the house. Such changes will inevitably have repercussions on the traditional status of women as homemakers and mothers as they increasingly enter the workforce.

By Islamic law, women occupy a lesser position than men. The testimony of two women, for example, is equivalent to that of one man (Quran 2:282), and the inheritance that a woman can receive is less than what men can receive (4:11). Whereas a man can divorce his wife for any reason, a woman can instigate divorce only for specific reasons. And whereas men can remarry immediately after divorce or a spouse's death, a woman must wait a prescribed period to see if she is pregnant, thereby establishing the child's biological lineage. A Muslim man can in theory marry a woman from another monotheistic religion; a Muslim woman, however, can marry only another Muslim (5:6).[17] Whereas a Muslim man, again in theory, can have up to four wives at the same time, a Muslim woman can have only one husband. Finally, sexual relations are at the man's command: "Go apart from women during the monthly course, and do not approach them until they are clean. When they have cleansed themselves, then come unto them as God has commanded you. Truly God loves those who repent, and He loves those who cleanse themselves. Your women are a tillage for you; so come unto your tillage as you wish, and forward for your souls; and fear God, and know that you shall meet Him. Give thou good tidings to the believers" (2:223–224).

Fundamentalist Constructions

Fundamentalist constructions of women—whether of the Muslim or non-Muslim variety—are based on the notion that men and women are equal, but that they need to occupy different spheres. Men, according to this model, support the family financially, and women, as mothers and wives, provide emotional well-being. Support for such a position is usually marshaled from the religious scriptures, which are appealed to as a reflection of the natural order—even though, as pointed out earlier, they were written by men most likely in order to legitimate their social, religious, and legal superiority—and as a way to separate further the sexes from each other. This separation often translates into a dynamic wherein women are considered both powerful and weak, to be feared and to be dominated at one and the same time.

The experience of Muslim women in fundamentalist or Islamist states is certainly not monolithic. At the most extreme end was Taliban-controlled Afghanistan, in which women were forced to wear the **burka** in public, were forbidden from working and being educated after the age of eight, and were faced with public flogging and execution for violations of Taliban laws.[18] At another spot much farther along the continuum is Iran, where there are female legislators in the Parliament and roughly 60 percent of university students are women, but where they are still forced to wear the veil.

Saudi Arabia, as noted in chapter 10, is the epicenter of the conservative Wahhabi (Salafi) movement. Women there, regardless of age, are required to have a male guardian in public. They can neither vote nor be elected to high positions in the government. Moreover, it is the only country in the world that prohibits women from driving. In 2011, the World Economic Forum's Global Gender Gap Report ranked Saudi Arabia 131st out of 135 countries for gender parity, and it was the only country to score a zero in the category of political empowerment for women.[19]

Western Feminism and Islam

It is important to be aware that patriarchy is certainly not confined solely to Islam. Western feminists, largely secular, have traditionally been interested in trying to show that men in all places throughout history have sought to control and oppress women, often using religion to legitimate their ambitions and power. Such feminists seek the liberation of women from the oppressive practices of religion and are often highly critical of all religious practices and beliefs. Mary Daly, one of the pioneers of feminist critiques of religion in general, was extremely critical of the Hindu practice of suttee, in which a widow immolates herself on her dead spouse's funeral pyre, but was criticized for projecting "Western" feminist ideas onto a practice and a culture about which, it was claimed, she knew relatively little.

A more recent generation of feminists, in a backlash against work like Daly's, are increasingly critical of what they perceive to be an imperialist mind-set that assumes superiority over non-Westerners or non-Europeans or "people of color." Using the rhetoric of postcolonial criticism, they point to the hubris of Western academics who are critical of religious and cultural practices of which they are largely ignorant, thereby further replicating colonialist critiques. Joan Wallach Scott, for example, argues that European attempts to ban the veil are racist, discriminatory, and intolerant of Muslim immigrants primarily from North Africa and thus are part of Europe's inability to integrate its former colonial subjects.[20] Other feminist scholars, such as Uma Narayan, have argued, however, that this new form of political correctness is based on the fear of being labeled a colonialist but in the end further silences criticism of misogynist cultural and religious practices.[21]

Contemporary Islamic Feminism

Largely in response to the secular tendencies of feminism, various religions have produced their own feminist theologies. One of the past issues with feminist critiques of religion was that the patriarchal structure of religion was presented as so monolithic that women's rights and their practice of religion became incompatible with each other. Feminist theologians, by contrast, seek to work within their religious systems to exact change in terms of creating new traditions, practices, interpretation of scriptures, and theologies. The goals of feminist theology include increasing the role of women among the clergy and religious authorities, reinterpreting male-dominated imagery and language about the deity or deities, determining women's place in relation to career and motherhood, and studying images of women in the religion's sacred texts. Within this context, Islamic feminism is concerned largely with the role of women in Islam and seeks the full equality of all Muslims, regardless of gender, in public and private life. Islamic feminists advocate both women's rights and a gender equality that they perceive to be grounded within an Islamic framework, but they recognize that they have been influenced by secular and Western feminist discourses and understand the role of Islamic feminism as part of an integrated global feminist movement. This position frequently leads conservative critics to label such movements as "Western" or "un-Islamic," thereby easily condemning and dismissing them.

Islamic feminists often highlight what they see as deeply rooted teachings of equality in the Quran and seek to question the patriarchal interpretation of later Islamic teaching by returning to the Quran and the hadith in order to create a more equal and just society. Many of these feminists are opposed to the veil and are frequently supportive of initiatives to ban the veil (for example, in France and Tunisia). Many are also in favor of reforming aspects of sharia dealing with personal and family law, especially as concerns polygyny, divorce, custody of children, maintenance, and marital property.

In places where Muslims form minorities (e.g., Europe, United States, Canada), many Islamic feminists argue that the sharia should not just be reformed to take the rights of women into consideration, but rejected completely.[22] Muslim women, they argue, should instead seek redress from the secular laws and courts of the countries concerned.

RIFFAT HASSAN

Riffat Hassan (b. 1943) was born in Lahore, Pakistan. She went on to receive a doctorate in philosophy in 1968 from Durham University in Great Britain with a dissertation on the thought of Muhammad Iqbal. After returning to Pakistan to teach, she immigrated to the United States in 1972. She is currently professor emerita in the Department of Religious Studies at the University of Louisville in Kentucky.

For Hassan, employing a trope that we have seen frequently in this chapter, the oppression of women in Muslim societies is not a religious issue, but a cultural one. If and when the Quran is properly understood, it becomes clear that it and the religion that flows from it sanctions freedom, not oppression:

> Given the centrality of the Quran to the lives of the majority of the more than one billion Muslims of the world, the critical question is: What, if anything, does the Quran say about human rights? I believe that the Qur'an is the *Magna Carta* of human rights and that a large part of its concern is to free human beings from the bondage of traditionalism, authoritarianism (religious, political, economic, or any other), tribalism, racism, sexism, slavery or anything else that prohibits or inhibits human beings from actualizing the Quranic vision of human destiny embodied in the classic proclamation: *"Towards Allah is thy limit."*[23]

Hassan contends that the Quran, instead of being rejected as the product of male elites, ought to be interpreted openly and pluralistically. It is a document that cannot be co-opted to sanction violations of human rights or other injustices because it is the word of God and as such (as the Mutazilites argued [chapter 7]) cannot be unjust.

In 1999, Hassan founded the International Network for the Rights of Female Victims of Violence in Pakistan,[24] a foundation that seeks to address the problem of honor killings. She argues that such killings are a distortion of Islam and that, in terms of theology, women should be seen as the equal of men because, as the Quran says, Adam and Eve and therefore men and women were created at the same time.

SHIRIN EBADI

Shirin Ebadi (b. 1947) was born in Hamadan, Iran, but shortly after birth her family moved to Tehran. In 1965, she entered the faculty of law at the University of Tehran and in 1969 passed the qualification exams to become a judge. In 1975, she became the first woman in Iran to preside over a legislative court. Following the Iranian Revolution of 1979, conservative elements decided that Islam did not allow women to become judges, so Ebadi was demoted to a secretarial position at the court where she had previously presided. She and other female judges protested and were assigned to the slightly higher position of "legal experts."

After taking early retirement, Ebadi began to write of the human rights struggle in Iran and in 1990 returned to public life as a human rights lawyer, defending political dissidents and women and children in physical abuse cases. She has been instrumental in the foundation of numerous organizations in Iran defending human rights, most notably the Center for the Defense of Human Rights. She writes in her memoir, for example, that "in the last 23 years, from the day I was stripped of my judgeship to the years of doing battle in the revolutionary courts of Tehran, I had repeated one refrain: an interpretation of Islam that is in harmony with equality and democracy is an authentic expression of faith. It is not religion that binds women, but the selective dictates of those who wish them cloistered. That belief, along with the conviction that change in Iran must come peacefully and from within, has underpinned my work."[25]

In 2003, Ebadi was awarded the Nobel Peace Prize "for her efforts for democracy and human rights. She has focused especially on the struggle for the rights of women and children."[26] She was the first Iranian and the first Muslim woman to receive the prize. The Iranian authorities allegedly confiscated her award, but the government has denied the charge, although it did criticize her for not wearing a veil when she accepted the award and in public communications inside Iran denigrated the award as little more than a political gesture by a pro-Western institution.

In recent years, Ebadi has lived in exile owing to the persecution of Iranian citizens who are critical of the government.

AMINA WADUD

Amina Wadud (b. 1952) is an African American convert to Islam. Born Mary Teasley in Bethesda, Maryland, Wadud was until recently a professor of religious studies at Virginia Commonwealth University.

Although Wadud has written much on the role of gender in Islam, she is perhaps most famous for an event that took place on March 18, 2005. On that day, she took on the role of imam and led a Friday prayer that included more than one hundred male and female Muslims. The event was sponsored by the now largely defunct Progressive Muslim Union and was heavily covered by international media. It also took place at the Cathedral Church of Saint John the Divine, the seat of the Episcopal bishop of New York, because three mosques had refused to host the service, and another venue withdrew its acceptance of the event after a bomb threat.

At issue was a woman functioning as an imam, something that broke with the tradition of having only male imams. Her detractors accused her of *shirk* (associating herself with God), thus of being un-Islamic. Her supporters argued that she did not go against Islamic legal teaching, only cultural custom. Although Wadud received death threats for her actions, she has subsequently functioned as a prayer leader at other congregational prayers and speaks internationally on issues related to Islam and gender.

This chapter has presented something of the complex intersection between Islam, women, and gender roles. It is perhaps not surprising that the three individuals examined at the end of this chapter now live outside the Islamic world. In the Islamic feminist desire to reform the religion, we witness the appeal to a perceived pristine Islam in evidence at the time of Muhammad and enshrined in a pure Quran untampered with by subsequent male interpretations that sought to exclude women. Whether this vision is accurate or not is impossible to determine. However, what is certain is that the appeals to an egalitarian Islam that promotes gender equality and human rights is an important part of constructing what some consider to be an authentic Muslim identity in the modern world.

NOTES

1. See, for example, Leila Ahmed, *Women and Gender in Islam: Historical Roots of a Modern Debate* (New Haven, Conn.: Yale University Press, 1992); and Fatima Mernissi, *The Veil and the Male Elite: A Feminist Interpretation of Women's Rights in Islam*, trans. Mary Jo Lakeland (Reading, Mass.: Addison-Wesley, 1991).

2. See, for example, the comments in Jane I. Smith, "Women in Islam: Equity, Equality, and the Search for the Natural Order," *Journal of the American Academy of Religion* 47 (1979): 517–537.

3. Quoted in "Wives of the Prophet Muhammad," Islamic Awareness, http://www.islamawareness.net/Muhammed/ibn_kathir_wives.html.

4. Denise A. Spellberg, *Politics, Gender, and the Islamic Past: The Legacy of A'isha bint Abi Bakr* (New York: Columbia University Press, 1994), 40.

5. This narrative account can be found in Muhammad Ibn Ishaq, *The Life of Muhammad: A Translation of the Ibn Ishaq's "Sirat Rasul Allah*," trans. Alfred Guillaume (1955; repr. Oxford: Oxford University Press, 2009), 493–499.

6. See, for example, Haleh Afshar, *Democracy in Islam* (London: Hansard, 2006).

7. Mary F. Thurlkill, *Chosen Among Women: Mary and Fatima in Medieval Christianity and Shi'ite Islam* (Notre Dame, Ind.: University of Notre Dame Press, 2008).

8. Annemarie Schimmel, *My Soul Is a Woman: The Feminine in Islam*, trans. Susan H. Ray (New York: Continuum, 1997), 15.

9. Farid al-Dian Attar, *Muslim Saints and Mystics*, trans. A. J. Arberry (Chicago: University of Chicago Press, 1996), 40.

10. Ahmed, *Women and Gender in Islam*, 1–14.

11. John L. Esposito, *What Everyone Needs to Know About Islam* (New York: Oxford University Press, 2002), 95–97. Interestingly, Esposito puts the veil under the rubric "customs and culture" as opposed to "faith and practice."

12. "Liberation by the Veil," Learning About Islam, http://www.al-islam.org/about/contributions/liberationbytheveil.html.

13. See, for example, Lois Beck, "The Religious Lives of Muslim Women," in Jane I. Smith, ed., *Women in Contemporary Muslim Societies* (Lewisburg, Pa.: Bucknell University Press, 1980), 27–60; and Robert A. Fernea and Elizabeth W. Fernea, "Variation in Religious Observance Among Islamic Women," in Nikki R. Keddie, ed., *Scholars, Saints, and Sufis: Muslim Religious Institutions in the Middle East Since 1500* (Berkeley: University of California Press, 1972), 385–401.

14. See the comments in John S. Hawley and Wayne Proudfoot, "Introduction," in John Stratton Hawley, ed., *Fundamentalism and Gender* (New York: Oxford University Press, 1994), 3–45.

15. United Nations Population Fund, "Violence Against Women and Girls," http://www.unfpa.org/swp/2000/english/ch03.html.

16. Andrew Rippin, *Muslims: Their Religious Beliefs and Practices*, 3rd ed. (New York: Routledge, 2005), 291.

17. See the discussion in Yohanan Friedman, *Tolerance and Coercion in Islam: Interfaith Relations in the Muslim Tradition* (Cambridge: Cambridge University Press, 2003), 161–163.

18. Physicians for Human Rights, "The Taliban's War on Women: A Health and Human Rights Crisis in Afghanistan," August 1998, http://physiciansforhumanrights. org/library/documents/reports/talibans-war-on-women.pdf.

19. Ricardo Hausmann, Laura D. Tyson, and Saadia Zahidi, *Global Gender Gap Report 2011* (Geneva: World Economic Foundation, 2011), 8–11, http://www3.weforum.org/ docs/WEF_GenderGap_Report_2011.pdf. The World Economic Foundation is a nonprofit foundation based in Switzerland that annually brings together top business leaders, international political leaders, intellectuals, and journalists to discuss what it considers to be some of the most pressing issues of the day.

20. Joan Wallach Scott, *The Politics of the Veil* (Princeton, N.J.: Princeton University Press, 2007).

21. Uma Narayan, "Essence of Culture and Sense of History: A Feminist Critique of Cultural Essentialism," in Uma Narayan and Sandra Harding, eds., *Decentering the Center: Philosophy for a Multicultural, Postcolonial, and Feminist World* (Bloomington: Indiana University Press, 2000), 80–100.

22. Perhaps the most recent example of the possible incorporation of sharia into the legal system of a non-Islamic state occurred in Ontario, Canada, where the province was considering implementing sharia tribunals that would be recognized by the regular courts.

23. Riffat Hassan, "Religious Human Rights in the Qur'an," http://www.oozebap. org/biblio/Religious_Human_Rights_in_the_Quran.rtf, italics in the original.

24. The foundation's Web site is at http://ecumene.org/INRFVVP.

25. Shirin Ebadi, *Iran Awakening: A Memoir of Revolution and Hope* (New York: Random House, 2006), 204.

26. "The Nobel Peace Prize 2003," http://nobelprize.org/nobel_prizes/peace/laureates/2003.

SUGGESTIONS FOR FURTHER READING

Ahmed, Leila. *Women and Gender in Islam: Historical Roots of a Modern Debate.* New Haven, Conn.: Yale University Press, 1992.

Ali, Kecia. *Marriage and Slavery in Early Islam.* Cambridge, Mass.: Harvard University Press, 2010.

Hassan, Riffat. "Feminism in Islam." In Arvind Sharma and Katherine K. Young, eds., *Feminism and World Religions*, 248–278. Albany: State University of New York Press, 1999.

——. "Is Islam a Help or Hindrance to Women's Development?" In Johan Meuleman, ed., *Islam in the Era of Globalization: Muslim Attitudes Towards Modernity and Identity*, 189–210. London: Routledge Curzon, 2002.

Mahmood, Saba. *Politics of Piety: The Islamic Revival and the Feminist Subject.* Princeton, N.J.: Princeton University Press, 2005.

Mernissi, Fatima. *The Veil and the Male Elite: A Feminist Interpretation of Women's Rights in Islam.* Translated by Mary Jo Lakeland. Reading, Mass.: Addison-Wesley, 1991.

Mir-Hosseini, Ziba. *Islam and Gender: The Religious Debate in Contemporary Iran*. Princeton, N.J.: Princeton University Press, 1999.

Narayan, Uma. "Essence of Culture and Sense of History: A Feminist Critique of Cultural Essentialism." In Uma Narayan and Sandra Harding, eds., *Decentering the Center: Philosophy for a Multicultural, Postcolonial, and Feminist World*, 80–100. Bloomington: Indiana University Press, 2000.

Schimmel, Annemarie. *My Soul Is a Woman: The Feminine in Islam*. Translated by Susan H. Ray. New York: Continuum, 1997.

Scott, Joan Wallach. *The Politics of the Veil*. Princeton, N.J.: Princeton University Press, 2007.

Spellberg, Denise A. *Politics, Gender, and the Islamic Past: The Legacy of A'isha bint Abi Bakr*. New York: Columbia University Press, 1994.

Stowasser, Barbar Freyer. *Women in the Qur'an: Traditions and Interpretation*. New York: Oxford University Press, 1996.

Thurlkill, Mary F. *Chosen Among Women: Mary and Fatima in Medieval Christianity and Shi'ite Islam*. Notre Dame, Ind.: University of Notre Dame Press, 2008.

Wadud, Amina. *Inside the Gender Jihad: Women's Reform in Islam*. Oxford: Oneworld, 2006.

——. *Qur'an and Woman: Rereading the Sacred Text from a Woman's Perspective*. New York: Oxford University Press, 1998.

Yazbeck Haddad, Yvonne, and John L. Esposito. *Islam, Gender, and Social Change*. New York: Oxford University Press, 1998.

12

ISLAM POST–SEPTEMBER 11

T HE EVENTS of September 11, 2001, still painfully etched in many people's minds, have played a crucial role in contemporary perceptions of Islam among both Muslims and non-Muslims. How, it was asked, could "religious" individuals fly planes filled with innocent passengers into buildings, killing thousands more? This question gave way to several others: "Who are these people," some asked, perhaps naively, "and why do they hate us?" With these questions, a public discourse on Islam—what its main teachings are, what its opinions on particular topics are, what it condones or does not—has been created. Contributions to this discourse are rarely neutral; they are dependent on the different political and ideological agendas of the actors involved, all of whom claim "expert" knowledge of what Islam *really* is.

This chapter's goal is to survey some of these voices with an eye toward understanding Islam at the present moment. In order to get as broad a picture as possible, it is important to examine the many actors responsible for manufacturing the competing versions of Islam and Muslim identities that currently dot the landscape of public discourse. The actors in the debate are both Muslims and non-Muslims, militant and apologetic or fearful; they come from the left and the right; and they are both liberal and conservative. What they all share—and this should come as no surprise given what has been show in the previous eleven chapters—is the need to define Islam in their own image: to emphasize those aspects of the tradition that best articulate their particular version of the religion and marginalize those aspects that do not.

Because of these myriad voices, it is important not to take one and hold it up as normative, thereby mistaking a part for the whole. Unfortunately, however, various commentators, politicians, and even scholars try to make liberal Islam or a militant Islam somehow representative of *the* Islam. It is necessary to be aware that contemporary Islam is a polyphony of voices that are rarely, if ever, in harmony with one another.

As witnessed throughout this study, numerous events in the past fifty or so years have demonstrated this multivocality: the Six-Day War with Israel in 1967, the Iranian Revolution in 1979, reactions to the Salman Rushdie "affair" in 1989. Muslim responses to such events have been anything but monolithic and show to just what extent the "Islamic world" is composed of competing visions, interests, and identities.

One of the enduring yet misplaced questions since the events of September 11 has been: Why hasn't Islam had a reformation? Both Christians and Jews have, with the result that in both of these traditions there exist both moderate and assimilationist voices that successfully counterbalance more fundamentalist ones. Implicit in the question of Islam's inability to produce a reformation is the notion that there is something the matter with the tradition as such. Moreover, such a question ignores the fact that—as we have seen time and again—Islam possesses under its large canopy many different worldviews and conceptions of what the religion is or should be. Some of these voices are reform minded, others are not. This diversity creates manifold Muslim identities and produces, as witnessed in chapters 10 and 11, a dynamic set of responses to the contemporary period. We have to be careful, of course, of assuming that one of these responses is the correct one simply because it fits our understanding of what Islam is or should be.

It is also important to remember that although certain militant groups and Muslims do bad things in the name of Islam (they, of course, consider such actions to be good and authentically Muslim), the truth is that the overwhelming majority of Muslims are like anyone else. They are trying to raise families, gain meaningful employment, take comfort in friendship and marriage, and make sense out of life using, in part, the religion bequeathed to them from their parents. The moment that we assume that Muslims are somehow different from some vaguely constructed "us," making them the proverbial Other, problems inevitably arise.

Militant Voices: The Case of al-Qaeda

Many non-Muslims tend to conflate Islam solely with militant Islam, per-haps owing to the headline-grabbing actions of groups that follow this type of Islam. Although transnational in scope, militant Islamic groups tend to have various political objectives that revolve largely around reas-serting Islam in the face of American imperialism and U.S. support for Israel and overthrowing various corrupt regimes in the Islamic world that are perceived to be "American–Zionist" puppet states. Such groups include, but are certainly not limited to, al-Qaeda (in Afghanistan, but now also in other areas), Hezbollah (in Lebanon), Hamas (in the Gaza Strip), Jaish-e-Muhammad and Lashkar-e-Taiba (in Pakistan), al-Shabab (in Somalia), and Jemaah Islamiyya (in Indonesia and Malaysia). All these groups are committed to ensuring that their vision of Islam replaces competing versions that they perceive to be too lax, popular, or mysti-cally inspired.

Despite the fact that many liberals, both Muslim and non-Muslim, con-sider groups such as al-Qaeda to be "hijackers" of a more peaceful version of Islam, the great paradox is that members of such groups consider them-selves to be not only Muslims, but the most authentic ones. And although most governments outlaw them as terrorist organizations, followers of such groups regard themselves as waging war (jihad, or at least one inter-pretation of it) on the West and their puppet states in the Islamic world.

Groups such as al-Qaeda envisage themselves as upholding the pure Islam practiced by Muhammad and his followers, the so-called *salaf* (from which we get the modern name "Salafi"), and the next generations. They see the use of violence as a valid and justifiable way to spread their version of Islam and as the duty of every believing Muslim. Whereas critics of the followers of this form of Islam may accuse them of hijacking the true and peace-loving Islam, those who struggle against the West in violent jihad accuse those Muslims who do not share this vision of collusion with the West (usually code for America and Israel) and, even worse, of infidelity. Osama bin Laden (1957–2011), the founder of al-Qaeda, which was respon-sible for the attacks on New York and Washington on September 11, 2001, stated, for example,

> Honorable and righteous scholars, this is your role. Today is your day. Our
> Islamic *umma* is confronting a very grave challenge and being subjected to ter-

rible aggression, and her rulers and many of her scholars have forsaken her. Who will lead and direct her, if not you?

Would we give the reins of our *umma* to secular, apostate opportunists? Our *umma* has despaired of all those politically and militarily bankrupt leaders, who have lost all credibility. She is looking to the divine scholars who lead her with inspiration and drive her on the right path and fight with her in the theaters and in the battlefields of *jihad* for the sake of God Almighty. If you do not dedicate yourselves to this task now, then what are you waiting for?

After the Crusaders' occupation of Saudi Arabia, the Jews' violation of Palestine and . . . the destruction and slaughter being meted out to Muslims in Chechnya today and Bosnia yesterday and throughout the world everyday, can matters get any worse?[1]

Here bin Laden laments the presence of American troops throughout the Islamic world, especially in Saudi Arabia (which includes the Holy Cities Mecca and Medina) and in Palestine, which includes Jerusalem (with Israel serving as the U.S. proxy in the Middle East)—the three holiest places in Islam. He calls upon conservative or Wahhabi clerics not to sanction this presence and not to lend the religious and intellectual support that is responsible for propping up what he considers to be corrupt regimes. The goal of such scholars, he says, should be to fight such regimes both legally and physically.

Suicide bombing is another instance in which the same thing can be interpreted in different ways. Many Muslims find such acts abhorrent, and many religious leaders, including the *fuquha* (legal scholars), have labeled such acts as illegal and contrary to the teachings of Islam. Religious leaders associated with militant groups, however, argue that the clerics who make this claim are ignorant of the religious law and are little more than employees of corrupt states (for example, the clerics associated with al-Azhar University in Cairo) and do the bidding of "infidels." These more radical or militant scholars point to fact that the killing of civilians is legitimate—allowable under law—under certain conditions. According to bin Laden,

Our prophet Muhammad was against the killing of women and children. When he saw the body of a non-Muslim woman during a war, he asked what the reason for killing her was. If a child is older than thirteen and bears arms against Muslims, killing him is permissible. The American people should remember they pay taxes to their government and they voted for their president. Their government makes weapons and provides them to Israel, which they use to kill Palestinian Muslims. Given that the American Congress is a committee that represents the people, the fact that it agrees with the actions of the American government proves that America in its entirety is responsible for the atrocities that it is committing against Muslims.[2]

Bin Laden here justifies the killing of innocents by arguing that in the modern world there are no longer such things as "innocents" (at least in the West). According to his worldview, the nature of public opinion and democratic elections make the entire American (or British or Canadian or Israeli) citizenry complicit in the fight against Islam because they support what the military does by paying taxes and voting in elections that further support military action.

Support for these types of groups comes from numerous constituencies. Some who join are part of the swelling number of unemployed in the Muslim world, where Islamist parties and more extreme militant groups (the line between them is often fine) produce a subversive discourse (e.g., a version of Islam) that is familiar. Another constituency, as recent headlines in America have shown, is Muslims in the West, some of whom feel tremendous dissatisfaction with "Western-style" materialism, racism, and xenophobia and who believe that America and Europe are at war with and thus kill Muslims throughout the world (e.g., in Bosnia, Iraq, Afghanistan, Palestine). Some of these individuals travel to secretive militant training camps in places such as Afghanistan, Yemen, and rural Pakistan with the aim of joining some global jihad against the West.

Muslims who disagree with this vision are labeled ignorant of their tradition and corrupt because of their willingness to engage in direct dialogue with "the West." Bin Laden once said, speaking of the Saudi regime specifically, although his sentiments are echoed in militant objections to virtually every other government in the Middle East (from Morocco to Egypt to Syria):

The Saudi regime has committed very serious acts of disobedience—worse than the sins and the offenses that are contrary to Islam, worse than oppressing slaves, depriving them of their rights and insulting their dignity, intelligence, and feelings, worse than squandering the general wealth of the nation. Millions of [dollars] flow into the bank accounts of the royals who wield executive power.

At the same time, public services are being reduced, our lands are being violated, and people are imposing themselves forcibly through business without compensation. It has got to the point where the regime has gone so far as to be clearly beyond the pale of Islam, allying itself with the infidel America and aiding it against Muslims, and making itself an equal to God by legislating on what is or is not permissible without consulting God.[3]

According to bin Laden and those like him, the Saudi ruling family is guilty of *shirk* and **takfir** (apostasy) because of their acts of disobedience. As such, they have ceased to be Muslims and to rule according to the tenets of Islam. The ironic result is that the Saudi regime, despite being one of the most conservative in the Muslim world, is here regarded as the object for jihad.

Interpreting the Events of September 11

Events such as those that occurred on September 11, 2001, present numerous obstacles to the student of religion. The most important one is: Were these individuals' actions religious? Or, perhaps framed slightly differently, are we to consider their actions as "Muslim" (however we define that), or, as some want to, do we label such actions as inauthentic and a distortion of the "real" Islam?[4] The danger of making their actions into a distortion or perversion, however, is that it risks overlooking how such actors use religious teachings to justify what they do. It makes them potentially too easy to dismiss, thereby undervaluing their so-called religious component.[5]

Another way to circumscribe such actions is to claim, as is commonly done in the Islamic world, that Muslims were not responsible for the attacks of September 11. On the contrary, and despite claims of responsibility by al-Qaeda, certain segments of the Muslim world contend that the U.S. Central Intelligence Agency (CIA) and the Israeli Mossad were the real perpetrators of the attacks as a way to discredit Islam and conquer Muslim (i.e., oil-producing) countries. In the aftermath of the attacks, for example, an infamous e-mail message circulated widely stating that Jews had been told to stay home on the day in question.

Such accusations of American and Israeli involvement are frequently heard not only for the attacks on September 11, but for various suicide bombings throughout the Muslim world. The Iranian government blamed "foreign elements," in particular the United States and Israel, for the recent suicide bombing at a Shiʿi mosque on July 15, 2010, the anniversary of the birth of Imam Husayn, in Zahedan, Iran, even though a Sunni militant group, Jundullah, claimed responsibility for the attack.[6]

The Internet is rife with conspiracy theories and half-truths on these issues and must therefore be used with caution. The best place to look for information on such events is reputable news sources (although, again, whether even reputable sources are unbiased is open to debate).[7] Many Internet sites, despite being glossy and expensive looking, may be the work of any number of groups with a particular ideological ax to grind. It is certainly fine to peruse such sites, but they should be treated as primary sources as opposed to secondary ones.

Perhaps adding to the conspiracy theorists' arsenal is the fact that the suitcase of the individual who is generally considered to be the ringleader of the September 11 attacks, Muhammad Atta, was checked only as far as Boston. He took two planes: one from Portland, Maine, to Boston, and then American Airlines 11, which was scheduled to fly from Boston to Los Angeles but instead was used as one of the weapons that destroyed the World Trade Center. The suitcase did not make it onto the plane that eventually crashed into the World Trade Center. Some have argued that the suitcase

MILITANT ISLAM AND THE INTERNET

Recent years have witnessed a rapid rise in the use of the Internet to spread the messages of militant and violent Muslim (and non-Muslim) groups. The result is that these messages are easily and readily accessible at the click of a mouse.

Many of these Internet preachers reach a wider and unprecedented audience than they would if they did not use the Internet to communicate their messages. American-born Anwar al-Awlaki, a former imam, posted his lectures and messages from his home base in Yemen until his death in September 2011. According to the U.S. government, he inspired many Islamic terrorists against the West. American-born Nidal Malik Hasan carried out an attack on the army base Fort Hood in Texas, and the Nigerian Umar Farouq Abdulmutallab (the so-called Christmas Day Bomber) attempted to blow up a plane bound from Amsterdam to Detroit on December 25, 2009—both had encountered al-Awlaki's "teachings" on the Internet and corresponded with him by e-mail.

Individuals such al-Awlaki use the Internet, among other reasons, to recruit and motivate potential terrorists to their cause, to raise funds, to coordinate actions, and—perhaps most important—to instill fear in their perceived enemies. The Internet's utility resides in its ease of access, lack of regulation, potentially large audiences, and ability to allow for a fast flow of information.

was a CIA plant, but it seems most likely that he intended it to be found because in it he had left both a will and a set of instructions about how the attack was to be carried out. Perhaps he intended for others to use these documents as a way to interpret and understand his life and actions. Both the will and the instructions assert repeatedly that he perceived himself to be a good Muslim. Just so there would be no debate concerning whether his actions were political as opposed to religious, he opened his will with the following:

> In the name of God all mighty
>> Death Certificate
>
> This is what I want to happen after my death. I am Mohamed the son of Mohamed Elamir awad Elsayed: I believe that prophet Mohamed is God's messenger and time will come no doubt about that [sic] and God will resurrect people who are in their graves. I wanted my family and everyone who reads this will to fear the Almighty God and don't get deceived by what is in life and to fear God and to follow God and his prophets if they are real believers. In my memory I want them to do what Ibrahim [Abraham] told his son to do, to die as a good Muslim.

Item 14 of the will states: "I should be laying on my right side. You should throw the dust on my body three times while saying from the dust, created you dust and to dust you will return. From the dust a new person will be created. After that everyone should mention God's name and that I died as a Muslim which [sic] is God's religion. Everyone who attends my funeral should ask that I will be forgiven for what I have done in the past (not this action)."[8] Such statements should make us cautious of being too hasty to write off the motivations of individuals who carry out attacks like the ones on September 11 as "un-Islamic" or crazed. Individuals like Muhammad Atta regard their actions as being true to the religion, and they therefore regard themselves as true, perhaps the only true, Muslims in a world of unbelief—practitioners of the faith who are prepared to die for their religion in the ultimate fight against the self-perceived forces of evil.

When we turn to the transcript of the September 11 attackers' instructions, we once again witness the role of religious language and terminology in justifying such acts. For instance, after the customary Muslim opening ("In the name of God, the most merciful, the most compassionate"), we read that on the night before the attacks, the perpetrators were to

Make an oath to die and renew your intentions. Shave excess hair from the body and wear cologne. Shower.

Make sure you know all aspects of the plan well, and expect the response, or a reaction, from the enemy.

Read al-Tawba and Anfal [traditional war chapters from the Quran] and reflect on their meanings and remember all of the things God has promised for the martyrs.

Remind your soul to listen and obey [all divine orders] and remember that you will face decisive situations that might prevent you from 100 per cent obedience, so tame your soul, purify it, convince it, make it understand, and incite it. God said, "Obey God and His messenger, and do not fight amongst yourselves or else you will fail. And be patient, for God is with the patient" [Quran 8:48].[9]

The Quranic references in such passages are unmistakable and quickly contradict the notion that these individuals were not Muslims. This latter claim, of course, is an ideological one that returns us to some of the theological debates as to who gets to count as a believer. Such debates are internal ones that revolve around notions of what others perceive to be authentically Muslim acts and behaviors: Although the September 11 attackers perceived themselves to be true Muslims, both Muslims and others critical of such actions deny this claim. If any more proof is needed as to the attackers' religious justification, consider the following statement:

You should feel complete tranquility, because the time between you and your marriage [in heaven] is very short. Afterwards begin the happy life, where God is satisfied with you, and eternal bliss "in the company of the prophets, the companions, the martyrs and the good people, who are all good company" [Quran 4: 71]. Ask God for his mercy and be optimistic, because [the Prophet], peace be upon him, used to prefer optimism in all his affairs. . . .

Bless your body with some verses of the Quran [done by reading verses into one's hands and then rubbing the hands over whatever is to be blessed], the luggage, clothes, the knife, your personal effects, your ID, passports, all your papers.

Check your weapon before you leave and long before you leave (you must make your knife sharp and must not discomfort your animal during the slaughter).[10]

In this quotation, we see many themes and motifs discussed in previous chapters. Muhammad is held up as the exemplar of moral and religious valor, someone whose actions are to be replicated (or indeed interpreted) by each generation. The Quran becomes not only an important document for what it says, but also a ritual object, something whose very words impart a sacramental quality to that which it touches, including the most mundane of objects such as knives and passports. Finally, this passage compares those to be killed on the airplanes (presumably the flight attendants) as animals whose throats are to be slit in a ritualized manner.

As disturbing as such a passage may be, it needs to be understood contextually. What we see is the shrewd use of Quranic verses and traditional terminology in the service of the murderous actions. This use does not mean, of course, that every Muslim agrees with the hijackers or that the entire Muslim tradition sanctions such activities. What it does tell us, however, is that these particular individuals—not unlike other individuals encountered in previous chapters—used select materials from the past to create an identity for themselves in the present. They and the larger al-Qaeda network of which they were a part envisaged themselves as the true heirs to Muhammad.

Although some people might not like to read this explanation, scholars of religion cannot pick and choose from the numerous voices within the contemporary Islamic world to indicate which ones are the most valid or the most authentic. Our goal must be both to understand whence such voices emanate and to explain how they use and interpret the tradition to achieve their ends, with which we may or may not happen to agree.

It is important to be aware that not all Muslims agree with the attackers' interpretations of Islam. As clarified in the coming sections, huge debates in the Muslim world discuss how to deal with groups such as al-Qaeda. Some Muslims, especially *some* young Muslims in the West and in Muslim countries, see such groups romantically and seek to join them and train with them. Other Muslims, although disagreeing with these groups' tactics, may nevertheless see them as sticking up for Muslims worldwide and drawing attention to the plight of oppressed Muslims—for instance, those in Palestine. Yet other Muslims, presumably the great majority, regard groups such as al-Qaeda as an abomination and a bastardization of what they perceive the true Islam to be. And for many of these latter Muslims, events such as the attacks on September 11 should lead to further examination and introspection regarding the future of Islam and its place in the modern world.

Islamophobia

The term "Islamophobia" has recently been coined to refer to prejudice and hatred directed against Muslims and Islam. Although one might make the case that Islamophobia has always been a constituent feature in defining the nature of Europe's interaction with Islam, the term itself is more customarily employed to refer to the post–September 11 period. In this regard, Islamophobia is the racist and discriminatory technique that claims, both explicitly and implicitly, that all Muslims are potential terrorists and that Islam is an extremely hostile and violent religion. It can be witnessed in the fact that the bad guys in movies and television produced after September 2001 have often been Arabs and that Muslims are frequently "racially" profiled at airports, border crossings, and so on.

Although this profiling of Arabs and Muslims has been in existence since at least the 1970s, the events of September 11 certainly exacerbated matters. However, some argue that Islamophobia is as much a fear that emerges from the increased number of Muslims in Europe and America as it is from the attacks, although the two are probably interconnected. Examples of Islamophobia range from the general, such as stereotyping Muslims at airports and firebombing mosques, to the more specific, such as the vote in November 2009 in Switzerland against the construction of minarets or objections to the construction of an Islamic center near Ground Zero in Lower Manhattan. There is some debate as to whether the movement to ban the veil (or at least the full face covering) in places such as France (chapter 11) is based on Islamophobia, as critics of the movement would charge, or on the traditional French notion of laïcité, or secular society, as proponents would claim.

There have been numerous criticisms of the term and concept "Islamophobia." Some critics argue that although hatred of Muslims is certainly real, it is just another variation on racism and hence does not require its own category. Perhaps the biggest criticism, however, is that this term is employed to censor criticism of Islam—not unlike cries of anti-Semitism that are invoked whenever people are critical of Israel and its policies. Anyone critical of Islam—its teachings on women or on the status of the non-Muslim—can potentially be labeled an Islamophobe. Even those who research the origins of Islam from a purely secular perspective are at risk of such charges because their approach might be perceived as insensitive

---

THE PARK 51 CONTROVERSY

Park 51 (originally given the name Cordoba House) is a planned thirteen-story Muslim community center to be located two blocks from the former World Trade Center site in Lower Manhattan, the focus of the attacks on September 11, 2001, often referred to as "Ground Zero." The proposed structure is frequently called the "Ground Zero mosque," although it is worth pointing out that neither is it a mosque, nor is it located at Ground Zero (nor would it even be visible from Ground Zero).

When this center was proposed, it created a great deal of controversy. Opponents of the Park 51 project have argued that erecting a mosque so close to Ground Zero would be offensive because the hijackers responsible for the attacks were Muslim and killed thousands in the name of Islam. Supporters, however, have argued that the center will be open to the general public and will ideally promote interfaith dialogue. They also argue that some of the victims were also Muslim and that many of the victims' families are in favor of the Park 51 project.

Prominent supporters and opponents of the project can be found among the families of the September 11 victims, the American and worldwide Muslim communities, and local and national politicians. It even became a highly polarized issue in 2010, during the midterm elections. The debate over Park 51 coincided with unexpected protests against new mosque constructions in other states, further leading to concerns that relations between Muslims and non-Muslims in the United States are once again deteriorating.

---

to Muslim belief and practices. A final example of the term's ambiguity is the controversy over the publication of the Danish cartoons depicting Muhammad. Critics labeled the cartoons a "classic" act of Islamophobia, whereas defenders argued that they were an exercise of free speech. The truth of the matter most likely resides, as it so often does, somewhere between the two arguments.

ISLAMOPHOBIA AMONG "NEOCON" COMMENTATORS

Neoconservativism is a right-wing movement that supports the use of American economic and military power to bring a particular version of democracy to other countries. In recent years, many in the so-called neocon movement see "militant Islam" as the biggest threat to American interests, both at home and abroad. According to neoconservatives, these militant Muslims seek to wage jihad on the West not only by violent means, by also by legal means through the use of the West's notion of political correctness and calls of Islamophobia.

Such commentators are usually very supportive of Israel and highly critical of the prospects of Palestinian statehood, and they are generally (but not always) behind active American involvement in the affairs of places such as Iraq and Afghanistan. All neocons, like the members of any other category, cannot be neatly placed under the same canopy, however, and range from the rather dull-witted (witness some of the commentators on Fox News) to the more sophisticated (such as Daniel Pipes).

DANIEL PIPES AND CAMPUS WATCH

Daniel Pipes (b. 1949) is a Harvard-trained historian who began his career specializing in the medieval Islamic period. In the mid-1980s, he left the academy and began commenting publicly on political affairs, especially Islam and Islamism, which he labels as "militant Islam," a threat to the global order in general and to America in particular: "As Islamists, they believe that their ways are superior and want to impose these on the country as a whole. In the short term, they promote Islam as a solution to the social and moral ills; in the long term, they work to turn the United States into not just a Muslim country but one run along militant Islamic lines. However outlandish this goal, it is one which in militant Islamic circles is widely assumed and much discussed."[11]

Pipes has also worked for various conservative think tanks. In 1990, he founded the Middle East Forum, whose self-stated goal is "to define and promote American interests in the Middle East and protect the Constitutional order from Middle Eastern threats."[12] Until 2010, Pipes also edited the forum's journal, *Middle East Quarterly*. Ephraim Karsh became the new editor and describes the journal's mandate as one of "questioning established wisdom, debunking popular myths, and providing an alternative perspective on the region's history and current affairs."[13]

In 2002, Pipes founded Campus Watch, a controversial organization whose goal, according to its Web site, is to address "five problems: analytical failures, the mixing of politics with scholarship, intolerance of alternative views, apologetics, and the abuse of power over students. Campus Watch fully respects the freedom of speech of those it debates while insisting on its own freedom to comment on their words and deeds."[14]

Whereas Pipes is concerned largely with radical Muslims in the Middle East Forum, Campus Watch sets its sights on scholars of Islam and the Middle East. To achieve its goals, it monitors what academics have to say in the classroom about both the religion and the region. It is particularly critical of what it perceives to be many scholars' liberal and anti-Israeli biases. According to its Web page, Campus Watch

- Gathers information on Middle East studies from public and private sources and makes this information available on its website, www.Campus-Watch.org
- Produces analyses of institutions, individual scholars, topics, events, and trends
- Makes its views known through the media—newspaper opeds, radio interviews, television interviews
- Invites student complaints of abuse, investigates their claims, and (when warranted) makes these known[15]

Critics refer to this activity as a form of academic McCarthyism.[16] Campus Watch replies, however, that its goal is not to police such discourses, but to ensure that alternate viewpoints on the Middle East are heard and included in the public debate.

Finally, in 2006 Middle East Forum launched Islamist Watch, whose stated goal is to "combat the ideas and institutions of nonviolent, radical Islam in the United States and other Western countries. It exposes the far-reaching goals of Islamists, works to reduce their power, and seeks to strengthen moderate Muslims."[17] Islamist Watch claims to educate the U.S. government, media, religious institutions, the academy, and the business world about "lawful Islamism," presumably Islamism that seeks to overthrow the status quo by legal means.

These organizations affiliated with Middle Eastern Forum are but a selection of various neocon sites on the Internet.[18] The goal of all these sites is to expose so-called real Islam, which is often equated with Islamism or "Islamo-fascism," a recently coined term used to denote militant Muslims' authoritarian nature.

IRSHAD MANJI'S *TROUBLE WITH ISLAM*

The theme of "empowering" moderate Muslims is a big one for many commentators dealing with the troubles besetting Islam today. Joining this chorus is Canadian Muslim journalist Irshad Manji. In light of the September 11 attacks, Manji has called for an end to "Islam's totalitarianism, particularly the gross human rights violations against women and religious minorities."[19] Her book *The Trouble with Islam Today: A Muslim's Call for Reform in Her Faith* has been translated into thirty languages and received widespread media attention. Manji is also the creator of the Emmy-nominated PBS documentary *Faith Without Fear*, which chronicles her journey to reconcile Islam with human rights and freedom.[20] Manji is a journalist by training and has no formal background in the academic study of Islam. Her Web site, however, presents her as a "scholar," and based on the fact that many are supportive of her attempts to reform Islam from within, she has been appointed as the director of the Moral Courage Project at New York University, which aims to develop leaders who will challenge so-called political correctness, intellectual conformity, and self-censorship.

Because Manji offers a critique from within the tradition, some liberal Muslims but also more frequently neoconservative commentators such as Daniel Pipes have labeled her a visionary. The tendency in Islamic studies circles, however, is to write her off as someone who, lacking the requisite academic and historical skills, largely misunderstands the complexity of Islam—although this criticism in itself may be considered problematic because it implies that academics/scholars are the only ones who can understand Islam. However we may see her, it is important to note that Manji's critical voice has reached an audience far wider than anything produced by scholars. Moreover, others frequently cite her as the moderate face of the tradition. Pipes, for example, argues that the views held by people like Manji ought to be included in the highest level of government discussion and taught in universities:

> Governments and leading institutions can do a lot. If you look at the situation today throughout the West including North America, you'll find that the Islamists, the radicals, are the ones invited into government circles who are generally in the media, are cited as authorities, who do the research in universities, who engage in discussions with the churches and so forth. It is important for all these institutions, governmental, academic, media and alike, to remove the recognition from the Islamists and give it to the moderate Muslims.[21]

Muslim Apologetics: The Need to Define a Liberal Islam

If one of the natural reactions to the events of September 11, 2001, has been a very critical assessment of Islam, an equally natural reaction has been to defend Islam, showing its intersection with principles such as liberalism, equality, and democracy. Although many practitioners may well want the heart of Islam to correspond to these values, such a construction functions on the same level as any other construction: it is the attempt to retrofit and impose a set of values deemed important in the modern period on Islam's earliest period. Time and again we have encountered various historical actors' attempt to construct an authentic Islam, so the use of this approach in defending Islam should come as no surprise.

Given the aftermath of the attacks on September 11 and other such events, there has been a tendency, as we have seen, to blame all Muslims for the activities of the few—to construct a monolithic Islam that sanctions violence against non-Muslims. The types of discourses produced by those examined in the previous section do much to create and sustain such hostility on a practical level. The individuals and groups discussed in this section attempt to counter claims that Islam is somehow inherently violent and that Muslims, more than practitioners of other religions, are prone to religious violence.

PROGRESSIVE MUSLIMS

Several organizations have served as the main vehicles to define Islam liberally and progressively, such as the Progressive Muslim Union, which was disbanded in 2006 and reconstituted in part as Muslims for Progressive Values. Perhaps there is no coincidence that many of these organizations have sprouted on American soil and are run largely by academics, many of them professors of Islamic studies. In a book reflecting these liberal and progressive values, *Progressive Muslims*, volume editor Omid Safi writes:

> [B]eing a progressive Muslim is the determination to hold Muslim societies accountable for justice and pluralism. It means openly and purposefully resisting, challenging, and overthrowing structures of tyranny and injustice

in these societies. At a general level, it means contesting injustices of gender apartheid (practiced by groups such as the Taliban), as well as the persecution of religious and ethnic minorities (undertaken by Saddam Hussein against the Kurds, etc.). It means exposing the violations of human rights and freedoms of the speech, press, religion, and the right to dissent in Muslim countries such as Saudi Arabia, Turkey, Iran, Pakistan, Sudan, Egypt, and others. More specifically it means embracing and implementing a different vision of Islam than that offered by Wahhabi and neo-Wahhabi groups.[22]

Implicit here is the assumption that there exists a liberal or progressive Islam that is somehow compatible with all these critiques. Not unlike Muslim feminists, progressive Muslims articulate this essential Islam, deriving it from the Quran and on the rare occasion from later Islamic sources, as compatible with modernity, liberal values, and so on. The flipside of this view is that the types of Islams practiced by the Taliban, Saddam Hussein, and Wahhabi and neo-Wahhabi groups are somehow inauthentic precisely because they stray from this self-styled "straight path." All these Islams, however, are constructed in the images of those doing the constructing, mirroring their concerns, issues, and socioeconomic positions. Even though they may be made uncomfortable by the comparison, both groups, the neo-Wahhabis and the progressive Muslims, are doing precisely the same thing: arguing that there exists an Islamic kernel somewhere in the ether or in a particular collection of texts and that their group can find it to provide the epistemological, religious, and intellectual categories to usher in the true brand of Islam.

TARIQ RAMADAN

Tariq Ramadan (b. 1962) is a Swiss-born scholar who presently teaches at St. Anthony's College in Oxford. The grandson of Hasan al-Banna, the founder of the Muslim Brotherhood in Egypt, Ramadan is a highly controversial figure. Critics accuse him of supporting Palestinian organizations that carry out suicide attacks against Israelis, of defending the stoning of adulterers, of promoting anti-Semitism, of speaking about peace only when it suits him, and so on. At the same time, however, many conservative Muslims have also attacked Ramadan for his liberal criticisms and his pointing the finger at many Muslims countries (e.g., Egypt, Saudi Arabia) for their violation of human rights and their overt violations of democratic principles.

In February 2004, Ramadan accepted a professorship at the University of Notre Dame, but the U.S. State Department revoked his nonimmigrant visa. The reason stated was the "ideological exclusion provision" of the USA PATRIOT Act. The persons instrumental in the denial of the visa to Ramadan included, not coincidentally, Daniel Pipes. Ramadan subsequently resigned his position at Notre Dame and took up his current one at Oxford. In January 2010, however, the ban on Ramadan's admittance to the United States was lifted.

In terms of his ideas, Tariq Ramadan seeks to create an independent Western Islam. This Islam, according to him, must not be anchored in the traditions of Islamic countries, but in the cultural reality of the West: "I do not represent all Muslims but I belong to the reformist trend. I aim to remain faithful to the principles of Islam, on the basis of scriptural sources, while taking into account the evolution of historical and geographical contexts . . . unlike literalists who merely rely on quoting verses, reformists must take the time to put things in perspective, to contextualize, and to suggest new understandings."[23]

This hermeneutic leads Ramadan to try and reinterpret traditional Islamic sources (e.g., Quran, hadith) for Muslims who live in the West and to show how a "Western" understanding of universal Islamic principles can help to integrate Muslims living in European and American societies. He claims that

> Western Muslims will play a decisive role in the evolution of Islam worldwide because of the nature and complexity of the challenges they face, and in this their responsibility is doubly essential. By reflecting on their faith, their principles and their identity within industrialized, secularized societies, they participate in the reflection the Muslim world must undertake on its relationship with the modern world, its order, and its disorder. . . . In my view, the future dialogue between civilizations will not take place at the geopolitical frontiers between "the West" and "Islam" but rather, paradoxically, within European and American societies.[24]

For Ramadan, American and European Muslims must engage in the reexamination of the fundamental texts of Islam and interpret them in light of their own cultural, intellectual, and social contexts. This reinterpretation, he believes, will create a "Western Islam" with the potential power to gain intellectual control of the tradition.

KAREN ARMSTRONG

I mention Karen Armstrong, a best-selling non-Muslim author, here as a way to show how religion is considered an internal and spiritual phenomenon unsullied by political and external forces. This way of speaking about religion has been customary at least since Friedrich Schleiermacher's critique of Kant's relegation of religion to the realm of the ethical, a critique popularized in religious studies circles by the works of scholars such as Rudolph Otto and Mircea Eliade. Armstrong, among others, works with the binary that religion when spiritualized does good in the world but when co-opted by politics can often be an agent of violence. In *Islam: A Short History*, for example, she writes that the "spiritual quest is an interior journey; it is a psychic rather than a political drama. It is preoccupied with liturgy, doctrine, contemplative disciplines and an exploration of the heart, not with the clash of current events . . . power struggles are not what religion is really about, but an unworthy distraction from the life of the spirit, which is conducted far from the maddening crowd, unseen, silent, and unobtrusive."[25]

Here Armstrong claims that religion is inherently peaceful and that when people do bad things in its name, they misunderstand the religion or attempt somehow to sully it or "hijack" it. Although this view of religion may be helpful if we are trying to understand events such as the attacks of September 11, it does not necessarily help us understand any better the statements of individuals such as Osama bin Laden and Muhammad Atta, who, as we have seen, view themselves as the true inheritors of Muhammad's message—a religious message. Armstrong's comments and indeed variations on them are commonplace and may make us feel better, but they do not help us understand or contextualize religious violence.

The Future

This chapter has examined some of the many responses to events such as the attacks that occurred on September 11, 2001. These events have put

Islam under a microscope, as it were. Many non-Muslims began to desire to learn more about the religion of Islam and how it makes Muslims "think." Such events have also forced many Muslims to consider or reconsider both the place of Islam in the modern world and how Islam can integrate with (or segregate itself from) non-Muslim societies.

Many of these latter questions relate to the role of civil society and how such a society can be realized and maintained using what are perceived to be authentic Muslim principles. What, for example, is the relationship between Islam and democracy or Islam and human rights? These questions and the debates that revolve around them are not entirely new. Indeed, the tensions between the state and Islam in the present period certainly resonated in the early and medieval periods when scholars and caliphs argued about who had the vested authority to lead the *umma*, a debate echoed in statements made by Osama bin Laden.

Although bin Laden's interpretation of Islam is certainly neither normative nor mainstream, it has functioned as a catalyst by which other Muslims (from fundamentalist to modernist to liberal and everything in between) have been forced to define and articulate their own visions of the tradition. It is for this reason that September 11 is so important: it has become a symbol against which various Muslim identities are being charted. In this regard, despite the ruminations of various conservative Muslim and non-Muslim commentators, September 11 is not the telos toward which Islam has been heading since the time of Muhammad. On the contrary, it is the point of departure for the future of Islam and the future of Muslim identities.

NOTES

1. Osama bin Laden, *Messages to the World: The Statements of Osama bin Laden*, trans. James Howarth, ed. Bruce Lawrence (London: Verso, 2005), 17.

2. Ibid., 140–141.

3. Ibid., 247–248.

4. See, for example, the comments in Karen Armstrong, *Islam: A Short History* (New York: Modern Library, 2000), 190.

5. On the "perversion" of these actions, see, for example, John A. Esposito, *The Islamic Threat: Myth or Reality?* 3rd ed. (1992; repr., New York: Oxford University Press, 1999), xii.

6. "Mass Funerals for Victims of Iran Mosque Bombings," *BBC News*, July 17, 2010, http://www.bbc.co.uk/news/world-middle-east-10672780.

7. Such Web sites include nytimes.com and bbc.co.uk.

8. For a facsimile copy of Muhammad Atta's will translated into English, see http://www.abc.net.au/4corners/atta/resources/documents/will1.htm.

9. A transcript of the instructions can be found in Bruce Lincoln, *Holy Terrors: Thinking About Religion After September 11* (Chicago: University of Chicago Press, 2003), appendix A, 93–98, quote on 93.

10. Ibid., 94.

11. Daniel Pipes, *Militant Islam Reaches America* (New York: Norton, 2002), 138.

12. The forum's Web site is at http://www.meforum.org.

13. "Efraim Karsh Appointed *Middle East Quarterly* Editor," Middle East Forum, press release, July 1, 2010, http://www.meforum.org/2681/efraim-karsh-appointed-middle-east-quarterly-editor.

14. "Campus Watch: Monitoring Middle East Studies on Campus," Campus Watch, http://www.campus-watch.org.

15. "What Campus Watch Does," in "About Campus Watch," Campus Watch, http://campus-watch.org/about.php.

16. See the comments in Joel Beinin, "Who's Watching the Watchers?" History News Network, September 30, 2002, http://hnn.us/articles/1001.html.

17. "About Islamist Watch: A Project of the Middle East Forum," http://www.islamist-watch.org/about.php.

18. Other, often less sophisticated sites include JihadWatch.com and frontpagemag.com.

19. Irshad Manji, *The Trouble with Islam: A Muslim's Call for Reform in Her Faith* (New York: St. Martin's Press, 2004), 3.

20. This documentary and other related materials can be found on Manji's official YouTube channel, IrshadManjiTV.

21. Daniel Pipes, "A Muslim Reformation?" September 28, 2003, http://www.danielpipes.org/1270/a-muslim-reformation.

22. Omid Safi, "Introduction: The Times They Are a Changin'—A Muslim Quest for Justice, Gender Equality, and Pluralism," in Omid Safi, ed., *Progressive Muslims: On Justice, Gender, and Pluralism* (Oxford: Oneworld, 2003), 2.

23. Tariq Ramadan, *What I Believe* (New York: Oxford University Press, 2010), 2.

24. Tariq Ramadan, *Western Muslims and the Future of Islam* (New York: Oxford University Press, 2004), 225–226.

25. Armstrong, *Islam*, ix.

SUGGESTIONS FOR FURTHER READING

Abou El Fadl, Khaled. *The Great Theft: Wrestling Islam from the Extremists*. San Francisco: Harper One, 2005.

Bin Laden, Osama. *Messages to the World: The Statements of Osama bin Laden*. Translated by James Howarth. Edited by Bruce Lawrence. London: Verso, 2005.

Gottschalk, Peter, and Gabriel Greenberg. *Islamophobia: Making Muslims the Enemy*. Lanham, Md.: Rowman & Littlefield, 2007.

Hughes, Aaron W. *Situating Islam: The Past and Future of an Academic Discipline*. London: Equinox, 2007.

Jamal, Amaney, and Nadine Naber. *Race and Arab Americans Before and After 9/11: From Invisible Citizens to Visible Subject*. Syracuse, N.Y.: Syracuse University Press, 2007.

Lincoln, Bruce. *Holy Terrors: Thinking About Religion After September 11*. Chicago: University of Chicago Press, 2003.

Manji, Irshad. *The Trouble with Islam: A Muslim's Call for Reform in Her Faith*. New York: St. Martin's Press, 2004.

McCutcheon, Russell T. *Religion and the Domestication of Dissent: Or, How to Live in a Less Than Perfect Nation*. London: Equinox, 2005.

Pipes, Daniel. *Militant Islam Reaches America*. New York: Norton, 2002.

Ramadan, Tariq. *Western Muslims and the Future of Islam*. New York: Oxford University Press, 2004.

——. *What I Believe*. New York: Oxford University Press, 2010.

Safi, Omid, ed. *Progressive Muslims: On Justice, Gender, and Pluralism*. Oxford: Oneworld, 2003.

GLOSSARY

ADHĀN   Call to prayer.

AHL AL-BAYT   Literally, "people of the house"; often used to refer to Muhammad's family.

AHL AL-TAṢAWWUF   "People of the Woolen Way" (i.e., Sufis).

ALLĀH   Arabic name for God.

AWRAH   The intimate parts of the body, for both men and women, that must be covered with clothing.

ĀYA   A verse of the Qurʾān; can also be used more generally to refer to any "sign" of God.

AYATOLLAH   Literally, "sign of God"; refers to the religious and legal scholars in Shīʿism.

BALKAFA   "Without (asking) how." Ibn Ḥanbals formulation that the Qurʾān's literal sense, including its anthropomorphisms, must be accepted.

BASMALAH   A statement that begins all of the chapters of the Qurʾān (except chapter 8): "In the name of God, the Merciful, the Compassionate"; also used as an invocation by many Muslims when they engage in certain activities.

BĀṬIN   Esoteric or hidden.

BEDOUIN   Desert-dwelling and ethnic Arab tribes.

BIDʿA   "Innovation"; often regarded as a heresy in the Islamic legal tradition.

BURQAʿ   A restrictive enveloping outer garment worn by women in some Muslim traditions for the purpose of hiding their entire face and body when out in public.

CALIPH   From *khalifat rasūl allāh* (successor of the Messenger of God). A term used to refer to a political successor of Muhammad, especially in the first three hundred years after his death.

DĀR AL-ḤARB   "The House of War"; refers to those countries/regions where Islamic law is not in place.

DĀR AL-ISLĀM   "The House of Islam"; refers to those countries where Muslims can practice their religion freely.

DAʿWA "The call"; the name employed to encourage non-Muslims to learn about Islam; proselytization.

DHAWQ "Taste"; the term Sufis use to refer to the immediacy of the mystical experience.

DHIKR "Remembering" or "mentioning" God; the rituals performed by Sufis to get nearer to God.

DHIMMĪ Non-Muslim minorities with legal rights and obligations in Muslim countries, provided they pay a poll tax (jizya).

DUʿĀʾ "Calling" on God; used for informal prayer (compared with the more formal prayer, ṣalāt).

FANĀʿ The mystic's "extinction" in God.

FATWĀ "Legal opinion" issued by Islamic legal scholars.

FIQH Jurisprudence or the science of ascertaining the religious law; fiqh practitioners are known as fuquhāʿ (sing., faqīh).

FITNA Civil war.

FIṬRA One's innate submitting nature.

GHAYBA Occultation or hiding of the last Imam in the Shīʿi tradition.

ḤADĪTH A tradition handed down and subsequently recorded that details some aspect of Muhammad's life.

ḤAJJ Annual pilgrimage to Mecca.

ḤARĀM A term designating any object or action that is prohibited to use or engage in according to Islamic law (opposite: ḥalāl).

ḤIJĀB The veil that some Muslim women choose to wear or are forced to wear (depending on time period, geography, and so on). Can also refer more generally to modesty and gender segregation.

HIJRA "Exodus" or migration of Muhammad and his followers from Mecca to Medina. This event marks the beginning of the Muslim calendar (622 C.E. = 1 A.H.).

ḤUNAFĀʿ Pre-Islamic Arabian monotheists; most likely a later theological construct (sing., ḥanīf).

ʿIBĀDĀT The "acts of worship" that Muslims are expected to perform.

IJMĀʿ "Consensus"; one of the four sources of Islamic law.

IJTIHĀD "Independent reasoning"; a principle in early Islamic jurisprudence.

ʿILM Scientific knowledge or, in the case of Shīʿism, the esoteric understanding of both the universe and the Qurʾān.

IMĀM Literally, "the one who stands in front" (i.e., in prayer). In Shīʿi Islam, designation of the legitimate successors to Muhammad; among Sunnīs, the designation of the community's religious leader.

ĪMĀN "Faith"; important religious virtue; one with "faith" is referred to as a muʿmin.

ISLĀM "Submission"—that is, to the will of God.

ISLAMISM An ideological movement that holds that Muslims must return to the "fundamentals" of their religion, take political power, and implement the sharīʿa to govern all aspects of life.

ISLAMOPHOBIA Prejudice or discrimination against Islam and Muslims.

ʿIṢMA "Infallibility." The state of sinlessness embodied by Muhammad and, in Shīʿism, by the Twelve Imams.

ISNĀD The "chain" of transmission that opens up a ḥadīth report and, according to Muslims, verifies it.

ISRĀʾ Muhammad's night journey from Mecca to Jerusalem. See also MIʿRĀJ.

JĀHILIYYA Period of ignorance that preceded the advent of Islam. Also used in the modern period to refer to personal ignorance of Islam (with a distinct moral connotation).

JIHĀD "Striving" or "exertion"; generally used to refer to "holy war" against infidels but can also refer to a personal inner "struggle" against one's passions and imperfections (*jihād al-nafs*).

JIZYA The poll tax paid by religious minorities to ensure their religious and political rights.

KAʿBA The black "cube" in Mecca. The holiest shrine in Islam; Muslims pray facing it and circumambulate it on the ḥajj.

KHAṬĪB The individuals who leads the Friday noon prayer and delivers the sermon (*khuṭba*) to the congregation

KUFR "Unbelief." An unbeliever is called a *kāfir* (pl., *kuffār*).

MADHHAB A school of law (pl., *madhāhib*).

MADRASA Traditionally an Islamic institute of higher learning; today often used to refer to any type of Islamic school.

MAHDĪ The "Guide" who will reveal himself in the messianic era.

MATN The textual report of the ḥadīth.

MIḤRĀB The "niche" in the wall that indicates the direction of the *kaʿba* in Mecca, toward which Muslims should face during prayer.

MINARET A tower that indicates a mosque.

MINBAR The pulpit upon which the *khaṭīb* delivers his sermon in the mosque.

MIʿRĀJ Muhammad's ascension to heaven. *See also* ISRĀʾ.

MONOTHEISM Belief in a single deity.

MUEZZIN The person who utters the call to prayer.

MUSLIM One who submits to the will of God.

MUʿTAZILITES A theological school popular in the eight and ninth centuries that emphasized human freedom and a rationalist understanding of the Qurʾān.

NAFS Ego; self; soul. The part of the self that the Sufi novice is supposed to overcome.

NASKH "Abrogation"; the legal principle whereby later verses or ḥadīth reports replace earlier ones.

NAṢṢ A Shīʿi Imam's explicit designation of his successor.

NIYYA The "intention" with which Muslims are supposed to undertake religious actions and obligations.

ORIENTALISM The study of the Orient. In the contemporary period, often used pejoratively to refer to the colonialist attempt to gain power over the "Orient" and especially the Muslim world.

POLYTHEISM Belief and worship of multiple gods or goddesses or both.

PURDAH The physical segregation of the sexes and the requirement that women cover their bodies and conceal their form. The Indian equivalent of *ḥijāb*.

QĀḌĪ A judge who rules based on Islamic law (sharīʿa).

QIBLA The direction (toward Mecca) that Muslims face in prayer.

QIYĀS Analogous situation for which a clear ruling has already been made, used by legists whenever a legal problem arises for which the Qurʾān and the Sunna cannot provide an answer.

RAKʿA The cycle of movements (standing, bowing, prostrating) during prayer.

RAMAḌĀN The month of fasting; believed by Muslims to be the month in which the Qurʾān was first revealed.

RAʿY "Personal opinion" (i.e., of the *fuquhāʾ*); one of the principles Islamic jurisprudence.

ṢAḤĀBA "Companions" of Muhammad.

SALAFĪ The pious ancestors, specifically the closest followers of Muhammad, usually the first three generations after the advent of Islam. In the modern period, refers to those who seek to return to the "pure" Islam of the first generations. Often another name for "fundamentalist" or "Wahhābī."

ṢALĀT   Prayer; proscribed five times a day.

ṢAWM   The fast that is proscribed during the month of Ramaḍān.

SHAHĀDA   The witnessing of one's faith ("There is no god but God, and Muhammad is His messenger"). One of the five pillars; uttered by the convert to signal his or her conversion; also uttered as part of the ritual prayer.

SHARĪ'A   Literally, the "path" or "way." Refers to Islamic law derived from the Qur'ān and Sunna.

SHIRK   "Associationism." The sin of associating something else (e.g., money, gods, power) with God.

SHŪRĀ   "Electoral council" of elders.

SĪRA   The biography of Muhammad.

SUNNA   The customs of a great or important individual. Usually refers to the "customs" of Muhammad emulated by later Muslims.

SŪRA   A chapter of the Qur'ān.

TAFSĪR   Interpretation of the Qur'ān.

TAḤRĪF   "Tampering"; the notion that other religious scriptures (e.g., the Hebrew and Christian Bibles) have been falsified.

TAKFĪR   Apostasy.

TAQIYYA   "Pious dissimulation"; a concept that sanctions the concealing of one's true religious obligations in the face of adversity.

TAQLĪD   The reliance on early legal judgments.

ṬARĪQA   The Sufi "way"; also used to refer to the various orders within Sufism.

TAWAKKUL   "Radical trust" (i.e., in God).

TAWḤĪD   The process of making one. Often used to designate monotheism.

TA'WĪL   Mystical or esoteric interpretation of the Qur'ān.

ULAMĀ'   The social class with expertise in legal and religious matters (sing., 'ālim).

UMMA   Worldwide community of Muslim believers.

UṢŪL AL-FIQH   The study of the origins, sources, and principles of Islamic law.

WAHHĀBĪ   A follower of Muhammad Ibn 'abd al-Wahhāb (d. 1787), the leader of a fundamentalist movement in Arabia that subsequently became the official religion of Saudi Arabia and has remained so to this day.

ẒĀHIR   Exoteric.

ZAKĀT   Alms; one of the so-called five pillars.

ZANDAQA   "Dualists"; often referring to Zoroastrians or Manicheans. In the later tradition, taking on the connotation of "heretic."

ZUHD   "Renunciation" or "asceticism"; used to describe the Sufis earliest lifestyle.

INDEX

…formation can be obtained
…Gtesting.com
…e USA
…220720
…0012B/936